CAUSE OF DEATH

CAUSE OF DEATH

FORENSIC FILES OF A MEDICAL EXAMINER

STEPHEN D. COHLE, MD
AND TOBIN T. BUHK

Prometheus Books

59 John Glenn Drive
Amherst, New York 14228-2197

Published 2007 by Prometheus Books

Inquiries should be addressed to
Prometheus Books
59 John Glenn Drive
Amherst, New York 14228–2197
VOICE: 716–691–0133, ext. 207
FAX: 716–564–2711
WWW.PROMETHEUSBOOKS.COM

11 10 09 08 07   5 4 3 2

Library of Congress Cataloging-in-Publication Data

Cohle, Stephen D.
    Cause of death : forensic files of a medical examiner / by Stephen D. Cohle and Tobin T. Buhk
        p. cm.
    Includes bibliographical references and index.
    ISBN 978–1–59102–447–7 (alk. paper)
    1. Forensic pathology. 2. Death—Causes. I. Buhk, Tobin T. II. Title.

RA1063.4.C64 2007
614'.1—dc22

2006035315

Printed in the United States on acid-free paper

CONTENTS

INTRODUCTION: SCENES

Late Spring 2004

Several smaller neighborhoods border the south side of Grand Rapids; in a large metropolitan area, one might call this area the near south side. It is not the inner city, but it is not suburban, either. Rows and rows of houses—older, brick houses from the early twentieth century—line wide streets shaded by oak and maple trees. The homes, despite wrinkles, pockmarks, and scars showing their age, manage to remain fashionable.

The small houses make ideal starter homes, a fact that has brought the young and the old to commingle here. Twenty-somethings—up-and-coming professionals who call this area home until they establish a client base or pay off mountainous student loans—live here alongside the elderly who never left. The twenty-somethings have invigorated these streets—infusing new blood into the neighborhoods in the form of laughing children who play on the narrow, cracked sidewalks—and the young urbanites have transformed house interiors, replacing dark wood with leather.

Along these streets, one finds an architectural tapestry as varied as the occupants who populate the homes; looking at the houses is like looking at a grove of trees in autumn, an endless variation of color, shape, and size. Here one finds all the personality traits missing in the modern cousins located in gated subdivisions: bay windows; hardwood floors; detached, single-car garages; gables; arches; columns in a variety of styles; and jack roofs that actually serve a purpose.

The residents are an odd mix of transients who come and go when they upgrade to larger homes; elderly who are too set in their ways figuratively, literally, or financially to move; and single parents or the unmarried who come to neighborhoods in which they can afford the housing.

And so a more sinister energy flows under Alger Heights as well, like a water table just below the foundations: a feeling of economic urgency. Some survive and move on to bigger and better locales and look back on their first homes with a fond sense of nostalgia. Some don't.

Some, like Sarah Coleman* (see below for an explanation about the use of the asterisk), never leave. Police would find her the afternoon her brother received a handwritten letter in neat, cursive writing postmarked the previous day. After reading the letter, he dropped it and ran for the phone to call 911. In the letter, Sarah Coleman says good-bye to her brother and his children and explains that she cannot pay the bills and that she will end her life and financial misery by gassing herself in her car.

Her car—a beige Caprice Classic from the late seventies but without a dent or scratch—sits inside of the single-car, detached garage. Two white pillows and a dark green blanket cover the backseat; a green garden hose, like a large, Day-Glo snake, lies on the garage floor next to the driver's side door, its tail affixed to the exhaust pipe with gunmetal gray electrical tape.

Sarah Coleman made herself a bed but never used it. If she had suffocated herself, she would have used the third-most-common method of suicide among women between the ages of forty-five and fifty-four (she was forty-seven). In 2003, a vast majority of women who committed suicide—46.4 percent, or almost four times the 12.2 percent who chose suffocation—elected to use poison. In other words, pills and an overdose. Nearly a third of all women aged forty-five to fifty-four shot themselves. At 56.6 percent, suicide by firearm was by far the most popular method of suicide for men in the same age range, with suffocation (18.3 percent) and poisoning (16.9 percent) the distant second and third choices.[1]

Her note to her brother did not contain an idle threat, as investigators would discover in her living room, where they would find a shocking image; although to the death scene investigator, one of a rotation of individuals who make a living in part by investigating scenes in which a death occurred, the scene may appear less than shocking.

*****

On that same afternoon in northern Michigan, a sheriff's deputy discovered a faded blue Ford pickup truck parked on the side of a dirt road under the shade of an oak whose branches extended over the two-track road.

As he walked toward the vehicle, he could make out the image—an outline at first—of a man slumped forward but sitting upright, his shoulders drooping and his eyes closed. He looked asleep—not an uncommon occurrence. Sometimes a third-shift worker, too tired to continue the long drive home, will park his car along the side of the road to catch a few winks before continuing.

This man—sixty-six-year-old Carl Vinson*—though, hadn't fallen asleep.

*****

The stories of Sarah Coleman and Carl Vinson would converge, as they would each travel to the Kent County Morgue for a detailed examination in the form of autopsy (see "Decompression," chapter 1).

The autopsy, although not required under Michigan law (see "What Killed Harry Freiburg?" chapter 3), becomes the essential last chapter in the stories of their lives and their deaths. It is the second stage in a four-stage process in a death investigation that includes (1) case history and scene investigation; (2) autopsy; (3) laboratory tests, such as toxicology screens; and (4) conclusions and determination of cause of death. While Sarah Coleman appeared to have committed suicide, what if her blood contained cyanide? Or a depressed skull fracture? The presence of the latter would ensure that her death, while an apparent suicide, was really a homicide in disguise. Carl Vinson's death appeared to the officer who found him to be the result of a massive heart attack or stroke. His rotund silhouette provides a clue, but in court this would be considered circumstantial evidence at best.

A few stab wounds along his spine, poison in his system, or a traumatic head injury would negate the idea that he died of natural causes.

Such surprises occur often. In the eighties, one of the medical examiners who preceded me did not want to conduct an autopsy on the victim of an apparent fatal car crash, until a stab wound was found in the victim's chest. The Kent County Morgue witnesses many examples where appearance conflicts with reality. Indeed, murderers often weave a forensic fiction to cover the facts. An apparent victim of a house fire has three bullet entrance wounds in the back; an autopsy of an apparent suicide victim (see "The Hand of God," chapter 10), reveals that she was shot in the head twice—an impossibility given the placement of the entrance wounds; and an apparent hanging suicide is proven in fact to be an accidental death, the result of a sexual act called the "choking game." The autopsy separates appearance from reality, fiction from fact.

And the autopsy serves purposes other than bringing murderers to justice. Recently, a young security guard was nearly severed in two when a heavy door fell on him. The plaintiffs in the subsequent civil suit will rely in part on the autopsy results to outline for the judge and/or the jury the extent of the injury so the court can determine the amount of money to award the survivors. The same would be true for victims of car accidents.

An autopsy can be instrumental in proving a person's guilt, but it can also prove someone's innocence. In another recent case, the reexamination of an infant revealed that the child died of natural causes and not the result of child abuse as originally thought by the pathologist who first examined the body. Larry Souter (see "Message in a Bottle," chapter 13) represents the worst manifestation of such a mistake.

Though most fans of *CSI* may understand the basic role of the medical examiner and forensic pathologist, few realize the differences between the appearance of the "telepathologist's" work and the reality of what occurs in a morgue. This book offers readers the opportunity to eavesdrop on my work as a medical examiner, but the story really begins four weeks before the discovery of Coleman and Vinson, in a gym. . . .

*****

Four weeks earlier . . .

A row of televisions tuned to various channels like chatty sentinels watch lifters eke out repetitions below. One television shows *Pumping Iron*, a documentary about Arnold Schwarzenegger's road to winning the 1980 Mr. Olympia title and others in the iron game. The grotesque images of extreme muscularity serve a healthy portion of incentive to the hard-core bodybuilders and power lifters who inhabit the gym, a dish of guilt to others.

Mirrors surrounding the room magically expand its size, creating a pleasant optical illusion of spaciousness; in reality, the room is a little larger than a three-car garage. The propped-open door in the corner admits the warm mid-April day into the room, and a swath of light runs diagonally across the rubber floor tiles. Conversations, always containing the words *sets* and *reps*, blend with the voices of the televisions and the clanking of forty-five-pound plates to create a cacophony unique to the free-weight room.

I notice him sitting on the edge of a bench press, penciling corrections on essays between sets. Tobin is a high school teacher who brings his grading with him when he frequents the gym. His familiar voice breaks through the din when he notices me.

"What's up, Doc?" he asks, slapping the manila file on the floor and rising to his feet.

If the gym had unwritten bylaws, the first item would read, "No discussions of work allowed"; people often lift to escape—a physical cathartic for the stresses of adult life.

Like swimmers caught in an undertow, though, curiosity pulls people toward the ubiquitous question about my profession: "How's work?" And this conversation is no different.

"How's work?" Tobin asks.

"Dead. But brisk," I respond.

Tobin, who knows my background, smiles at the irony in this statement. I am the medical examiner and chief forensic pathologist for Kent County.

"Just out of curiosity, Doc, do you watch *CSI?*" Tobin is curious if real medical examiners enjoy shows that feature their fictional counterparts.

"I've seen a few episodes here and there. The other night, I caught a piece of a *Crossing Jordan* episode, but I didn't watch all of it. So far-fetched."

"How so?"

"A case, solved and neatly packaged in a one-hour segment, but this is not the reality of pathology." I tell an anecdote to illustrate.

A few years ago, I conducted an autopsy on a man, a respected member of the community, who had had a torrid, adulterous affair with an exotic dancer. He was found dead in the month of January, lying under a tree; curiously, no outward signs of suicide were apparent. His family, devastated, found a note which suggested that the guilt of the affair drove him to suicide. As is normal for all suicide cases, I conducted an autopsy to determine the cause of death. The toxicology screen of his blood and other body fluids revealed nothing but the presence of a tranquilizer, at a "therapeutic level"—a dose that shouldn't have killed him. The autopsy revealed that the man died of exposure. He froze to death, casting suffi-cient doubt that the death was suicidal; I ruled the manner of death as "Undetermined."

"A strange way to leave the world," Tobin notes, shaking his head. "I wonder what happened."

"Sometimes, you search for answers, but you don't find any."

"You should write a book." He chuckles. "I can only imagine the sto-ries you have to tell."

THE SIGHTS, THE SOUNDS, THE SMELLS

In the 1984 comedy *This Is Spinal Tap*, Rob Reiner's character, director Marty di Bergi, in his preface to the film, explains that in his "rockumen-tary," he wants to bring to the audience "the sights, the sounds, the smells of a hardworking rock band." Robin Williams's character Shawn, the psy-chologist in *Good Will Hunting*, reiterates the importance of experiential knowledge to Matt Damon's character, Will. A person can read about the Sistine Chapel, he explains to the film's namesake character, but unless a person experiences it firsthand, he cannot possibly know what it smells like.

How can a book create this experience for the reader? Unless the reader happens to be a homicide detective or an acquaintance of a forensic pathologist, he or she will remain relegated to televised reality or books about celebrity autopsies or fantastic cases worked by high-profile pathologists. The reader cannot literally enter the morgue, yet the cases detailed in the chapters of this work offer another possibility: they permit the reader to attend autopsies by proxy. Each chapter contains one or two of my actual cases, autopsied by me, a real-life medical examiner and forensic pathologist. Through each chapter, the reader will experience "the sights, the sounds, the smells . . ."

Years of watching televised "reality" clogs the mind like plaque building up in the arteries of the brain. In the following chapters, readers will discover the points at which fiction and reality converge and diverge. The cases also illustrate the truth in the cliché that "the truth is stranger than fiction." And this is what makes this book unique.

Readers can find a number of books by noted forensic pathologists describing their most fascinating and bizarre cases. Equally plentiful are forensic reference books overloaded with complex terminology. The "True Crime" section of any bookstore would yield a dozen volumes at any given time. While the following narrative contains actual cases, all of which captivate for various reasons, we wanted more than a forensic "casebook"; we wanted to bring the reader into the morgue, to experience the sights, sounds, and smells of forensic medicine; into the world of forensic pathology, a world different from but often more interesting than the image conjured by television "reality." And I wanted a medium to ask the questions that any reader might.

Enter Tobin Buhk, a high school teacher and freelance writer with an interest in forensic pathology. Tobin, who wanted to pursue a medical career in college but chose a different direction, contemplated a career change to an RN or a paramedic. He wanted to "test the waters" by volunteering in the morgue, which made him the ideal medium through which to tell this story.

Anyone who watches television shows like *CSI* knows a little about forensic medicine and may be able to identify basic terms like rigor mortis. A smaller group of avid fans might even be able to explain what lividity is. And an even smaller group may be able to explain how rigor mortis indicates time of death and how lividity indicates placement of the body postmortem. Yet television fails to capture the reality of forensic medicine; in the following pages, inside a real morgue, readers will see things few could ever imagine—things not often, if ever, depicted on television dramas:

What is a "stinker" and what does one smell like?

How can a pathologist dispel the stench of decomposition using nothing but a 12-gauge veterinarian needle and a disposable lighter?

Why would a pathologist remove the eyes of a child who died as the result of a shaking and blows to the head?

Why would a pathologist remove the skin of a victim's thumb?

What metaphor do pathologists use to describe stab wounds?

What is the "golden hour" as it relates to closed head injuries?

How can drowning and a house fire be used to cover up murder?

What is the tattoo design of choice for many risk takers?

How can insects be used to match victims with perpetrators?

In the pages of this book, readers will find the ultimate *Law & Order* episode, but instead of being a passive observer on the couch cradling a bucket of popcorn (in fact, you might not want to eat once you enter this world), you will enter a world few but the initiated are permitted to observe. You will step inside the morgue and participate by proxy, like a tourist of sorts, with the chief medical examiner for Kent County, Michigan, playing the role of tour guide through the world of forensic pathology.

To further create an experiential feel to the text, we've added another unique twist to teach you by proxy. Tobin, to learn about the medical world, shadowed me on call for a year, and his interest in medical science evolved into an interest in telling the stories of a medical examiner. As someone who experienced forensic pathology for the first time, Tobin's questions, concerns, fears, and preconceived notions mirror those of the uninitiated public; like the vast majority of you who have picked up this book, his only previous experience with the underworld of the morgue comes from snippets of television programs. By the time we reach chapter 13, Tobin will have moved from being a passive observer to an active volunteer, answering phones, noting organ weights, sketching wounds, and taking tissue samples.

The following chapters detail actual cases I autopsied and Tobin observed as he visited the morgue several times during the span of a year. What follows is a tour of the world of forensic pathology; we will take you into the morgue, into the circumstances of the victims who find their way into the morgue, and into the their bodies, which harbor the evidence of the forces that led to their demise. You will also be brought into the lives of the professionals whose task consists of answering questions posed by the circumstances, by the families of the deceased, and by the victims themselves. This narrative does not take place in Manhattan or downtown Chicago or Detroit, but in the medium-size, midwestern city of Grand Rapids, Michigan. The following cases do not involve cannibal killers, serial poisoners, or ax murderers. What follows is something far more captivating. What follows is reality.

In the pages to follow, you will watch the business of the morgue, but you will also experience what it feels like to take a tissue sample, hold a human lung, feel the interior of a damaged lung, smell the faint scent of wintergreen Lorann oil, and hear the sound of wet branches snapping when the rib cutters sever the ribs. Few people, except practitioners, have the opportunity to venture into such a place.

There you will experience the uncensored, unabashed, unadulterated world of a medical examiner, just by turning the page.

VARIETY IS THE SPICE OF DEATH

An infinite variety of people exist in the world, and they leave the world in an infinite variety of ways. Homicide, suicide, natural causes, accidental death: these are generic terms that fail to capture the brutal and often bizarre ways that victims reach the morgue. One murder victim came to the morgue encased in a block of ice. Another was chipped from a block of concrete. One victim's killers tried to dismember him. Another killer decapitated and skinned his victim's head.

CSI fans will find much of interest since each chapter contains an "interchapter" of a past case, culled from twenty plus years as a forensic pathologist and medical examiner; these are shocking cases that provide worthy bases for any fictionalized crime drama—cases that may send screenwriters scrambling for their pens:

- A distraught housewife who investigators believed committed suicide, until they discovered two bullet wounds in her head. This depressed wife commits suicide, but how did she shoot herself in the head twice? Or did someone else pull the trigger? (See chapter 10, "The Hand of God.")
- An inmate at a maximum-security prison falls from the third tier of cells and dies from a fatal head injury. An examination reveals a fresh stab wound in his back, so was his "accident" a murder? (See chapter 7, "The Museum of Tattoos.")
- Over a three-day period, an unlicensed physician prescribes his patient over two hundred prescription painkillers, among other medications, and shortly after, she dies. But did she die from this drug cocktail? (See chapter 12, "Bad Medicine.")
- The body of a woman floats to the surface of a lake with sixty pounds of cinder block and chain attached to her legs; her hands are bound behind her back, and duct tape covers her eyes and her mouth. Her killer faces the death penalty if the prosecution can answer one question: Did she drown? (See chapter 4, "The Oxford Lake Death Penalty Case.")
- A bottle convicts a man of first-degree murder after an early-

morning liaison turns deadly for his paramour. Thirteen years later, he walks out of his cell a free man. Why? (See chapter 13, "Message in a Bottle.")

- A worker for the only plant in the United States licensed to produce anthrax dies, the victim of a heart attack. But what caused his heart to stop beating? This question would erupt into a battle between the victim's widow and the Department of Defense. (See chapter 9, "David versus Goliath.")
- A husband admits to strangling his wife but claims that it was an accident, a sex game gone awry. But was it murder? (See chapter 4, "The Rough Sex Case.")
- A driver faces a second-degree murder charge if the prosecution can answer one, vital question: Was his victim a person? (See chapter 6, "The Shortest Chapter.")
- A nineteen-year-old college student's revels have ended after fraternity brothers find him unconscious the morning after a party. He dies later that day, but what killed him? (See chapter 11, "Cyanotic.")

The medical examiner answers these and other questions—unique questions posed by those who cannot speak. He provides answers to those left to reassemble lives fractured by a death. Imagine a room with two doors, one representing the past and the other the future; the room represents the present. But the doors pose a problem. One cannot be opened unless the other is closed. The door to the past, while open, creates a vacuum that keeps the door to the future sealed. Without answers, families cannot close the door to the past and open the door to their future.

Medical examiners help to provide the answers demanded by loved ones and those who speak for a society that rests upon a foundation cemented by justice. In the case of a homicide, the dead can provide vital clues that help to answer the questions How? and Who? Without the answers to these questions, the guilty party may go unpunished, while the victim and the victim's family are left without closure. Without justice, the cement of our society, its foundation, crumbles under its own weight.

If death represents a dividing line between this world and the next, or between something and nothing, or just represents a boundary that some label "the end," most people live on one side of the boundary. A select few work along the margin between life and death. In the pages that follow, we bring you into the forensic pathologist's world to confront the reality of existence along the boundary between life and death. And while on this journey, we hope you will experience the notion of pathos.

In his *Poetics*, the Greek philosopher Aristotle described tragedy, which he maintained must "excite pity and fear" in the observer; this pity and fear results from observing the suffering endured by the play's protagonist. The confluence of drama and life takes place as the audience becomes enrapt with the character's suffering. Life is a drama, and any study of forensic pathology underlines this fact.

One need look no further than a human anatomy chart to discover the inner workings of the human machine, and one chart fits all. All humans, with variation, possess the same machinery. The forensic pathologist must examine the machinery of the deceased to determine why and how the machine stopped functioning, but often little or no definitive evidence exists. As a result, the forensic pathologist must examine facets of the victim's life and the circumstances of the victim's death, and thereby enter that person's human drama. Therefore, a study of forensic pathology is to a degree one type of study of the human drama, namely, human tragedy.

The Greek word for suffering, *pathos*, provides the basis for the word *pathology*. It is an appropriate etymology. A study of forensic pathology is a study of pathos.

Yet reader beware: "reality" does not win beauty pageants. People make incredibly bad choices and do hideous things to themselves and each other. And there are the victims, the pathos of whose stories becomes lost in translation from reality to television and film. They come to the morgue in a variety of ways: they drink too much or overdose on drugs, drive recklessly, shoot, throttle, garrote, asphyxiate, strike, and knife each other or themselves. And each comes with a story—a tragedy to be sure, but one not staged for an audience. A study of forensic pathology is a study of pathos, but don't take our word for it . . . take a look, turn the page. . . .

A NOTE ABOUT VICTIMS AND ANONYMITY

Although the following pages contain many cases that would make excellent fodder for television screenplays, strictly speaking this is not a *CSI*-type book. Rather, much of the power of this book comes from the forensic mysteries posed by victims of heart attacks, closed head injuries, and other accidents. It would appear callous, to say the least, if the authors exposed the identity of someone's grandmother who died of a heart attack. Grandma and her surviving relatives deserve their privacy. Yet these types of cases, rather than those of crazed serial killers, form the basis of the forensic pathologist's work, and it is from such cases that this work derives its power.

The cases that led to significant court action and resulted in significant press coverage are unaltered (all of the interchapter cases and the autopsy of Richard Sullivan, which is detailed in chapter 4, "Red Sky in the Morning"). In other cases, such as victims of heart attacks, suicides, and accidental deaths, to prevent what some may see as a breach in medicolegal ethics, and out of respect for the deceased and their families, we have protected the identity of the victims and those related to the cases. Information not germane to the forensic science, such as names and circumstances, has been altered. Victims who have been given pseudonyms are marked with an "*" upon the first mention of their names. The forensic science, though, and, most important, the morgue scenes described in the following chapters are genuine and unaltered and occurred exactly as depicted.

To underscore the fact that the victims are real people whose ends often came abruptly and in many cases tragically and are not just objects to be studied and marveled at, victims have been given names and identities. They are people, and these are their stories.

DECOMPRESSION

Late Spring 2004
Spectrum Health, Blodgett Campus
East Grand Rapids, Michigan

I use the word *decompression* when referring to an outsider's first foray into the morgue, that moment when the living come in contact with the dead. The word seems appropriate for the experience. Divers decompress to remove noxious gases that can make them sick. In this chapter, Tobin will enter the morgue for the first time; he will decompress. He will begin a one-year tour of duty in the Kent County Morgue to learn about the world of the forensic pathologist from the inside. His exploration began with a telephone call last night.

*****

Last night, fate had cooperated with our project, and somewhere in Kent County an accident or a homicide has provided a subject.

"We have a body," I inform Tobin, deciding to leave the details for the morning, to let the possibilities linger in his mind; I couldn't resist the temptation to raise the drama.

"Great," Tobin responds, his voice flat, devoid of inflection, a tone

21

that belies the delight inherent in his word choice, "great," as if the news has stunned him. "Ah, I don't mean to say I'm glad someone died," he adds to temper what appears his misplaced enthusiasm. He doesn't want to sound too enthusiastic, like some morbid death-junkie, but I know he's thrilled he will see an autopsy. It is an awkward emotion he will experience many times in the next eight months.

"Have you ever had hepatitis shots?" I ask.

"No." A long pause ensues, pregnant with the anxiety I can sense building. I can almost hear him breathing.

No immunization for hepatitis. Today, just about every parent has his/her child immunized against hepatitis B, but these immunizations did not become common medical practice until relatively recently.

"Is this a problem?" he asks.

"Doesn't matter. We use maximum precautions."

"The nervousness bordering on panic feels like a kidney stone rolling in my stomach, Doc."

"When my assistant opens the skull," I explain, trying to calm his fears, "you'll stand in the corner. Hepatitis may become briefly aerosolized with the dust when sawing through the skull."

"Are you sure this won't be a problem?" Tobin asks. The prospect of leaving the morgue with anything other than memories terrifies him.

"There's always a risk." My response doesn't make him feel much better. "But I'm not sure that one can even catch hepatitis this way. I never got hepatitis shots."

Perhaps now he feels better, much better, at least until I finish the story. "I have the antibodies for hepatitis B, so I must have contacted it at one point, but I don't know how. I must have cut myself with an infected knife."

Now his fears become intensified; the stone has begun to pitch in the acids washing against his stomach like waves crashing against a beach. Nonetheless, he's determined, but I imagine he won't sleep much tonight.

We agree to meet in the hospital lobby at eight the next morning.

*****

It is a rainy morning in mid-May; a light drizzle falls from the sky, covering everything with a bright sheen. A heavy blanket of clouds that look like steel wool covers the sky. Symbolic weather, a device so effectively used by authors and Hollywood directors to indicate the psychology of characters or to foreshadow events. Edgar Allen Poe used storms to parallel the mental decay of Roderick Usher in a short story familiar to most school kids, "The Fall of the House of Usher." Shakespeare used stormy weather to great effect in *Macbeth*—the stormy weather always presages and in most cases directly precedes a death. A thunderstorm accompanies the murder of King Duncan, for instance.

For a week now, rain has bombarded Grand Rapids like the eighth plague, swelling the Grand River to a near-record-high 19.5 feet above its normal level. Today, the tapping of the rain eerily provides mood music for Tobin's first journey into the underworld.

Just beyond the parking ramp, the postmodern architecture of Spectrum Health, Blodgett Campus, looms. Formerly, it was Blodgett Memorial Medical Center until it merged with Butterworth Hospital in downtown Grand Rapids to form Spectrum Health. The structure is nestled in the middle of the area's most prestigious suburb, called East Grand Rapids, the home of former president Gerald R. Ford.

The old and new wings coexist, a common juxtaposition that never ceases to impress; the old, red brick a remnant of the days when the Model T was cutting-edge technology, the burnished, brown stainless-steel skin of the modern wing, draped over a poured concrete skeleton, a visual symbol of the space-age technology that grew up with it. Today, the façade looks like a mausoleum. Why did the architects choose such a cold, clinical look? Certainly not to create a becalming effect in visitors and patients. This scenery seems fitting for the drama that will develop this morning; Tobin has come here to research the everyday workings of a real-life forensic pathology laboratory, but in entering the morgue, he will enter a play without an ending, a play for which the ending has not yet been written.

As he gazes up at the hospital's façade, a cloud passes over the sun, creating a brief eclipse. He remembers that someone died last night or he would not be here, and his smile melts away with the sun.

He takes a sip of tea, to relax. He's tired and needs the caffeine, but the butterflies in his stomach have had more than enough. He arrived far too early on Saturday morning to view his first autopsy. He slept little last night; somewhere during his REM sleep, he would later tell me, a nightmare emerged that in retrospect seemed like a bad horror film from the fifties—plenty terrifying at the time, though. I chuckled as months later he recounted the nightmare, although I understand the mental pathology that created it. Countless students from high school kids to medical interns have visited the morgue and watched autopsies, and every one brings with him some preconceived notion of this world, usually born of years watching television thrillers such as *CSI*.

An exotic dancer was stretched out on a stainless-steel table in a stainless-steel room, still in the miniskirt and fishnet stockings native to her trade, her torso covered with blood from the autopsy. The medical examiner, with one deft movement, managed to remove her breastplate (!) with a hideous sucking sound. Tobin watched the macabre tableau from a corner in the room, noting down each detail, when to the shock of everyone in the room, the deceased turned her head, opened her eyes, and began to speak. In a clear soprano, she uttered, "So, Doctor, what happened to me?" as if an interested observer more than a victim. (If this dream followed the cliché of the old horror film, she would have spoken in a pained, raspy horse-whisper.) The whites of her eyes were bright red.

Funny how the mind works, absorbing information, melding that information with images already stored somewhere in the human hard drive, and producing new combinations, which seem often to emerge during the deepest of sleep. Last night in his unconscious hours, Tobin's mind regurgitated a twisted version of a case I had described to him in an earlier conversation: the story of the man who exposed himself to the elements as a method of ending the guilt incurred over his adulterous affair with an exotic dancer. Last night, he saw the dancer, or the image of the dancer his mind had woven.

Those who lack experience think in stereotype. Tobin's first trip into the morgue would prove the veracity of this statement. Without live experience, one reverts to images engineered for television programs or movies. To this point, for instance, Tobin has never viewed a live autopsy; when he thinks of a morgue and the scene of an autopsy, his mind may conjure images of a stainless-steel room and blood-spattered walls (notice the word choice here), and a wall of drawers, each containing one body covered by a bedsheet. A medical examiner opens one of the drawers and pulls back the sheet to reveal . . .

Like most people, Tobin has never seen a pathology lab. He has never even seen a dead body, even a dead relative in a coffin at a funeral.

An analogy will help explain what he will soon experience. Museums tend to objectify the past; people become mere artifacts. The effect is heightened by those fortunate enough to visit or enter historical sites. Divers who visit shipwrecks, for example, subconsciously objectify the wreck, forgetting that a tragedy of some sort sent the oxidizing pile of metal to the bottom with at least some loss of life probable, each victim's story a tragedy. It becomes too easy to romanticize about the artifact, the human element buried under the silt and dust covering the wreck, until the appearance of a shiny white porcelain toilet, glistening like a tooth under the beam of a dive light, provides a sharp reminder that humans once worked and perhaps played here, a sharp reminder that we are all human.

Watching fictional medical examiners on television is like diving on that wreck—the television screen becomes the lens through which the viewer sees a distorted version of reality. Entering the morgue, though, is like all of a sudden coming across that porcelain toilet on the wreck; the visitor can hear, feel, and smell the experience as the human tragedy becomes real. Although it becomes natural to objectify, as a forensic pathologist, you don't ever want to forget the human element, just as a doctor would not want to think of his patients as objects, but as living, breathing people.

The first foray into the morgue, like the first dive on a shipwreck, is the most powerful experience because the observer will not objectify as a practitioner might—although the first-time visitor often wants to steel his nerves by telling himself that the figure on the slab in the morgue is a clay figure. Yet reality will strike Tobin like a cold bucket of water; like many others who enter this world for the first time, he will see these victims not as objects but as people, as someone's father, sister, or child. He may want to forget this reality, but along his journey he will hear a phantom voice, like the collective voice of the deceased who ended their life's stories a floor below us, whisper in his ear that he won't.

At 8:15, I arrive at Spectrum. The hospital is a quiet place this morning, with few bodies moving through the central lobby. I spot Tobin on one of the couches in the lobby, dressed in black jeans, tennis shoes, and a button-down shirt; perhaps there is some message in his black jeans, or perhaps he just didn't know what to wear, although he doesn't have to worry about impressing the people he will soon meet. His attire presents a marked contrast to my pale blue hospital scrub pants topped with a gray T-shirt that bears the word "Atlanta" in bright red letters.

"I don't know about you," I say, "but I can't work without breakfast."

From the quizzical expression on his face, I can predict his dilemma. Breakfast? Should he or shouldn't he? He doesn't want to leave his breakfast on the morgue floor.

"I don't mind telling you, Doc, it's been like a kidney stone rolling around in my stomach all week. I'm nervous as hell."

A grin and a few words will increase the drama a bit. "You should be."

"Should I eat?" His Adam's apple rises, like his blood pressure I suspect, and falls, and he swallows.

"Well, you should eat something."

He decides to take the doctor's advice and makes himself a cup of black tea and selects a croissant from the hospital's self-serve cafeteria— a reserved, safe breakfast; I select something with a little more substance: oatmeal and sausage.

After a little casual conversation, curiosity has bested him. "What subject will you examine this morning?" Tobin asks. Already, somewhat subconsciously, as if his mind contains some defense mechanism that objectifies human death, he has become accustomed to referring to victims as "subjects." It is an attractive defense mechanism.

"*Subjects.* We have two."

Tobin's first experience in the morgue will be a double feature.

The first subject, a sixty-six-year-old male from a northern Michigan county, was found dead in his car, the victim of an apparent heart attack. The second subject, a forty-seven-year-old female from Grand Rapids, is an apparent suicide victim, and thus an autopsy becomes necessary to ensure that her suicide was, in fact, a suicide and not a homicide.

In a few minutes, Tobin will visit these two.

"Are you sure I'll be alright without the hepatitis shots?" Tobin asks between sips of the tea that he cradles between his palms (he hasn't touched his croissant). The question has remained on his mind since we last spoke, like an itch that he can't scratch.

He flinches. "It's like I can feel an invisible bug crawling up my leg."

Although that invisible bug he feels crawling up his leg most likely won't bite him if he follows the necessary precautions, it isn't invisible. It's real. . . .

THORNS!

Remember the scene in *The Wizard of Oz* in which Dorothy and her three companions must pass through a field of pink flowers to reach Oz? The flowers are a trap laid by the Wicked Witch of the West to waylay the trio and prevent them from reaching the Emerald City; with a magic spell, she has turned the flowers into opiates that will put them to sleep.

Now imagine the field filled, not with pink flowers, but with raspberry bushes, tangles of branches, each covered with thorns, reaching out and grabbing at clothes like hungry fingers. A number of dangerous viruses inhabit these raspberry bushes, and one tiny scratch from a thorn could lead to a terminal infection. In fact, merely walking through the field could result in an infection. Imagine this scene, and you imagine the tremendous risks medical examiners assume each day on the job. Pathology is one of the most dangerous branches of the medical profession.

If pathologists signed liability waivers, the documents would be the length of a telephone book and contain a virtual alphabet of germs and viruses that arise during the business we do in the morgue, from the common and treatable to the rare, exotic, and incurable. The names of the insidious critters that crawl in with victims are as scary as the bugs themselves: anthrax; blastomycosis; coccidioidomycosis; diphtheria; a variety of hemorrhagic fevers; hepatitis A, B, and C; human immunodeficiency virus (HIV); legionella; meningococcus; plague; streptococcus; rabies; rickettsiosis; tuberculosis; tularemia; and a host of others.

Many factors cause the increased risk, especially the type of clientele that frequents the world's morgues: pathologists will see more intravenous drug users than others in the medical profession, and blood-borne pathogens such as hepatitis and HIV often plague this population. Microorganisms that inhabit the blood cause the greatest risk to pathologists, since medical examiners work closely with blood and items, such as clothes, that contain blood. For this reason, pathologists often face a greater risk than the physicians who attended the infected patients before death. Any contact with infected blood could lead to an infection. Some of the viruses possess an amazing resilience: hepatitis B can live for as long as a week, even in dried blood. Even the dried crimson streaks on the barrel of the dry-erase marker we use to log organ weights could contain hepatitis virus.

The easiest path to acquiring an infection in the morgue is sustaining a cut from one of the "thorns" that from every corner of the morgue tug at the clothes and skin of pathology department personnel. The morgue's "thorns" primarily consist of the cutting implements we use: scalpels, long knives, and the oscillating blades of the Stryker saws used to cut skulls. An errant cut or slice that penetrates the latex gloves and skin underneath could be a fatal error. And one need not apply much force to create a deep cut with the ultrasharp blades. Combine an exhausted pathologist with a sharp blade, and this scenario could easily occur.

Other "thorns" exist as well in the bodies of the victims; shards of bone from compound fractures, cracked ribs, glass or objects embedded in wounds, such as knife blades—all could cause an accidental cut and lead to an infection.

As I explained earlier to Tobin, somewhere along the way, I must have cut myself, perhaps with a scalpel, because, despite never receiving the sequence of hepatitis immunization shots, I have acquired the antibodies for hepatitis B.

Joel Talsma, with six months experience, the youngest member of the department, tells a harrowing story: during his third autopsy, he sustained a cut on his thumb that required several stitches. The victim's case history read like a résumé of drug use, including heroin, so a blood serology test followed Talsma's cut: the victim's blood tested positive for hepatitis B and C.

Immunizations combat hepatitis B, but no such immunization exists for hepatitis C; Joel's error could have been a deadly one—although after six months and periodic tests, he has not contracted the hepatitis C bug. He smiles nervously when recounting the story; the weekend following the cut, he traveled to Maine on vacation, where he wondered if a deadly disease had taken root in his system. Hepatitis can live for a long, long time in blood. Some evidence suggests that hepatitis can even remain virile in formalin-fixed slides. Yet a very small percentage of those exposed to hepatitis C actually contract the illness.

One does not have to sustain a cut to contract an infection during an autopsy. Swallowing or inhaling an infected drop of blood could lead to an "occupationally acquired" disease; even a drop of blood splashed into an eye (the reason for the plastic face shield on autopsy masks) could prove fatal. Some viruses in the form of "infectious aerosols" can float in the air; swallowing or inhaling them can lead to an infection. When the Stryker saw contacts skull, it throws into the air wisps of bone dust that appear as tiny puffs of white smoke; this bone dust can carry into the air hepatitis as well as other infectious agents, including tuberculosis—one of the most common pathogens transmitted in infectious aerosols. The eyes are a quick inroad to the circulatory system, so contact with infected dust or fluid could also lead to an infection. To prevent this possibility, pathology personnel use facemasks with a wedge-shaped plastic visors.

Dissecting infected lungs can expose medical examiners to tuberculosis. True medical horror stories abound of medical students who, after completing a pathology cycle, test positive on a tuberculin skin test. Paul Davison, the Kent County medical examiner's team's most seasoned pathology assistant, had an experience that underlines the risk of contracting tuberculosis from infected subjects; in the late eighties, he assisted in the autopsy of a patient infected by tuberculosis (TB).

"When we opened his lungs, I knew right away he had TB," Davison explains. A few months later, Paul tested positive and took medication for a year to counteract the exposure. A stealthy bug, tuberculosis often remains undetected until death, often infecting a patient with little or no symptoms. A person could carry TB and not know it.

TB can hover in the air for a protracted period of time, infecting those in the environment. Outbreaks can occur if and when air inhabited by TB escapes the morgue (one reason that we keep the door secured with a key-code entry); one notable outbreak occurred in the Los Angeles Coroner's office when infected air escaped because of poor ventilation. Anyone who visits the Kent County Morgue will see the rather conspicuous sign above the scale: "No Eating or Drinking in the Morgue." At first sight, the sign's message might seem strange—who would want to eat or drink in the morgue? The prohibition exists not to prevent those with iron constitutions from enjoying a cup of coffee in the morning, but to prevent a possible infection; with each sip, infectious agents could enter the lungs. Pathologists of the past used to mask the smell of decomposition by smoking cigars. Yet, pathologists now realize, each inhalation could lead to an infection if microscopic, aerosolized bugs enter the lungs.

Morgue personnel also face the risk of another thorn—toxins. The most common toxic agent encountered in the morgue—formaldehyde—enters not as an unwelcome interloper but as a tool for preserving remains. Yet long-term and overexposure to this chemical can produce a variety of problems from mild skin irritation to lung cancer. As a rule of thumb, if one can smell formaldehyde, which produces an odor only in dangerous amounts, the exposure has exceeded the maximum safe limit set by the Occupational Safety and Health Administration (OSHA).

Other toxins, such as cyanide, sometimes enter the morgue as interlopers. Cyanide ingested by a suicide victim creates a major risk to those performing the autopsy. The victim's stomach converts cyanide into a dangerous, poisonous substance called hydrocyanic gas, which, when inhaled, can prove fatal. Opening and dissecting a stomach that contains hydrocyanic gas places morgue personnel at risk. Likewise, commercial pesticides such as metallic phosphides present in a victim's stomach can pose a risk; inhalation of these substances could leave the medical examiner feeling queasy and with a headache.

Of course, medical science and knowledge continually evolve. During the sixteenth century, outbreaks of black plague periodically occurred throughout Europe, leaving the era's doctors stymied and desperate for a solution. Wild theories circulated. Some believed that wearing garlands of garlic might ward off the plague (interestingly, the garlic may have isolated the wearer and thus kept him from the plague), while others believed that a peeled onion placed strategically in an infected place would absorb the infection. Pathologists once experienced a "dark age" as well—until the nineteen eighties, practitioners sometimes did not wear masks or gloves while handling human remains. I have a photograph of myself next to a body, and you can see that I'm examining the body with ungloved hands. As a result, dangerous exposures occurred. My natural hepatitis immunization offers the proof.

Forensic pathologists face the constant risk of occupational exposure to dangerous pathogens, but this risk may not be the greatest one they face. The profession of medical examiner also poses a more insidious risk, an emotional risk that few people realize.

Forensic pathologists deal with innumerable tragic situations. In fact, almost every death is tragic. The ones that get to you the most are the deaths of children, especially the ones the same age as your own children. You get a sick feeling in your stomach, followed by relief that it wasn't your kid, then guilt for feeling that way. The absolute worst are the child abuse cases. It's a tribute to human monstrosity that an adult could hit, kick, scald, slam, or otherwise maim a helpless child. Your gut reaction is you'd like to have just five minutes with the perpetrator in a closed room; let them try it on someone their own size.

All you can do is take a deep breath and realize that these emotions are useless; the best thing you can do for the dead child is to perform a thorough autopsy, document the injuries, and collect evidence in order to present testimony to put the murderer away and to prevent him/her from ever injuring another child.

You also empathize with the parents of the dead child (whether the death was homicidal, accidental, or natural), but your feelings of sadness must be controlled if you are to do your job. You have to build an emotional wall around yourself, and, while you remember that the body you are examining was a person with people who loved him/her, if your emotions get the better of you, you can't be objective and you'll do no one any good. You might cause harm.

This isolation of emotions can take its toll in your personal life. When you're dealing with your own loved ones, especially your spouse, you must remember to become a loving human being again and let yourself out of that self-imposed state of emotional isolation. I know what happens if you don't. It's cost me two marriages.

*****

After we finish breakfast, I lead Tobin to the basement floor of the hospital, where the morgue is located. We figuratively as well as literally enter the underworld, and as we travel through beige cinder-block corridors, Tobin has now become a tourist with several well-known literary parallels. In Greek mythology, Hercules traveled to the underworld to complete one of his twelve labors—to conquer and bring to the surface a three-headed dog called Cerberus—and in Dante's *The Divine Comedy*, the Roman writer Virgil, as tour guide, leads Dante through the various layers of Hell.

After a few turns, we reach the morgue, guarded by key-code access. The gray, steel door hides an entirely new world—a fascinating, wondrous, yet terrible world. Tobin is about to enter a *Law & Order* episode . . . for real.

And, as the yellow symbol on the door reminds us, we are about to enter a biohazardous zone.

A steel plate on the door reads

Area BA
Room 48

"Why would someone need this type of security in a morgue?" Tobin asks. "Wait, don't say it. Because people are dying to get in." His nervousness masked by a cliché joke.

"Because it contains evidence."

The morgue suite consists of several small rooms constructed of beige cinder block similar to the architecture most would associate with schools. The relatively low ceilings give the rooms and the sole passage linking the rooms together a compressed, boxed-in feeling. Taken together, the suite feels like a bomb shelter or a bunker.

Waiting in the conference room is an older man in a three-piece suit, a funeral director from Alcona County who made the three-hour drive to bring in the sixty-six-year-old man found dead in a car. Blodgett's pathologists have agreements to do selected autopsies for many northern and western Michigan counties that do not have forensic pathologists of their own. Inside a glass case on one side of the room sit various caliber bullets lined up like soldiers at inspection. The man explains that he will wait for the body in the conference room.

I lead Tobin down the small corridor past a bathroom and into the morgue itself—lined with beige tiles—where the sight of the two bodies, fully clothed, lying on the stainless-steel tables, stops him in his tracks at the entrance to the morgue. The upbeat sound of the jazz music emanating from the stereo on one side of the room must seem incongruous to the first-time visitor. Perhaps Tobin would find something from Wagner more appropriate. A strong odor of disinfectant fills the room (not the stench of death that one might associate with the stereotypical image).

After a few seconds of surveying the scene in silence, Tobin manages to utter in a hushed voice, "And there they are." He is speaking in hushed tones, like one might use in a church or a library.

"I wanted you to decompress," I tell him. Tobin stands silently looking at the body on the table nearest the corridor.

Decompression—the perfect word for this context. Divers also refer to this process of removing harmful gases from their systems accumulated during dives as "off-gassing." Tobin is now in the process of decompressing, of becoming acclimated to the world of forensic pathology, a world that will bridge the gap between the living and the dead.

I introduce him to Jason Chatman, who will assist in this morning's autopsies, and then leave to change in the adjacent bathroom, giving Tobin time to survey the scene and ask Jason a few questions.

Along one side of the morgue, a large stainless-steel door leads to the cooler. Two desks, one with a computer, are situated on either side of the cooler door. The opposite wall contains two workstations, which look like giant stainless-steel workbenches; between them, suspended from the ceiling, a large scale for weighing organs dangles. Along another wall, a doorway leads to an evidence room. Tobin's examination of the morgue is only cursory; the bodies captivate his attention. They lie on two large, stainless-steel tables that glitter under the fluorescent lights. Each table contains a large basin at one end, the plumbing of each basin plunging into the tiled floor beneath.

He circles the steel tables containing the bodies. The bodies come to the morgue exactly as they are found at the scene—these two are fully clothed. The victim lying on the table nearest to him—the apparent heart attack victim named Carl Vinson*—is wearing blue jean shorts and a checkered short-sleeve, button-down shirt, unbuttoned to reveal two EKG pads still adhered to his chest where an attempt to revive him occurred. A thick layer of hair covers his chest and abdomen like steel-gray lichen, and even while prone, his abdomen protrudes—in life, this man was never cheated at mealtimes. His deep-set eyes, framed by bushy, gray eyebrows that jut out from his brow ridge like weeds jutting over a cliff, are closed and, while not smiling, he has a placid expression that suggests he died not an altogether painful death. The dark, brunette roots under his gray hair indicate his hair color before age took control. His head is propped up by a large white plastic block—a large sign tacked onto one of the two bulletin boards on either side of the refrigerator door warns "Security: Please make sure that the Funeral Homes do not take our head blocks," which is somewhat of a problem. A reddish purple bruise-like discoloration covers the back of his neck and head.

A few feet away on a second table lies a woman—the apparent suicide victim—Sarah Coleman.* A red plastic bag covers her head—the bag, fastened onto her head with gray electrical tape, obscures her features and creates a good deal of suspense as one wonders what she looks like under the makeshift shroud. At first glance, the uninitiated visitor might surmise that she shot herself in the head and the police covered her head with the plastic bag to secure the mess. As explained later, though, this is not the case. She is wearing a white, striped blouse, purple shorts, and Reebok tennis shoes, and her hands are almost clenched, like she's clawing at the air.

"So is it Dr. Chatman?" Tobin asks.

---

*Denotes the first use of a pseudonym in each chapter. To maintain the privacy of victims and in the interest of good taste and professional ethics, some victims are given pseudonyms and some nonessential facts of their cases are changed. The circumstances of their deaths and the forensic science are real and unchanged. Victims from cases that led to significant court action are not given pseudonyms.

"Mr. Chatman," he replies.

"Does this ever bother you, or have you become somewhat numbed to the sight of dead bodies?" Tobin, somewhat numb himself, asks Jason. Perhaps after the initial shock, the sight of the bodies doesn't bother him as much as he thinks it should, and this realization bothers him. But the cutting has yet to begin.

He shakes his head. Chatman, the twenty-nine-year-old assistant, viewed his first autopsy as a sophomore in high school, which served as a precursor to his health science degree from Grand Valley State University, a Grand Rapids–based institution. After college, he went to work in the morgue, where he has assisted in autopsies for the last four years. One thing does still bother him, though, he explains—a child or an infant, such as a Sudden Infant Death Syndrome (SIDS) or a victim of child abuse. For Tobin, the mere thought of a child stretched out on one of the morgue's two stainless-steel autopsy tables creates an eerie sensation on the back of his neck, like a cold, invisible finger lightly running to the base of his skull as he thanks the fates that today he will see no children.

"They don't smell like I expected," Tobin remarks.

Jason explains that these bodies are "fresh" (both found yesterday, Friday), and therefore they lack the usual stench associated with putrefaction. Instead, the heavy disinfectant in the morgue pervades, preempting all other odors, hanging in the air like a clinical Glade without the pleasant smell of flora.

I toss Tobin a gown and slip covers for his shoes.

"Why do I need these for my shoes?" Tobin asks, bewildered.

Everyone who enters the morgue wears shoe covers to shield the shoes from the spots of blood that may get onto the floor during the autopsy. This prevents a pair of bloody shoes that might leave friends and family wondering, and also prevents the potential spread of diseases like hepatitis.

As Tobin slips the coverings over his shoes and begins tying his gown, Jason Chatman hands him a surgical mask that he slips over his ears and that covers his nose and mouth; a plastic visor shields his eyes. The clock on the wall reads 9AM—time to begin. Tobin sits in the chair in the corner of the room where he can observe the proceedings and jot notes on a yellow legal pad.

And the procedure begins . . .

Jason begins the process with a superficial examination: taking measurements and snapping shots of the body with a Sony Mavica digital camera—pending the conclusion of each autopsy, each subject is a potential murder victim. Before the autopsy, Jason collects an assortment of evidence that would prove useful should Vinson have met his end in any other way than a natural death. A search through his pockets turns up some personal papers that Jason places on the table used to hold the evidence. The personal papers, like a slap in the face, remind one that this man had a story extending beyond the margins of the autopsy table.

While Jason removes Vinson's clothes, I begin the narration of the circumstances of Vinson's case into a handheld recording device that looks like a cellular phone. "Sixty-six-year-old, Caucasian male, 227 pounds, found slumped over in an automobile . . ."

Jason places each item removed into a large, green plastic bag and tucks the bag under the table. More digital photos of the nude corpse with the Sony Mavica follow, and every detail, such as the absence of earrings, is noted for the record. The next detail noted is the purple blob on the man's left shoulder—a faded tattoo that looks like an oak leaf. The blob excites Tobin's curiosity, lifting him from the chair.

"A tattoo," he notes as he leans in to study the blob. "The lettering . . . looks like Chinese script."

In fact, the lettering is a phrase in Vietnamese, which, together with the man's age, suggests that he acquired the tattoo during America's campaign in Southeast Asia, approximately thirty to thirty-five years ago.

Next, Jason will extract various bodily fluids. Tobin cringes as Jason sticks the hypodermic needle into Vinson's right eye to collect the eye fluid, or vitreous humor. This fluid will provide an accurate measure of the level of ethanol in the system when the fluids are sent to the toxicology lab for an analysis. The level of ethanol would indicate if Vinson died from an overdose of alcohol. The vitreous humor is also used to determine the level of electrolytes (e.g., potassium, calcium, sodium, chloride, and so on) and glucose, which would indicate if the victim suffered from diabetes or if he was dehydrated when he died.

Tobin watches, his mouth agape, as Jason produces an oversized hypodermic needle about eight inches in length. He studies Vinson's hip and then jabs the needle into the crease between the upper thigh and the torso—blood from the femoral vein is collected and sent to the toxicology lab. Blood tells no lies, and the subsequent toxicology screen will indicate if Vinson had taken anything prior to death that might alter the probability that he died a natural death. If the toxicology screen reveals the presence of narcotics beyond a clinical (nonlethal) dose, a drug overdose or even homicide must be considered.

A sample of DNA is collected, just in case, on a special card. The card, subdivided into four sections, each section containing a circular drop of Vinson's blood, looks like the four of hearts in an oversized deck of playing cards or a wild card in an UNO deck.

Jason removes the head block; he and I pull Vinson onto his side to examine the underside of his torso. The autopsy routine always includes an examination of the victim's back for gunshot or knife wounds. We've had cases that appear like natural deaths until we look at the back and find a knife wound. Like the back of his head and neck, Vinson's entire back has a dark purple, bruised appearance caused by a process known as *lividity*. Without the blood pressure caused by a heart pumping, gravity pulls the blood to that part of the body nearest the ground. The presence of lividity provides the forensic pathologist with a clue as to the position of the body at the time of death. If a victim dies while lying prone, the back of his torso, head, and neck will appear purple. Lividity in the face and front of the torso would indicate the victim died while lying facedown. Lividity along one side of the body would indicate that the victim died while lying on his side. Vinson, the lividity suggests, died on his back.

Tobin moves back to a safe distance, back to the chair in the corner of the morgue, while Jason begins the Y-incision. With a scalpel, he draws a red line from the left shoulder to a spot over the sternum (breastbone), from the right shoulder to the same spot, and from the spot over the sternum to just above the pubic hair, creating the "Y." The scalpel cuts through the epidermis with ease.

At first, the cut looks like a thick line drawn by a red Magic Marker; as Jason extends the cut, the line opens to reveal the bright yellow fatty tissue under the skin, and a line of blood runs down each shoulder, creating a small, viscous pool on the table. The relative lack of blood often strikes visitors like Tobin as surprising; preconceived notions of the autopsy often have blood bursting from cuts, splattering the walls, but again, without the body's engine working to create pressure, the body's life fluid remains static.

Jason pulls aside the flaps of skin created by the incision—he places the triangular flap at the top over Vinson's face. Under the epidermis, the muscle looks like raw meat as the dirty white bone of the rib cage and breastplate or sternum come into view. With a long-handled "rib cutter," shears with a curved end or beak, which look exactly like a shears used to prune hedges, Jason digs into the rib cage and begins snapping through the ribs, making sounds like the crunching of wet twigs. He moves through the ribs with relative ease; after he finishes severing the ribs, with his fingers he pulls out the breastplate and places it into a large, shiny steel bowl, like an oversized wok, positioned between Vinson's legs. A strong, bitter, pungent smell begins to hover in the air.

Jason begins to remove the internal organs, beginning with the heart and lungs, which he removes as one entity—a blood-red mass that he places into another bowl. Next, the liver, then the kidneys, which are a deep purple color and the size of a small fist. He will eventually remove everything, placing the organs into steel bowls and setting them on a workstation, where they will be dissected in search of how Vinson died. Tobin rises from his seat, growing braver with each moment, and begins to drift toward the autopsy table as Jason begins work on the intestines, which look like a pile of moist hot dogs.

As Jason continues to remove the intestines, Tobin drifts toward the workstation where the examination of Vinson's internal organs has begun; first, each organ is weighed, the weight noted on the white board next to the workstation, and then each is dissected with a long-bladed knife that looks like a long, thin meat cleaver. After the autopsy, the weights will be entered on the official report.

Next to the workstation on which the dissection occurs is a cabinet containing medical paraphernalia, such as boxes of empty cassettes used to collect organ samples, and a collection of bottles. The bottles, lined up like silent sentinels standing at attention, silently eavesdrop on the proceedings in the morgue; a one-liter bottle of Absolut vodka in front commands attention and is often the first one of the collection recognized.

"Liquor bottles?" Tobin, who has come to stand behind my shoulder to observe the dissection of the internal organs, has noticed the bottles, his inner musings seeping into verbal expression. The bottles provide the ultimate conversation piece, because visitors to the morgue always find the presence of the liquor bottles bizarre and incongruous, suggesting a forensic pathologist's "sideboard" from which he will take a few sips during a tough case.

Far from incongruous, though, the bottles provide a common denominator for how many victims enter the morgue, feet first. Each came in with a victim, most carried by an intoxicated individual who fell, sustaining a fatal head injury. They fell, but they protected the booze.

"Each bottle in that cabinet tells a story," Jason adds. Not all of them bad stories, though. "One of the bottles," Jason points to a bottle of Thunderbird apple-flavored wine, "was used to celebrate Doc's fiftieth birthday." It is unopened.

Much of the examination of organs is "exclusion." The body's *context*—the scene of the death—provides a preliminary suggestion of cause of death. Context is everything, and it is a concept that will reappear throughout the following chapters. This victim's context, found slumped over in his car and with a history of hypertension, would suggest he may have died of a "fatal cardiac arrhythmia," but this *mode* of death leaves no trace, so a detailed examination of the organs must occur to exclude any other possibility. Each organ will be weighed, dissected, and examined.

As each organ is examined, evidence for a "fatal cardiac arrhythmia" mounts. The kidneys exhibit signs of hypertension. A normal kidney would have a shiny surface; the surface of this kidney is pitted and refracts light—a sure sign of hypertension or diabetes. I slice through the kidney, creating cross sections, each of which is examined. During the examination of each organ, a small piece is cut and placed into a Ball jar filled with formaldehyde and labeled with Vinson's assigned number, EA-xx-xxx (each autopsy subject is assigned a seven-digit number for reference).

The "stock jar" will contain pieces of the internal organs; the hospital will store the stock jar for three years in case the need for further evidence arises, after which time the jar's contents will be disposed of. Five hundred and fifty autopsies a year, five hundred and fifty Ball "stock jars"— the reader can only imagine where the hospital keeps 1,650 jars and what the "stock room" must look like . . . walls and walls filled with the jars. A long line of bright pink plastic boxes called cassettes sits on a nearby shelf; into these cassettes is placed a piece of each organ: from these, glass slides for microscopic examination will be prepared.

The base of the workstation contains three pedals that look like piano pedals. The pedals trigger the recording device located at the top of the workstation, which looks like a giant calculator covered with a blood-spattered plastic sheet. At the beginning of the examination, I input Vinson's assigned number and so begins the oral record of the autopsy. With the three pedals, labeled "record," "play," and "replay," I control the information input into the official record.

Vinson's heart also supports the fact that he suffered from hypertension, which adds to the mounting evidence that he died, not from something as yet unrecognized, such as ingestion of arsenic or an overdose of heroin, but of a fatal cardiac arrhythmia, which is one condition that can arise from a hypertensive heart.

A heart attack is a generic term for a myocardial infarct, or permanent damage (scarring) in the heart muscle (myocardium). With an inadequate blood flow to the myocardium, often caused by blockage in the coronary arteries, the heart does not receive sufficient oxygen. Starved of oxygen, it begins to die.

The presence of one or more myocardial infarcts indicates that the victim suffered from one or more events that led to a reduced blood flow, which can include blockage of a coronary artery from atherosclerosis— often with a superimposed blot clot or spasm (narrowing of the artery caused by the contraction of the smooth muscle in the vessel wall).

Myocardial infarcts can also lead to many nonlethal maladies. A ventricular tachyarrhythmia is a rapid heartbeat that begins in the two lower chambers of the heart, called ventricles; a supraventricular tachycardia (SVT) is a rapid heartbeat that comes from the atria, AV nodes, or both, which lie above the ventricles; an atrial fibrillation is an irregular, often rapid heartbeat; and an atrial flutter is a rapid contraction in the upper chambers called atria, despite a regular heartbeat.

Whether or not an infarct is present, heart muscle deprived of oxygen can be the source of a lethal arrhythmia, either ventricular tachycardia or ventricular fibrillation.

Because heart attack is the number one cause of death in America, the Kent County Morgue receives a number of victims each year taken by this physiological culprit. The evidence in Vinson's body suggests that he will become another notch in this fiend's stick of casualties.

Hypertension creates an abnormally large heart. The heart is weighed, then placed onto the workstation, where the mass, the noblest organ associated with human emotion since humans first began expressing emotions with words, looks like a slab of raw meat, a raw steak: a blend of red shades encircled by a ring of white.

The weight is noted on the white board; at 570 grams, Vinson's heart is enlarged—another characteristic of hypertension—far beyond the range of 370–380 grams that would be considered normal for a man of his size. With no obesity present, the heart should account for approximately 0.5 percent (or 1/200) of the total body mass.

As I begin the dissection of Vinson's heart, a putrid, sour stench fills the room—directly behind, Jason is opening the intestines in the washbasin at the end of the autopsy table. Tobin, still standing behind me, tries to breathe through his nose, but the smell seems to have descended like a cloud. Again, his thoughts become audible as he utters, "What is that stench?"

"Feces," Jason informs, "and this guy is full of it," he says as he stretches out the intestines, foot by foot, and slices through them. "Even more than Dr. Cohle."

This banter during the autopsy underlines the matter-of-fact procedure of the work, but it also acts as an emotional buffer; how could a person do this type of work if he dwelled on the fact that the body on the table could be a friend, a relative, or a lover?

Jason chuckles as Tobin retreats to the other side of the morgue, where he stands next to the table on which lies Sarah Coleman, the apparent suicide victim.

The room is well ventilated, Jason explains to Tobin, with the noxious vapors pushed by air pressure toward the corner of the room—where he's standing. So, in a second attempt to escape the stench, Tobin moves back toward the entrance to the morgue.

The time has arrived for Jason to open the skull to access Vinson's brain; it is time for Tobin to retreat to avoid any bone dust and potential hepatitis infection. He sinks farther back into the corridor leading into the autopsy room when he notices Jason reaching for the Stryker saw resting in a cradle under the table on which Vinson's body is lying.

Jason slices across Vinson's head with a scalpel, his incision slicing through the scalp to the bone; with a ripping sound, he pulls the face forward and down to expose the top of the skull where he will excise the calvarium (skull cap) and access the brain. With a high-pitched whirring sound, the saw cuts through the skull. Wisps of dust form small clouds in the air and tiny pieces of skull fly as he works the Stryker saw through the skull. The saw, which looks like a tiny circular saw with a disk the size of a silver dollar for a blade, is unique—its blade moves back and forth. The Stryker is also used for removing casts.

Jason's forearms flex as he works the Stryker across the top of the skull, called the calvarium. After a few minutes of intense labor, he removes the calvarium to expose the brain, off-white with the appearance of cauliflower or coral. The brain looks like . . . well, a brain. Jason probes inside the skull and removes the brain, placing it in a bowl and setting it onto the workstation surface. He replaces the Stryker into its niche below one end of the autopsy table.

While the brain is weighed and its weight recorded on the white board next to the workstation, Jason removes a thin, white sheet coating the inside of Vinson's skull—the dura. Under the dura—the membrane that separates the brain from the inside of the skull—Jason will search for signs of skull fractures. He doesn't expect to find any—with the context in which the body was found and Vinson's medical history, the cause of death appears to be heart disease, supported by the forensic evidence of hypertension: the pitted surface of the kidneys and the enlarged heart. Yet the autopsy protocol requires that no dura remains left unturned . . . just in case. And the brain could provide additional evidence that Vinson succumbed to the ravages of heart disease. Under the brain, the skull is a pale blue-white color with a central indentation where the spinal column begins.

Using a long-bladed knife, I breadloaf the brain into cross sections and examine each carefully for any evidence that may support the theory that Vinson died from a fatal cardiac arrhythmia or any evidence that could counter it. Without the obstruction of bone, the blade slices through the brain easily and without sound. Each of the slices is examined, one of which contains a spot—a greenish yellow blot about half the size of a dime—dead brain tissue called an infarct. This is a telltale sign that at one point Vinson had suffered from a stroke and more evidence to support the theory that he died from a fatal cardiac arrhythmia.

Ninety minutes later, case closed: Vinson officially joins the alarming number of American men who die each year of a fatal heart arrhythmia— his heart ceased beating effectively. A heart arrhythmia is a disturbance in the regular rhythm of the heartbeat that may be harmless and occur without problem or may prove fatal and result in sudden death. It is estimated that over two million Americans suffer from an irregular heartbeat (called atrial fibrillation) of some type. According to the American Heart Association, most who suffer from arrhythmias suffer from atrial fibrillation, which occurs more often in men than women regardless of age. Interestingly, the presence of atrial fibrillation, or an ineffective "quivering" of the atria, increases the risk of a stroke by a factor of five, and causes 15 to 20 percent of all strokes. An estimated 335,000 sudden cardiac deaths caused by coronary disease occur each year.[1] With his cause of death established, Vinson became another victim claimed by the mass murderer known as hypertension.

Back on the autopsy table, Vinson's body awaits the final procedure of the autopsy. The large, gaping hole left by the Y-incision reveals an empty trunk cavity, which makes Vinson's body look like an empty shell—like the being once inside molted and left this shell of flesh as a reminder of its presence. A red-tinged flap of skin, the underside of the face, is stretched downward to reveal a gaping hole in the skull, also empty. As I look at the clock, I realize that it took just ninety minutes to hollow out a human being completely and examine the parts that make this amazing biological machine function.

Jason readies the corpse for the final phase of the autopsy by lining the trunk cavity with a large, white plastic bag. The bag, called the entrail bag, will hold the dissected organs to which will be added embalming fluid. The preserved, dissected organs will be buried with the body. I bring each bowl containing the dissected organs (minus the pieces placed in the stock jars and the cassettes but including the cross sections of the brain) and pour it into the bag-lined cavity. After the last bowl, Jason replaces the breastplate and closes the three flaps of skin created by the Y-incision.

Using a long spool of white string and a long needle, Jason begins stitching closed the Y-incision. The needle perforates the skin with a popping sound, and after a few stitches, the string has turned from stark white to bright pink. Next, he stuffs a handful of cotton into the skull, to absorb any fluids, replaces the section of skull, and closes the incision. With a large bottle, he next douses the corpse with a pink fluid and scrubs the body to remove any bloodstains that the autopsy may have left. He explains how carefully they try to keep the body clean for the funeral home. The blood and foam funnel into a tube that runs into the floor and from the floor it runs into the city sewer system, which again raises the specter of blood-borne pathogens. Jason wraps the corpse in a white sheet and lifts the bundle of sheet onto a red velvet bag lying open on another table. Vinson will wear this red velvet shroud to the funeral home.

Jason wheels the gurney into the refrigerator; the funeral director in the snappy suit waiting in the adjacent room will collect the body from the refrigerator's entrance to the hospital corridor. As Jason moves the corpse, I open the refrigerator door so Tobin can see how fiction and reality diverge. Years of watching *Law & Order* shows has in many viewers preprogrammed the image of a stainless-steel wall containing drawers like file cabinet drawers that slide forward. This refrigerator, though, is just a dimly lit room, the size of a small bedroom, with shelves lining the back wall on which rests another body wrapped in a white sheet, like a cocoon waiting to be opened in the morgue.

"The refrigerator seems small, very small," Tobin remarks, as Jason rolls his eyes.

While a curious spectator for the first autopsy, Tobin will not escape an autopsy without a job. Most visitors to the morgue are assigned a duty, which pulls them over the invisible line between observer and practitioner. For today, Tobin's job will consist of jotting down the organ weights as I read them from the board. This is a harmless job, but it is difficult to write with a ballpoint pen while wearing the latex gloves.

In preparation for the second autopsy, Jason takes measurements of subject two, the suicide victim who entered the morgue with a gift-wrapped head (her head masked by a red plastic bag and a few circles of duct tape). Next, he photographs the body, snapping pictures with the morgue's resident digital camera. He takes several pictures of the red bag fastened to her head by the dirty gray tape.

After he finishes, the dictation begins, as the details of the apparent suicide victim, a forty-seven-year-old white female, are noted into the handheld recording device.

"Why the red bag? Did she shoot herself?" Tobin asks, wondering if investigators covered her head with the bag to contain bodily fluids.

"No," I respond. "Death by asphyxiation." The victims arrive at the morgue exactly as they are found—in this case, with the suicide weapon, the red bag, still in place.

"Asphyxiation," Tobin mutters and looks at the red plastic bag covering her head, sealed around her mouth—her death mask and the method she chose to end her earthly existence. "Seems like an odd way to go," he remarks.

"We see this method with older subjects," I explain. "It's not common, but we have seen cases in which the subject hanged himself with his feet on the floor."

"Where there's a will, there's a way," Jason interjects with a cliché perfectly suited for the context.

"How many suicide victims leave notes?" Jason asks Tobin. "Take a guess."

Tobin shrugs. "Forty percent."

Jason shakes his head. "Between eighteen and twenty percent."

The number is surprisingly low.

Sarah Coleman, though, did leave a note, a letter really, detailing her reasons for ending her own life. Her note is her final line of dialogue; the autopsy made necessary by suicide marks the end of her life's tragedy.

Reading the copy of Sarah Coleman's suicide note makes a person feel guilty, like you're eavesdropping—hell, you are eavesdropping—on an intensely personal letter, a front-row seat to the final act of Sarah Coleman's tragedy. Drenched with pathos, the note slaps you in the face with its raw, intimate humanity. Articulate vocabulary and neat hand-writing suggest that in life Coleman was an educated and intelligent woman. The note, sent to her brother and his family, contains her rationale for the suicide; she explains that she has decided to take her own life because of her ailing financial situation. Coleman details the method she has chosen to die: carbon monoxide inhalation in her automobile—an old beige Caprice Classic. Police found the car in her garage prepared for a suicide attempt, then found Coleman slumped over in a chair in the living room of her Grand Rapids home, her head covered by the bag. Why she chose to suffocate herself with a plastic bag is a mystery that will never be solved.

Jason snaps a few photographs of her death mask before he removes the plastic bag—a moment filled with anticipation as one wonders what she looks like under the makeshift mask. He cuts the duct tape and snaps a few more digital photographs. Like Vinson, her eyes are closed, her mop of wavy auburn hair, streaked with renegade strands of gray, seems disheveled, and under a long, curved nose, her mouth hangs agape as if gasping for a breath. Compared with the serene expression on Vinson's face, suggesting he passed peacefully, her facial expression suggests that she didn't, that her chosen method of suicide created a degree of agony. A white, crystalline cloud—frothy pulmonary edema—fills her mouth. The presence of the froth, coupled with her hands, which appear clenched, presents a picture of a violent death; the presence of the froth, though, does not indicate a violent death, but that she died of depression of the respiratory center of her brain—a similar mechanism to a drug overdose. In other words, the part of her brain that controls respiration ceased functioning. Jason disappears into one of the adjacent rooms and returns with a white plastic bag—an evidence bag.

Jason places Sarah Coleman's death mask inside the evidence bag and then begins to undress her. He removes her tennis shoes, socks, blouse, shorts, and purple underwear; he places each item into a large plastic bag and then tucks the bag under the autopsy table. As Jason undresses her, I explain to Tobin what I will look for in this examination of subject two; again I will look for any evidence to contradict the apparent cause of death—asphyxia by suffocation.

Jason and I turn her body onto its side to examine the back. Like Vinson, her back appears mottled with bruises, the result of the blood pulled downward by gravity as she lay prone in the morgue. Next, the collection of body fluids—vitreous humor from the eye socket, blood from the hip. Jason makes the Y-incision, with a scalpel drawing a line down her torso to a spot just above the pubic hair.

From the first cut, her autopsy is procedure, routine, as nothing contradicts the finding of death by asphyxiation. At just under an hour, Coleman's autopsy takes much less time than Vinson's, because Vinson had more physical ailments, each of which required careful examination. Coleman committed suicide—asphyxia by suffocation—and nothing in the autopsy contradicted this finding. Nor did the autopsy reveal the existence of any disease; if Sarah Coleman hadn't ended her life prematurely, she most likely would have lived a long, healthy existence.

As Jason stitches up the incisions, Tobin falls back into the desk chair and picks up the suicide note encased in a plastic sheet. He appears exhausted, the emotional strain of viewing his first autopsy leeching away his physical strength. "In many ways," he observes as he notices me standing behind him, "the suicide note is harder to take than the cutting, although none of this bothers me as much as I think it should bother me, and this in turn bothers me."

"Each subject that comes into the morgue is a tragedy," I explain, "and you don't want to forget that fact, but when you leave the morgue, you want to leave those tragedies behind; you can't let them ruin your life." Still, Tobin won't forget the images he saw today—they will remain indelibly stamped in his memory.

"Next time," I pat Tobin on the back, "we're going to get you more involved."

Time to disrobe.

No established, prescribed order for removing the scrubs exists, but Tobin, motivated by a morbid fear of contracting some contagion during his visit to the morgue, decides on an order that will least likely bring him in contact with any spots of blood: first, the blue gown goes into the laundry hamper, then the booties covering the shoes, the latex gloves, and finally the mask, which goes into the biohazard hamper for disposal.

From the hampers, he travels down the corridor to the bathroom; he washes his hands with the special antibacterial soap by the sink, and then again with the regular liquid soap from a wall dispenser.

We emerge from the morgue around noon. We find our way through the labyrinth of cinder-block tunnels to the hospital entrance. The rain-drenched morning has melded into a sunny day (another interesting instance of symbolism), the remnants of the morning's precipitation evident in the humidity that has descended on the city in place of the rain. Tobin's pace seems to be quickening as he nears his car. He's spent part of the day with the dead, now all he wants is to rush home to spend the remainder of it with the living.

A few weeks later, Tobin would recount the barrage of emotions he experienced the evening after he viewed his first autopsy; his are typical emotions experienced by first-time visitors to the morgue. He felt traumatized. A depression, like a high tide, overcame him most of the evening, and the smell of the deceased enveloped him; he seemed to wear it like a shirt, and periodically all Saturday night, wafts of the pungent, sweet odor coursed through his consciousness. And he could not, despite a bath and a shower, wash away the smell of the latex, and he began to wonder if he ever would.

CONTRASTS

Early Summer 2004
Spectrum Health, Blodgett Campus
East Grand Rapids, Michigan

Two victims.

One black. One white.

One young. One middle-aged.

One wanted to die; the other didn't.

While one common thread ties together their tragic deaths, their stories contrast.

Indeed, such contrasts appear often in life—and in death. One need only enter the Kent County Morgue, in which this morning two victims lie, to realize the contrasts; although one common thread binds together their deaths, their stories provide a drastic example of the contrasts often found on the other side of the gray security door that separates the Kent County Morgue from the outside world.

Ottawa County sheriff's deputies arrested Kevin Gilchrist* after they caught him driving under the influence (his third such offense) Thursday night and in possession of a concealed weapon (a pistol). He may have had a bit of an Edward Hyde in him when he drank heavily, as he allegedly had fired the weapon sometime before police arrested him (in fact, the phrase *Jekyll and Hyde* is often used to describe the effects of alcohol on some people who become "mean" drunks).

Gilchrist found himself a resident of the county, replete with a cell and a roommate, who left the cell Friday afternoon to visit the jail's dayroom. Ten minutes later, another inmate discovered Gilchrist, a torn bedsheet around his neck attached to the upper frame of the cell's bunk bed. His faint pulse would disappear minutes later.

During the investigation into Gilchrist's death, officials claimed that although he appeared despondent, he gave no indication of being suicidal, thus they did not place him on suicide watch. The façade, it appears, does not always indicate what lies beyond.

Robert Perry,* in contrast to Kevin Gilchrist, did not want to leave the world as suddenly as he did. Like Gilchrist, the night he died he reveled in alcohol, attending a party on the west side of town with his friends. He excused himself to use the bathroom, as he most likely did often that night, but never returned. About fifteen minutes later, his friends would find him sprawled out on the bathroom floor, unconscious. Realizing Perry suffered from something more severe than an alcohol-induced blackout, they rushed him to the hospital, where to their shock he died shortly thereafter.

These two victims, unlikely roommates, this morning share the autopsy room in the Kent County Morgue, both victims of violent deaths.

On this sunny, cool morning of what will become a hot, humid afternoon, Tobin is waiting in the hospital lobby, legal pad in one hand and pen in the other, at eight thirty—our agreed-upon meeting time. We make our way down the stairs into the cinder-block-lined corridor leading to the morgue. The Grim Reaper once again had a busy night last night, and in the morgue below, two victims await examination. The Kent County Morgue itself, like the two victims lying on the autopsy tables under the bright, fluorescent lights, is a study of contrasts, of comedy and tragedy.

*****

Imagine a scene of two teachers passing in the hallway between classes.

"Did you read the article about the German couple who placed their child on an Internet auction for one Euro?" one of the teachers asks the other. The other shakes her head, curious about her colleague's question.

"One Euro," she explains, "equals a dollar and eighteen cents." Her expression seems pregnant with disgust. "Can you believe they would charge *that* much?" The colleague could hear her laughing all the way down the hall and around the corner, a good cathartic laughter that would allow her to stand in front of a class of twenty-five teenagers. Whatever works. Every profession utilizes "black" or "dark" humor so its practitioners may complete their jobs and maintain a certain degree of sanity.

Humor and *morgue*—two terms that seem in dramatic contrast—are two words that conjure images that when placed next to each other create instant juxtaposition. This odd combination can be found in the images tacked onto the bulletin boards covering one of the autopsy room's walls. Yet, despite the two bodies lying on the tables behind, this juxtaposition seems less like a contrast and more like a couple who have been married a long, long time.

The gallows humor present in the morgue is symbolized by a series of papers taped to the wall that separates the autopsy room from the refrigerator that keeps morgue customers on ice. Most of the clippings tacked onto the bulletin board are comics, and together they provide an interesting glimpse into the "dark" humor that circulates in the world of forensic pathology. The comics provide the levity in a place drenched with seriousness.

A few examples of "morgue humor":

A photocopied comic shows a doctor briefing a grief-stricken wife next to a hospital bed containing her husband. "'He's one tough cookie. I've never seen anyone bounce back from an autopsy before.'"

A *Far Side* comic depicts two thieves dressed in black among a roomful of gurneys, each containing a body covered by a sheet, each with a pair of feet protruding. The comic carries the lone caption, "Pickpockets of the Rue Morgue."

In another comic, two buzzards stand over a body covered by a sheet on a gurney; the image stands over the caption containing one scavenger's comment, "'On the off-chance that the patient doesn't make it, I'll meet you down in the morgue for lunch.'"

"'No, I don't want to live forever, but I damn sure don't want to be dead forever, either,'" one retiree says to another as they sit on a porch in their rocking chairs.

The next comic contains the image of a doctor seated behind a large desk, sporting a dour look. "'Before we try assisted suicide, Mrs. Rose, let's give the aspirin a chance.'"

"Struck from behind, all right . . . and from my first examination of the wound, I'd say that was done by some kind of heavy, blunt object." The comic contains the image of a man lying prone in a bowling pin factory.

The bulletin board next to the one containing these comics has tacked onto it bits and pieces relevant to the business of the morgue. The two bulletin boards seem to illustrate the odd marriage of levity and serious-ness—the juxtaposition that pervades the morgue and lives within its practitioners.

The first item on the more serious bulletin board is a photocopied sheet titled the "Glasgow Coma Scale," which is a test performed in hos-pital triage to determine the extent of a patient's consciousness—talk about a transition from the comic about a man beaned in a bowling pin factory! Fate again—this comic oddly and eerily foreshadows one of the victims lying on the autopsy table behind. (See below for an explanation about this scale.)

Another photocopy carries the title "Normal Heart Weight"—a chart useful in determining if a victim suffered from an enlarged heart, which presents potential evidence of heart disease. This scale, for example, indi-cated that Carl Vinson, one of the victims in the previous chapter, suffered from a seriously enlarged heart.

Normal Heart Weight

2x body weight in grams	
Males	0.45–0.5% of body weight
Females	0.40–0.45% of body weight
1 SD =	28g for women
1 SD =	35g for men
2 SD are physiologic	

NOTE: SD = Standard Deviations

*****

A relaxing bouncy rhythm appears in the air, almost a cue that work is about to begin, as Jason Chatman selects the music for this morning's proceedings. The first autopsy will be accompanied by a soundtrack provided courtesy of the Allman Brothers.

The first subject to be examined today, Kevin Gilchrist, arrived from Ottawa County, a neighboring county bordering Kent County to the east and Lake Michigan to the west. Gilchrist, a forty-two-year-old white male, apparently committed suicide while a resident of Ottawa County Jail, where charges of marijuana possession and a third Driving under the Influence (DUI) charge sent him. To the chagrin of his jailors, who left Gilchrist alone for a mere ten minutes, the despondent prisoner created a makeshift noose with bedsheets, wrapped one end around his neck, attached the other end to the upper frame of a bunk bed, and slid downward. Another prisoner happened by Gilchrist's cell and discovered his body. Unlike the condemned convict dropped from the gallows, the procedure chosen by the deceased didn't cause a dislocated vertebra that severed the spinal cord, creating a painless death; instead, Gilchrist died of asphyxia.

His corpse arrived this morning with an escort, an Ottawa County sheriff's deputy with short, spiked blond hair and a facial expression that does not hide a certain anxiety. Gilchrist lies on the autopsy table, his bright orange, county-issued jumpsuit starkly contrasting against the glittering stainless-steel autopsy table. At six feet four inches and 200 pounds, in life he would have looked down upon a number of people, the authors included. His well-trimmed reddish blond beard balances, in a symmetry that an artist could appreciate, the boundary of hair that rings the bare top of his scalp. The jumpsuit is torn down the middle to reveal two EKG pads still on his chest, which look like silver smoker's patches. Patches of dark hair cover his chest except for a conspicuous section on the upper left side where an attempt was made to "kick-start" his heart. His eyes are closed, and a circular, white plastic bite-guard resembling the plastic cork in a bottle of Andre champagne is clenched in his mouth—mute testament, despite Gilchrist's desire and willingness to depart the world of the living, that Ottawa County sheriffs last night wanted to prevent him from "going gently into that good night."

The image of Gilchrist and his makeshift noose has its fictional parallel in a sequence in *The Shawshank Redemption* when Andy DuFresne, serving two life sentences for murders he didn't commit, obtains a length of rope, and his friend, Red, passes an uneasy night wondering if Andy will use the rope to do himself in. Gilchrist, it appears, had all the rope he needed on his bed.

His circumstances have their real-life parallel in Sarah Coleman (see the previous chapter, "Decompression") and her method of suicide—fastening a plastic bag over her head with electrical tape—"where there's a will, there's a way." Gilchrist illustrates the truth in the cliché, since he literally hanged himself in such a way that should at any time he decide to abort the attempt, he could have simply placed his feet on the floor and stood up. The difference between life and death for Sarah Coleman meant poking her finger through the plastic bag. Except she didn't, and Kevin Gilchrist didn't stand up, not because he couldn't but because he didn't want to. He apparently wanted out of life's circus badly enough to endure asphyxia. The method is common; according to statistics published by the National Center for Health Statistics (NCHS), "suffocation suicides" are outnumbered only by "firearm suicides."[1]

Again, "Where there's a will, there's a way." Indeed, people have chosen methods that would make even Gilchrist's example seem mild. Brutus's wife, Portia, committed suicide by "swallowing fire" after her husband participated in Julius Caesar's assassination and fled Rome; centuries later, a Polish woman committed suicide by feeding herself, over a protracted period of several months, 3 knives, 101 pins, 20 nails, 3 pieces of glass, and (among other things such as a few rosary beads and spoons) 19 coins. A Parisian woman chose an even more bizarre way of leaving this world: she bled herself with a hundred leeches.[2] Another infamous case involves a man who positioned the blade of a knife between his forehead and a tree and, by repeatedly ramming his forehead, drove the knife into his brain.[3]

Just as the autopsy procedure begins, a knock on the door to the morgue suite brings Rebecca, a twenty-something undergraduate from Ferris State University who aspires to become a pathologist. The blonde-haired student visits the morgue often as a volunteer to observe and learn from the work of the forensic pathologist. She helps herself to a surgical gown from the linen cabinet and, a few minutes later, looks like she's ready to step into the OR.

In fact, on many occasions, the morgue becomes a "teaching" hospital for countless interns and students. This morning, Rebecca, one of a legion of college volunteers who is allowed periodic access to the morgue to learn about pathology, will observe the autopsies.

Rebecca helps Jason lift Gilchrist onto his side; while we always examine the back of each subject, we also, as a point of procedure, photograph the backs of all subjects who die in police custody.

"How do you tell the difference between a hanging and a homicide made to look like a suicide by hanging?" Tobin asks. The possibility of a murder staged to appear like a suicide by hanging or asphyxiation has occurred to numerous screenwriters. One *Law & Order Special Victims Unit* episode titled "Ridicule" involves a woman found hanging from the ceiling fan in her bedroom. Investigators presume she hanged herself, when, in fact, the woman's murder was staged to appear as an accidental autoerotic hanging (see "Safe Sex" below).

Suicides by hanging create a "signature" pattern of marks around the neck, usually an inverted "V" on the back of the neck, from the rope's suspension. The pressure from the rope often causes petechiae, which are tiny broken blood vessels—red dots on the face, eyelids, and mouth lining. In contrast, a homicide by strangulation would produce different markings: a straight line across the back of the neck caused by the item used to cut off the air supply—a garrote made from a belt or a cord.

Often during homicides, the perpetrator will leave bruises and contusions around the neck—a testimony to the ferocity of the terminal struggle; the attack may also damage the internal neck structures, particularly the hyoid bone (discussed below). For this reason, I will closely examine Gilchrist's neck structures, although I will find no marks on Gilchrist's neck because he used a bedsheet and was hanging for only a few minutes.

On occasion, asphyxia can occur by accident, if, for example, a factory worker's gold necklace pulls him into a machine and strangles him. There is one type of behavior—not as uncommon as one might think— that sometimes leads to death by asphyxia, sometimes by accident . . . and sometimes not.

SAFE SEX?

Police find Joe Simpson,* wearing nothing but a pair of boxer shorts, on his knees and slumped forward, a rope tightened around his neck. The other end of the rope is fastened to a steel loop jutting out of the stud near the top of the wall behind him; the tension on the rope has left Simpson in a position that makes it look like he was praying when he died.

A suicide? A homicide? An accidental death? Perhaps all three, even though it may sound inconceivable that one scenario could appear to be a suicide but actually be an accidental death that is also a homicide.

Back to Simpson. The death scene investigator, who studies scenes in which deaths take place and acts as the eyes and ears of the medical examiner who may not visit scenes, takes stock of the scene. At first, Simpson's demise appears an act of suicide (albeit with his knees on the ground) via asphyxia, but the crime scene investigator knows better. Although uncommon, he has seen similar cases before, particularly in the nineteen eighties. Several aspects of the scene seem to argue with the supposition that the victim wanted to end his life. Investigators can find no note, and Simpson's friends report that just yesterday he seemed vibrant and happy, not despondent, which one would associate with suicide. And he had just earned a promotion to Software Engineer Grade 3.

On the floor in front of Simpson sits a mirror, reflecting every movement, and pornographic magazines laid open flank the mirror on all four sides. Upon closer examination, the investigator notices a leather band around Simpson's neck, under the rope, used to protect the skin from any damage he may have to explain to his friends and family. Next to Simpson's right arm, another rope sways slightly. The rope ends in a knot that looks like a highway interchange located by the ring in the wall. The crime scene investigator recognizes the configuration as a safety release, a "self-rescue mechanism" often employed by those engaged in such activity, and suspects that one tug of the rope would send Simpson face first into the beige carpet. The investigator jots a few notes that he will send to the medical examiner.

For the medical examiner and forensic pathologist, this scenario, called sexual asphyxia, often presents a sticky situation but illustrates the notion that "context is everything." Forensic pathologists use the autopsy as a vehicle to determine three facets of a case: the physiological reason for death (the *mechanism* of death), the agent (*cause*) of death (e.g., a gun, knife, rope for suffocation), and the *manner* in which the deceased left this world (e.g., suicide, homicide, natural causes, accident, or undetermined). In making determinations about the manner of death, this context is crucial.

Context—the circumstances in which the body was found—provides a working theory. The pathologist then explores the victim's body to exclude any other possibility and thus prove the theory by default. The evidence gathered at the scene provides a theory; Simpson didn't commit suicide—his death resulted from an accident while engaged in autoerotic behavior. Yet some cases provide a quagmire into which forensic pathologists sometimes must wander. Consider a death by Russian roulette, a classic example of the subjectivity in forensic pathology and manner determination. When playing a game that requires a player to place a revolver loaded with just one bullet against his head and pull the trigger, and during his turn the gun discharges and kills him, did he in fact commit suicide or die of an accident? One could argue that only suicidal maniacs would play such a game.

Sexual asphyxia can be another example of a forensic quagmire. Sexual asphyxia is a type of sexual behavior with a twist: those who participate in sexual asphyxia find the sensation of suffocation sexually stimulating, usually accompanied by a sexual act such as masturbation. Asphyxia is achieved with a plastic bag, chemicals, a partner's hands, or most commonly, a noose fashioned from a rope, a necktie, or a sheet. This practice may occur as *autoerotic* behavior (defined as sexual activity occurring while one is alone) or as a sexual act in which one partner assists in the suffocation/strangulation (using a plastic bag or a garrote) of his/her partner. In either case, death sometimes results from miscalculation. During autoerotic sexual asphyxia, the subject often leaves himself an "out," or a safety release, as Simpson did, but if he passes out before he can release the "chokehold," asphyxia results.

As a classification, sexual asphyxia is relatively new, but acts involving the practice have occurred for a long time and have found their way into contemporary literature. The Marquis de Sade, that cad of cads, wrote a novel called *Justine* (published in 1791), which includes references to sexual asphyxia as practiced by the character Roland.

The practice has not gone unnoticed in recent fiction. For example, in Michael Crichton's book *Rising Sun* and in the subsequent movie adaptation, the murder victim engages in this practice.

Autoerotic asphyxia as a sex game is not new, but it isn't old, either; young people still engage in such forms of sexual adventure. Some call it the "choking game."[4] The dynamic is simple. One applies pressure to the carotid artery with anything from a rope to a belt to a chain, and a feeling of faintness results. When the pressure is released, the blood rushes back to the head, causing a euphoric feeling or lightheadedness lasting for a few seconds. Some people smoke crack, some inject heroin, and some choke themselves (or others). The popularity of the "choking game" is a matter of speculation, but many deaths once ruled suicides might in fact have been accidental.

An autopsy on Simpson would reveal similar damage as Kevin Gilchrist sustained in his jail cell hanging, but how does the medical examiner differentiate between suicide and accidental death? Context.

Did the victim leave a note or make any overtures toward suicide? Is the victim wearing little or no clothes? Is there any evidence of masturbation or ejaculation, such as the presence of semen? Is there a mirror and/or pornography on the scene? Did the deceased prepare any devices as safeguards? Does any evidence or history suggest that the victim regularly engaged in sexual asphyxia?

But sometimes it takes two to tango; sexual asphyxia sometimes occurs during a sexual act between two people, with one partner assisting in the suffocation of the other, perhaps by holding a bag over the partner's head. And in this game, miscalculation may lead to a fatal error—the asphyxiated passes out and does not revive. The presence of a second person makes a significant difference in the determination of manner of death. The medical examiner cannot rule the subsequent death a suicide or a natural death, because, although unintentional, a person caused the accident, which may place the death into the category of homicide. So sometimes an accident is indeed a homicide.

Of course, clever killers have attempted to dress murders in the clothes of sexual asphyxia. In one case (see "The Rough Sex Case," chapter 4), a husband, whose intimacy with his wife always involved asphyxia, contended that his wife died as the result of misadventure—a tragic accident that resulted from rough sex. Yet the bruises that covered her arms and torso suggested something more than rough sex—they suggested homicide.

In addition, strangulation homicides usually result in a different type of damage (see below) to the neck structures than strangulation accidents. And of course, an accidental death usually would leave telltale clues—context is everything.

*****

Only about a quarter of all suicide victims leave notes. Like Sarah Coleman, Kevin Gilchrist left a note. The terse note (just a short paragraph), in simple vocabulary, penned in a sloppy handwriting, presents a stark contrast to Coleman's articulate prose and neat handwriting.

As Jason begins the Y-incision, the Ottawa County sheriff's deputy retreats into the corridor leading to the autopsy room, far enough away to be out of sight of the autopsy. Jason asks him if he doesn't like the sight of blood; he explains that he once saw a child autopsied and the experience left him "shaken."

After making the Y-incision, Jason spends some time excising the neck structures—the key element in this autopsy. With his scalpel, Jason cuts underneath the neck to remove the tongue, which he will leave connected to the heart, lungs, trachea, and larynx; he places the conglomeration, consisting of the wine-dark lungs and bright-red heart at one end and the pale, pink tongue at the other, into one of the large bowls placed between Gilchrist's legs. When removed from the body, the tongue (which we don't usually see in its entirety) looks surprisingly large. Rebecca lifts the bowl and places it on the workstation. Each organ is weighed and dissected, with pieces of organs deposited into the stock jar assigned to Gilchrist and the pink cassettes that will travel to various laboratories for analysis after the autopsy.

The first item to be examined is the hyoid bone located in the throat structure. The diameter of a silver dollar, the hyoid structure, the only bone in the human body not touching other bones, consists of three fused portions that together form a horseshoe. The hyoid bone provides the pathologist a vital piece of evidence in making a final determination as to cause of death. In a homicide by strangulation, fractures of the hyoid usually occur at the end of the bones forming the sides of the horseshoe, called the cornua. Place your hand across your throat and squeeze your thumb and forefinger, and you'll feel the pressure that in a homicide could cause damage to the hyoid bone. The constricting neck structures exert pressure on the ends of the hyoid structure, and fractures sometimes result, especially in older victims.

I pick up the hyoid and, holding each end, gently tug as if pulling on a wishbone. It's a bit loose, but not fractured. The looseness occurs at the joint of the bone forming the base of the horseshoe and one of the sides, and it does not indicate a fracture; hanging with bedsheets would not usually cause a fracture to the hyoid. Finding a fracture of the hyoid bone, in a hanging, would call into question the suicide manner, and suggest homicide, because the pressure needed to fracture the hyoid would not likely occur in a suicide when the deceased hanged himself with a sheet.

The music changes; for the next forty-five minutes, we will work to the sound of Simon and Garfunkel. After a few minutes, the duo's classic tune "Homeward Bound" fills the room with a pleasing, mellifluous, and calming sound.

"Interesting," I note as I remove the liver from the bowl and place it onto the cutting board.

"What?" Tobin asks. He and Rebecca huddle closer to me as I begin to cut the liver into sections.

"He was an alcoholic."

"How can you tell from looking at the liver?" Tobin wonders.

"The color," Rebecca responds. She has seen the livers of others who have abused alcohol. "It's usually a dark brown. Quite lovely, actually," Rebecca adds. To Tobin, her word choice, "lovely," paired with a human liver, seems odd, incongruous, a snatch of dialogue lifted from Dr. Hannibal Lecter. Gilchrist's liver is a dull yellow—the color of a legal pad.

Yet this yellowing does not indicate that the decedent suffered from cirrhosis. Cirrhosis is scarring of the liver. This liver exhibits a condition known as "fatty change," which appears in some but not all alcoholics.

A great many people at one time or another have gone on a drinking binge, and now some might be panicking at the possibility that their livers look like this damaged one. Binge drinking, though, does not necessarily lead to such damage, so don't worry about that binge or two you experienced your freshman year of college, or in high school, or whenever. Only the livers of alcoholics, obese people, and diabetics show fatty change, and not in all alcoholics at that. Excessive amounts of alcohol over time can damage a healthy liver; fat accumulates in damaged liver cells, and the yellow fat within the liver cells causes the dull-yellow, telltale color.

Anyone who has experienced a binge in the past (and who most likely endured berating from some caring loved one—"you'll damage your liver") will know about the nauseous and deep, morning-after depression that follows the previous night's revels. Did the effects of alcohol influence Gilchrist's decision to end his life?

At this point, the phone rings. "Answer the phone, will you, Tobin?" I ask. "Just answer it 'autopsy room.'"

On the other end of the telephone line, a nervous Kent County sheriff's deputy wants to know if they need a law enforcement officer to witness the autopsy of the second subject, a twenty-five-year-old black male who died of a closed head injury; the deputy didn't think he could make it or find anyone at the last minute to take his place. If he wanted to observe, he would have appeared in the morgue at 7:30 this morning. He just doesn't want to come to the morgue. Who can blame him?

"Broken ribs," Jason announces as he examines Gilchrist's empty chest cavity.

"A little knowledge is a dangerous thing, which makes you just a little dangerous," I kid Jason, as he notes down on the white board "4th, 5th, 6th ribs broken" under the organ weights scrawled at the top of the board. It would be unlikely that Gilchrist broke a few ribs while in the process of asphyxiating himself, but if someone beat him in police custody, maybe.

At hearing about the broken ribs, the nervous Ottawa County sheriff's deputy who came to observe moved to the end of the corridor, his eyes widening like a deer in headlights. But jail personnel did try to resuscitate Gilchrist after they found him; the deputy explains that rescue personnel pushed on his chest in an attempt to kick-start his heart, and in the process broke a few ribs—not at all uncommon and, in fact, a frequent occurrence with CPR; no sinister jailhouse shenanigans here.

The deputy's shoulders droop a bit as I discuss the autopsy and inform "Deer in Headlights" that I found nothing to call into suspicion the conclusion that death occurred by asphyxia by hanging, that no forensic evidence suggested negligence or wrongdoing on the part of officials.

Of course, that war would be waged in the public forum of discussion, with the *Grand Rapids Press* offering a short article on the case that evening. The article briefly detailed the circumstances of the suicide, but between the lines of the text one could detect the paranoia of litigation. The article explained that county jailers assess each prisoner's mental state in a "screening process" and that, except for his state of intoxication, the victim offered little about which to worry. If the results of their review suggest that a prisoner poses a suicide risk, they remove certain materials from that prisoner's cell. Did the officials at the Ottawa County Jail feel the pressure of a hand around their necks—the invisible hand of pending litigation?

The grip they might feel is not just figurative and not invisible, either; it has a face—the face of a man who, just shy of two years earlier, lay on this autopsy table. Jeffrey Clark died of dehydration while a resident of the state. According to the prison psychologist's notes, Clark flooded his cell. As a result, prison officials shut off the water to his cell.[5] Through negligence or miscalculation, Clark died; an autopsy confirmed that he died of dehydration. Clark's death led to an investigation and numerous allegations of negligence and cruelty.

While Gilchrist apparently wanted to end his life, death pulled Robert Perry from his earthly existence. Substance use would also play a role in his demise; apart from this commonality, their tragic stories couldn't be different. Perry's situation is reminiscent of a monument in London's Westminster Abbey, a monument to Lady Elizabeth Nightingale, commissioned by her grieving husband and designed by the famous sculptor Roubiliac in 1761. The monument depicts Joseph Nightingale attempting to fight off death personified as a grim reaper figure wielding a spear (a skull cloaked in a rope) who has come to claim Elizabeth. Death, in Roubiliac's terrifying sculpture, attacks the couple from below and looks ready to pull Elizabeth off of the monument and to the underworld with him. The image, according to legend, so frightened a grave robber that the thief dropped his crowbar as he fled the scene. Today, visitors are protected from the monument, which sits in a portion of the abbey usually closed to the general public.

Last night, the Grim Reaper came calling on Robert Perry, and no one—not Perry's friends, paramedics, or doctors—could scare him away.

As Jason takes measurements, I peruse the hospital report that accompanied Perry's body to the morgue. Last night, he had been doing what many young people do—partying with his friends. His party, though, would end with a fall in the bathroom that would result in blunt-force trauma to his head, with which nature began a process that, despite their best efforts, physicians couldn't reverse.

His friends brought him to the emergency room last night and informed the attending physician that they found him sprawled out on the bathroom floor, unconscious. Tests revealed the presence of alcohol and cannibinoids (marijuana) in his system. With the aid of smelling salts, he came to, but spoke gibberish, which prompted the doctor to suspect a closed head injury. Next the doctor administered a look, feel, listen test to obtain a Glasgow Coma Scale score—a common procedure for patients with suspected closed head injuries.

Glasgow Coma Scale

EYES OPEN

Never	1
To pain	2
To verbal stimuli	3
Spontaneously	4

BEST VERBAL RESPONSE

No response	1
Incomprehensible sounds	2
Inappropriate words	3
Disoriented and converses	4
Oriented and converses	5

BEST MOTOR RESPONSE

No response	1
Extension (decerebrate rigidity)	2
Flexion abnorma (decorticate rigidity)	3
Flexion withdrawal	4
Localizes pain	5
Obeys	6

Total 3–15

His score, a nine out of a possible fifteen, meant that he probably had a closed head injury, so off for a CT scan to look at potential damage. Perry, the report notes, with an "altered mental status," was belligerent and refused the test.

Thirty to forty minutes later, the report, which reads like a horrific, clinical diary of a man's final hour, mentions that the attending physician repeated tests and obtained a Glasgow Coma Scale score of three, which meant he didn't respond to any type of stimuli. A study of the chart tacked to the bulletin board on the morgue wall (see above) reveals that Perry's score of three was the lowest score obtainable, and indicates that he didn't open his eyes and had no verbal or motor response.

Shortly thereafter, Perry died.

Jason need not undress Perry, who arrived at the morgue as naked as the day he arrived on earth, except for a list of devices used by the hospital in a desperate fight to save his life the night before, which today make him look like an experiment of Dr. Frankenstein. Jason cuts the end off the long white tube—the catheter—that protrudes from his penis and waits until the pale, yellow urine stops emptying onto Perry's leg. He pulls the catheter free. Next, he turns his attention to another white tube protruding from just above the left clavicle at the base of Perry's neck— he pulls out a long wire that hospital personnel used to monitor the heart.

At six feet and 235 pounds, Perry has the physique of a linebacker. His eyes are closed and his face seems oddly absent of expression. He kept his hair short, almost shaved, but a shaved patch breaks the crescent-shaped hairline; in the middle of the shaved patch, at the top of his forehead, is a short incision about an inch in length, which is stitched closed. Later in the procedure, as Jason removes the brain, it becomes clear that this incision went through the skull and was used by hospital personnel to monitor both the pressure inside his skull and the results of their attempts to lower that pressure.

As Jason removes the various medical apparatus attached to the twenty-five-year-old, I begin narrating specifics into the handheld recording device: twenty-five-year-old black male, apparently died from a head wound, found unconscious on bathroom floor, a possible fall.

Robert Perry was an excellent candidate for an "organ harvest." His organs were viable for donation because he was kept alive on life support for a time. Physicians will take the desired organs, while he's on life support but after he's pronounced dead, and leave the rest for examination during the autopsy, as long as the organs they take do not contain evidence as to cause of death.

Since Perry died of a head wound, one might think that we need only examine the head and the brain to determine the cause and type of head injury, but a complete autopsy is always performed. If there's been an organ harvest, we autopsy the head and whatever is left.

The family apparently refused the organ harvest, though.

"Do you see many organ harvests?" asks Tobin, who has been standing next to Perry's body and watching the examination intently.

"Hospitals are desperate for organs. They'll even take organs from people with a history of intravenous drug abuse," I explain.

By now its time for another compact disk change, and Jason plucks another disk from the wall formed by stacks of CDs on either side of the stereo; this time, Dave Matthews Band will supply the soundtrack for Mr. Perry's autopsy.

Thirty minutes later, a dissection of Perry's internal organs reveals no significant disease or defect. The absence of disease or defect underlines the tragedy of Perry's death; if a massive tumor or severely blocked arteries in the twenty-five-year-old had been discovered, one might be tempted to say that the Grim Reaper misread his calendar and visited Perry a few years ahead of schedule. But Perry most likely would have enjoyed a long life unhampered by physical illness.

Although the dissection of Perry's internal organs is routine procedure, his death is not devoid of mystery. The circumstances in which he was found—his alleged accident occurring without witnesses—create the need for an autopsy. Did he sustain his fatal head wound as the result of a fall? Or did someone hit him, during an assault? Or did his death result from a cerebral aneurysm?

"What do you suspect caused his death?" Tobin asks.

"We need to take a look in his noggin," I explain. "That is the key in this case."

Jason fires up the Stryker saw. After a few minutes, with a tug and the ripping sound that accompanies the face peeling from the skull, he has exposed the skull. While procedure dictates the rhythm of an autopsy, the circumstances of some cases require extra steps. Jason removed the entire neck structures of Kevin Gilchrist, including the tongue, because the mortal wound he inflicted upon himself involved the constriction of the neck structures with a torn bedsheet.

No matter what the suspected cause of death, though, the same basic procedures occur in all autopsies. Perry died from something that went awry in his skull, but even if he died from a stab wound that pierced his heart, we would still examine his head using the same protocol, which includes pulling down the back and front sides of the scalp for examination. Jason incises the scalp in the rear of Robert Perry's head and tugs the scalp rearward and down, accompanied by the same ghastly ripping sound as the scalp comes free of the bone, so the entire outside of the skull can be examined. Jason snaps several digital photographs of the skull before he begins to excise a crescent-shaped section of skull necessary to remove the brain.

Jason reaches into the skull with both hands as he loosens and attempts to remove the brain. Unlike in many other autopsies, in which a few strategic swipes of the scalpel allow him to easily remove the body's nerve center, Jason appears to struggle and announces that the brain "is really soft." A "soft brain" results from decomposition, caused when the body exists at body temperature (98.6° F) for several hours without an oxygen supply to the brain—like hamburger left sitting out.

Despite the softness, Jason manages to remove the brain, which he weighs and sets on the workstation. As I conduct a cursory examination of the brain, Jason removes the dura (the protective lining separating the brain from the skull) in order to study the inside of the skull for the presence of fractures.

Perry most likely died from compression and herniation of the brain stem. When a person hits his head, the momentum continues to move the brain, causing it to collide with the skull. The collision causes bruising and swelling of the brain. As a result, the brain of a man who sustained a fatal head injury in a fall would exhibit a certain pattern of bruising on the brain, so I will look for the telltale pattern.

"Tobin, this is the brain stem, and it controls body functions. In a sense, it is the boss." I turn the brain onto its side and point to a section at the bottom—the brain stem—which is swollen. Imagine slicing off the top half inch from a softball—the swollen brain stem resembles this slice of the softball, protruding from the underside of the brain. This section sits inside a funnel-shaped hole in the base of the skull called the foramen magnum.

"So he died when his brain stem swelled?" Tobin asks. He shuffles over to Perry's body, where Jason is peeling away the dura lining the skull to reveal the bluish white bone. From a bird's-eye view of the skull, almost in the center of the skull's bottom is the foramen magnum—where the brain stem exits the skull and gives rise to the spinal cord.

Tobin has a favorite saying—"the asshole is boss"—that emanates from an elderly relative who suffers from some severe gastrointestinal problems; indeed, one with such a malady may be inclined to believe that "the asshole is boss." To some degree, especially for those who have suffered from what can only be described as torturous problems in their plumbing, this might be true; in fact, though, the brain stem is boss, and Perry's case underlines this essential fact. If one considers the human body as a very well-lubricated machine with the heart as the engine, then in this comparison the brain becomes the computer. The power source of this CPU, the brain stem, sits at the bottom rear of the brain over the foramen magnum and controls the function of bodily organs.

Swelling in the brain stem forces it into the cavity of the foramen magnum, compressing and subsequently preventing it from functioning properly. The heart is thus kept from beating and pumping blood, which in turn denies the brain its supply of oxygen. Without blood supplying oxygen to the brain tissues, lights out; death is imminent. Indeed, the brain stem is boss.

But when Perry struck his head on something in that bathroom, did nature begin a process that even the finest physicians using cutting-edge technology couldn't reverse? In such cases, doctors have the "golden hour" in which to diagnose and set to work treatments that would reverse the process. Part of the treatment would include evacuating a blood clot from the skull, usually via a hole or two, and administering medicine designed to keep the brain from swelling: mannitol, an osmotic agent, and steroids to prevent swelling.

At the point Perry hit his head, grains of sand began to fall from a "golden" hourglass; forty-five minutes after he arrived at the hospital, the last grain fell—nature, in this case, conquered human effort.

"Take a look at this," Jason says, and I lean over to examine the underside of Perry's skull.

"Jason discovered a fracture," I shout. The presence of the fracture is pleasing because it is the last link in a chain of evidence that negates an ugly surprise such as a homicide.

"Why?" Rebecca asks, confused at my reaction to Jason's discovery. She watches as Jason snaps a few digital pictures of the fracture.

"This makes us feel better about an accident as opposed to an assault. Take a look."

A hairline fracture, like a line drawn with a pencil, extends for about an inch and a half about midway up the back of the skull. Hard to believe that the force of 235 pounds striking the rim of a bathtub or even the tiled floor would not do more damage than this fracture.

Yet the existing skull damage fits the theory that Perry fell and hit the back of his head, sustaining what would become a fatal blow. An assault would be less likely to leave a linear fracture and, in many cases, would result in depressed fractures, which, on the inside to the skull, would look like an inverted pockmark. If someone, for example, had hit Perry on the back of the head with a hammer, the hammer would leave a depressed fracture. With wounds caused by such excessively hard blows, fractures would extend or radiate from the depression like tiny cracks in an eggshell.

Blunt-force trauma to the head can also leave superficial evidence that might appear upon examination. The scalp, for instance, may be damaged (although the object that strikes the victim's head may leave a telltale imprint; for example, falling and hitting the comparatively dull edge of a bathtub may leave little damage to the scalp, while several blows to the head with a hammer would leave extensive, distinctive marks).

The victim's eyes can also provide evidence. Severe blows to the head can cause bleeding inside the skull, called subdural hematoma (under the dura, or protective membrane lining the skull), which can compress the brain. As a result of the compression, the pupil of the eye on the side of the hemorrhage will dilate, a condition often referred to as a "blown pupil." In the crime drama *Heat*, Al Pacino's character, Vincent Hannah, a robbery-homicide detective, describes to his arch rival, played by Robert De Niro, a recurring nightmare that plagues him, in which victims of head wounds sit around a table and stare at him with "eight ball hemorrhages," speechless. The eight ball hemorrhages" are the dilated or blown pupils that follow severe blows to the head.

Since blown pupils can occur with many types of head trauma, their presence only suggests that the victim sustained some type of head wound, not what the type of head wound might be. So the type of fracture is the key piece of forensic evidence in determining what type of blow the victim sustained and the subsequent cause of death. An accidental fall would have likely resulted in this "linear" crack running a more or less straight, vertical line along the back of Perry's skull—not the case with a blow from an object such as a hammer or a lead pipe.

While the discovery of a depressed fracture would signal a potential homicide and make interesting fodder for a *Law & Order* or a *Crossing Jordan* episode, this victim died from an accident. This fact does not deprive the case of some mystery. On what did Perry strike his head? Sustaining a fatal injury in the bathroom may at first seem unlikely, but on second thought, doesn't the bathroom present a prime location for a terrible accident to occur? People bathe, shave, and defecate in the bathroom. We all frequent this (usually) small room from time to time. The sixteenth-century French philosopher Michel de Montaigne once said, "Even on the most exalted throne in the world we are only sitting on our own bottom" ("*Et au plus eslevé throne du monde, si ne sommes assis que sus nôstre cul*").[6] In fact, Elvis, the King, died in his bathroom (he was found with his face buried in the shag carpet).

And the typical bathroom offers a number of hard edges on which a person who loses consciousness could strike his/her head: the edge of the sink, the edge of the bathtub, plumbing fixtures in the tub, the toilet seat, the toilet tank, and others.

You may have heard someone being ridiculed for having a soft brain, but in this case, it is literally true; the brain is too soft to dissect today. A few seconds later, Jason appears with a white gallon bucket filled with formaldehyde. After a week of submersion, the formaldehyde will solidify the brain, and I will section it. (After eventually dissecting the brain, I did find the pattern of bruising expected from an accidental fall). With this declaration, the autopsy concludes.

An odd object dangles in the air above the floor scale next to one of the autopsy tables—a wire skeleton a little larger than a Barbie doll. The figure presents an almost comical shape that adds to the humor represented by the comics on the bulletin board that began this experience in the autopsy room. In the literary world, an author creates juxtaposition, two images that often appear contradictory placed side-by-side, to illustrate a point.

The point created by the juxtaposition of humor and death? That pathologists and their assistants are ordinary people doing everyday jobs that bring them face to face with extraordinarily bad situations. Humor is the narcotic that makes it all palpable to the psyche. Such contrasts appear often in the Kent County Morgue.

"Are you going to the gym today?" Rebecca asks in casual conversation as we walk toward the hospital cafe.

"Dead lifts," I respond. "My favorite."

Rebecca laughs.

*****

Twenty minutes later, the scene shifts to the hospital café with Jason, Tobin, Rebecca, and me eating lunch; it seems odd that Tobin could eat lunch after observing two autopsies performed. He has got his sea legs, so to speak. Lunch conversation focuses on the trip to Las Vegas that Jason and I have planned for the fall until gravity pulls the conversation back into the realm of medicine and pathology as Tobin asks a question many ask when they discover my profession.

"Why did you chose pathology, or did it choose you?"

If you had one question to ask a medical examiner, you may very well ask this question. What would drive someone to devote his professional existence to the dead?

Many want to know what force or forces lead a person into a profession such as forensic pathology.

One of the more frustrating and rewarding aspects of being a medical examiner and forensic pathologist is the interactions I have with the families of the deceased. It is satisfying if I can explain why the patient died, if I can assert that the victim didn't suffer, and if I can transmit to the surviving family members the implications of diseases that we diagnose at autopsy. Once I even got a fruit basket from a grateful family.

On the other hand, some families have agendas. They'd like us to opine that their loved one died of malpractice or from an accident that was someone else's fault. They would like us to state that their loved one suffered miserably after the injury in order to increase a payment from the defendant for pain and suffering. They may believe (or want to believe) that the contact gunshot wound of the head had to have been received while the victim was cleaning the gun (they're unable to explain why one would hold the gun to his temple or insert the barrel in his mouth in order to clean the gun). Or they may claim that the 250 antidepressant tablets the deceased ingested were taken because she forgot that she had already taken the daily dose.

Finally, the family (and the forensic pathologist) may be frustrated when the medical examiner is unable to determine a cause of death. Such indeterminable causes can occur because of decomposition, a subtle cause with no anatomic correlate, or poisoning by an unusual drug or toxin not identifiable on the routine drug screen. Without a specific cause of death, closure is harder to come by.

I *chose* pathology because I like to think, sometimes at length, about aspects of a case, and in clinical medicine there's pressure to move on to the next patient. Sometimes there's a need to do more testing or obtain more history from the patient, but there may not be time to do so. Also, actually seeing diseases or injuries with the naked eye or under the microscope is more intellectually satisfying than using indirect methods (lab tests or x-rays) for making a diagnosis. So many of the diseases seen by clinical doctors are mundane and, while treatable, are not curable. In forensic pathology, we are in charge of what tests are done, and the extent of an evaluation. We don't have to ask permission from an insurance company or an HMO to do tests or perform procedures.

"That's why I like to write fiction," Tobin responds after a pause. "Because I can control all of the variables."

WHAT KILLED HARRY FREIBURG?*

Midsummer 2004
Byron Center, Michigan

C arl Sandburg once personified Chicago as the "city with the wide shoulders"—his nod to the hardworking residents of the city that skirts the southwestern edge of Lake Michigan. Take I-94 due east to 196, which runs along the western edge of Lake Michigan. Two and a half hours later, you'll find yourself in Grand Rapids, Michigan. And if Chicago is the "city with the wide shoulders," Grand Rapids is an adolescent who has overgrown his clothes. In fact, as Tobin travels south on 131, the north-south artery that bisects Grand Rapids, from either side of the highway a Las Vegas kaleidoscope of neon street signs illuminates the steel gray of a July evening in Michigan. This is Kent County, a pastiche of bedroom communities and suburbs, with the city of Grand Rapids at its center. And this is the capital of my professional domain, which includes counties throughout the state and consists of approximately two million people.

I live in Byron Center, a bedroom community at the extreme southern edge of the metropolitan area. This evening Tobin and I will discuss the drama of the medical examiner's professional life, the world of a medical examiner, and the gritty world of forensic pathology. Fifteen years ago, most of the area through which I traveled between the hospital and my home consisted of wide-open, vacant, and in most cases forested land.

Grand Rapids has certainly grown, but the culture has yet to catch up with the suburban sprawl. While the younger set complain of boredom— that social ennui brought on by a lack of what Chicago possesses— twenty-somethings herald the city as the place to raise a family. Ironically, this creates a vicious whirlpool effect, sucking nightlife into the vortex of family life and conservative values. (As of this writing, Grand Rapids residents have vehemently opposed the construction of an Indian reservation casino in Gun Lake, about thirty miles south of Grand Rapids, and several attempts to place an adult nightclub in the downtown, metropolitan area have been about as welcome as a keg in a temperance meeting. These efforts, needless to say, have failed.)

One of the benefits of conservative West Michigan is that, while each year Detroit competes for the highest per capita murder rate in the United States, Grand Rapids experiences relatively few violent crimes and even fewer homicides. The Kent County medical examiner's staff conducts approximately 550 autopsies per year, and, of these, only 5 to 10 percent arise from homicides—fewer than five homicides per month—whereas the latest statistics indicate that Detroit averages approximately a homicide a day. According to one detective interviewed, Ottawa County averages an unbelievably meager two to three homicides per year! Such statistics draw families to the area, and the presence of families tends to keep the area free from crime.

Tobin arrived at twenty minutes after eight.

"Wasn't sure which house, Doc," he says, as he steps inside the foyer, a black canvas bag slung over his shoulder, in it a laptop computer on which he will type notes this evening. "But you left me a clue—your car": the black Porsche Boxster in the open garage with the personalized license plate that reads "4ENSIC." Once inside the kitchen, Tobin is greeted by three resident cats of the house: Nemo, Celia, and Remington; each makes an appearance in the kitchen before disappearing into the room from whence it came.

Devotees of murder mysteries know that a search through the

victim's abode is a sine qua non because the living quarters of a person can provide vital clues about the occupant's personality. Tobin examines my living room, which offers a glimpse into my private life. Books line shelves on either side of the room, and above the fireplace mantel, a large painting depicts the only Civil War battle that took place in my hometown of Carthage, Missouri.

A Bose Wave radio and a copy of *Meditations* by Marcus Aurelius occupy one of the room's coffee tables. In an adjacent room, a computer stands ready for a game of online chess, a daily occurrence to which I have become addicted over the years.

Books, mostly fiction, fill the bookcase; works by Stephen King and Patricia Cornwell outnumber the rest. The number of Stephen King thrillers paired with my profession might lead a person to conclude that I like the macabre.

"You like Stephen King," Tobin muses as he scans the book spines, browsing through their titles.

"Most of those belong to my soon-to-be ex," I explain.

"Do you have a favorite author?"

"I like Kinky Friedman—a country-western singer who writes murder mysteries—Tom Clancy, and John Grisham."

Tobin settles into one of the wooden chairs around the dining table; he pushes to the side a gallon-sized tub of whey protein on top of a *Coin Prices* magazine to make room for his laptop computer. Each of these objects represents one of my many interests. An avid weight lifter with a four-day-a-week habit, I rarely miss a workout and I often engage in competitive power lifting.

"You're a numismatist." Tobin has noticed the *Coin Prices* magazine.

"When I was a kid," I explain. "And this is what a nerd I was: I used to purchase rolls of coins from the bank and search through the rolls for the coins I needed. I completed almost an entire collection of Jefferson nickels this way, except for the 1950-D, of course."

Eventually, the discussion drifts toward my work.

"What's the difference between a medical examiner and a coroner?" Tobin asks, firing off his first question of the evening.

Many people mistakenly refer to me as a coroner, but I am in fact a medical examiner, and the two terms, while referring to the same type of work, are not interchangeable. I serve as the chief medical examiner of Kent County (in the first year of my second term) but also as a forensic pathologist. In 1969, Michigan enacted its Medical Examiner Law abolishing coroners (some states still have coroners who, by definition, need no medical expertise). Coroners, who are elected to their posts, can thus be laypeople.

Medical examiners must be physicians. Each of Michigan's eighty-three counties must have its own medical examiner, all of whom must be licensed medical doctors (possess an MD degree or be a doctor of osteopathy who has a DO degree). Surprisingly, the Michigan Medical Examiner Law does not require its medical examiners to have any prior death-investigation experience or training. Many of Michigan's medical examiners are family practice physicians, whereas in some other states, medical examiners must be forensic pathologists.

The duties of the medical examiner consist of investigating the following kinds of deaths: all accidents, suicides, homicides, unexpected deaths, deaths (mother or fetus) related to nonmedical abortions, deaths that occur in police custody, and any death for which six voters from the county sign a petition for investigation. A death investigation, though, does not necessarily involve an autopsy. An investigation might consist of traveling to the scene, examining the circumstances surrounding the death, or receiving information about the death over the phone. The medical examiner has the authority to order an autopsy if he or she deems it necessary and to appoint lay (nonmedical) investigators, which I do. Unlike my theatrical counterparts on such television shows as *Law & Order* and *Crossing Jordan*, I do not travel to crime scenes. I used to visit crime scenes, but as chief medical examiner, I delegate most of this to members of my staff, such as Paul Davison, who are called medical examiner investigators and conduct on-site visits and analyses. Shockingly, the Michigan Medical Examiner Law does *not* mandate an autopsy in any circumstance; the determination to conduct an autopsy is at the sole discretion of the medical examiner, who can authorize an autopsy in *any* circumstance.

"You could get away with murder," Tobin remarks; his mind spinning as he conjures up various scenarios. The Medical Examiner Law provides the perfect shield to the medical examiner if he had murder on his mind. In such a twisted scenario, the medical examiner would simply not order an autopsy. A Michigan medical examiner, if of a homicidal bent, could literally get away with murder!

"Funny you should mention that," I reply.

THE PERFECT MURDER

In 1990, my staff and I examined the exhumed body of a woman—the wife of a physician—who died from a vague, mysterious infection never characterized. She was found dead by the babysitter. Upon hearing of his wife's death, her physician husband returned to the scene (their home) and convinced the elderly medical examiner not to order an autopsy and to certify the death as due to pulmonary embolus—a blood clot that travels through the heart and lodges in the pulmonary artery, obstructs blood flow, and ultimately causes death.

The victim, who had no "risk factors" for what physicians call PE (pulmonary embolus), was buried in 1980, over twenty-five years ago, after a superficial exam had occurred but no autopsy was conducted. Prior to his wife's death, the husband had acquired a girlfriend to whom he told the strange and untrue tale that he worked for the Central Intelligence Agency and that his previous family was his cover. Nearly ten years after the death of his wife under suspicious circumstances and now married to the girlfriend, the man began to threaten her. Fearing for her life, she reported his threats to the police. In the years after the burial, a nurse who worked at the hospital in which the wife died came forward and stated that she witnessed the husband injecting a "cloudy fluid" into the wife's IV bag. Coincidentally, a book called *Blood and Money* was published in 1980—the same year the wife died of the uncharacterized infection. *Blood and Money*, a nonfiction book, details the death of a plastic surgeon's wife, poisoned with dangerous virulent bacteria, which had also been injected. I suspected that the physician may have read the book and decided to dispatch his wife in the manner described in *Blood and Money*—a copycat murder.

The man's threats toward his new wife prompted authorities to reopen the case of his previous wife's death, and in 1990 I conducted an autopsy on her well-preserved remains. I found no indication of pulmonary embolus, but neither did I identify another cause of death. There was no evidence that would indicate she died a violent, traumatic death (such as blunt-force trauma, stabbing, shooting, poisoning), and if the physician who conjured stories about life as a spy in fact murdered his wife, the law lacked the evidence needed to punish him for it. Michigan's Medical Examiner Law and the man's devious manipulation of this law may well have allowed him to get away with murder. An autopsy of the wife's body at the time of her death may well have determined the cause. If indeed the death resulted from some less-than-virtuous action on the part of her physician husband, he would have been charged with murder.

*****

Other factors influence a medical examiner's decision to conduct an autopsy, such as deaths unexplained by their medical or scene history or the circumstances surrounding the death, or accidental deaths that could result from and can expose a dangerous work environment. In addition, in such cases as suicides, the medical examiner's determination of cause of death makes cents (forgive the cheap pun) as well. Most life insurance policies become null and void in cases of suicide, which makes sense; if they didn't, the seriously depressed would purchase monstrous policies and leave a fortune to their heirs.

After two bottles of peach-flavored tea, the hour has grown late. I have scheduled an online chess match with a Russian friend. I must stay up late for our midnight match and my opponent must awake early.

"Thanks," Tobin says as he makes his way toward the black Toyota Corolla parked in the driveway.

"Oh, I should show you my tattoo collection," I say almost as an afterthought.

"Tattoo collection?" Tobin stops and smiles. The very possibility piques his interest.

"Two albums of photographs," I explain, realizing the oddness of my first statement. "Some really interesting tattoos, each with a story." What people do to themselves never ceases to amaze me.

But the tattoo collection is a story for another time (see chapter 7). It's late and in the morgue, awaiting examination, is a victim who died in a house fire under mysterious circumstances. Tomorrow, an autopsy will take place to determine what killed Harry Freiburg.*

Midsummer 2004
Spectrum Health, Blodgett Campus
East Grand Rapids, Michigan

A wave of heat has descended on West Michigan, covering the region like a blanket under which the hot, humid atmosphere hovers, accompanied by a discernable haze and a palpable odor of damp vegetation. One can feel the squeeze of the humidity, even at this early hour—eight in the morning—and can taste the moisture dangling in the saturated air. Twenty minutes ago, the bank marquee en route to Spectrum West read seventy degrees—a harbinger of another ninety-degree afternoon. School kids on respite from a hectic school year and outdoor enthusiasts will welcome another hot day, since Michigan has suffered from an unseasonably cool summer until the past week. Many flock to the yellow sandy beaches fringing the entire west coast of Michigan—heralded as some of the finest sandy beaches in America, if not the world. The heat even makes a dip in Lake Michigan, often liquid ice even in the summer months, desirable. Others flee inside to breathe the canned atmosphere of air conditioners.

Lately, Saturday has become double-feature day at the morgue, with two victims stretched out on the stainless-steel tables a floor below—one died as the result of a house fire; the other, a "recreational" drug overdose. The notion of a burn victim makes the mind go wild conjuring images; the sickly image of a blackened crust, like the skin on an overdone hot dog cooked over an open fire, has proved the predominant one.

Tobin makes his way across the roadway separating the parking structure from the hospital, wearing black jeans and a white button-down Polo shirt. I arrive about thirty minutes later than expected, at about nine in the morning of what promises to be a nice day in the Midwest. Baseball weather.

Across Lake Michigan—the "Big Lake" as residents of western Michigan refer to it—a baseball game in Milwaukee will begin just about the time when we will finish with the two autopsies scheduled for today, a game I will miss. I consult with the Milwaukee County medical examiner regarding cardiovascular cases—I specialize in cardiovascular pathology (see chapter 8, Broken Hearts)—and I expected to travel to the city across the lake today. I told my would-be hosts that I would love to see a major league game, so this afternoon they would have obliged, but a lack of cases there has kept me in Grand Rapids today. After a brief greeting and an apology for my tardiness, I explain that just one victim awaits—the second victim, who inadvertently took an overdose of drugs, has not yet arrived at the morgue.

An Ottawa County sheriff's detective waits in the meeting room that makes up part of the morgue suite; he will observe the autopsy because Freiburg died under suspicious circumstances. Meanwhile, today's assistant, Joel, briefs two undergraduate science students who will observe today's autopsies. There will be five to observe as I conduct the autopsy on Mr. Freiburg.

Tobin listens intently as the Ottawa County detective briefs us about the enigmatic case of Mr. Harry Freiburg, the forty-year-old victim of a house fire in Holland, Michigan, a small but bustling city along the western shore of Lake Michigan and a thirty-minute drive from downtown Grand Rapids. Like the Ottawa County sheriff who accompanied the body of Kevin Gilchrist, the county inmate who hanged himself from the upper frame of a prison bunk bed with prison-issued bedsheets, this detective—an older man with two decades of experience guiding his crime scene hypotheses—sports a short haircut reminiscent of Parris Island and other Marine Corps training camps. The detective has a boyish face that has escaped the cosmetic ravages caused by twenty years on the job, but a hint of gray has infected the blond strands and belies his youthful appearance.

The officer produces an 8½-by-11-inch color photograph of the bathroom in which firemen found Freiburg sprawled out, unconscious, and in respiratory and cardiac arrest Thursday at approximately 8:30 in the evening. They managed to resuscitate Freiburg and take him to a local hospital. Emergency personnel transferred the victim to Spectrum Hospital in Grand Rapids because he was in urgent need of the facility's high-tech burn unit. Nonetheless, at 2:49 PM on Friday, Freiburg succumbed to his injuries.

Last night (Friday), the local evening news ran the story about the victim of a house fire in Holland, with cause of death "yet to be determined." In a few minutes, we will meet the victim in an attempt to answer the questions raised about his last moments of life in order to determine what killed him.

The detective explains several "troubling" facts of the case, facts that call into question the notion that the fire was an accident. First, he explains, Freiburg was found lying in the bathroom, but this room didn't exhibit the kind of fire damage that would have caused the burns covering 55 percent of his body. Investigators pinpointed the origin of the fire as the loveseat in the living room, and fire personnel managed to control the fire before it reached the bathroom.

The photograph of the bathroom looks like an earthquake shook the room for an hour but does not look like a fire hollowed it out. In far too many house fires, the residents become victims because they don't maintain the smoke alarms, and the smoke and carbon monoxide from the fire chokes and asphyxiates them before they can flee the flames. These are cheap deaths indeed, since they might well be prevented but for the cost of two AA batteries. Despite the low-rent neighborhood, the landlord had installed new smoke alarms and a carbon monoxide censor. Neighbors reported hearing the fire alarms well before the blaze—enough time for Freiburg to flee the house—yet he apparently didn't react when the alarms sounded. Why? The lack of fire damage to the bathroom would indicate that he received his burns elsewhere then fled to the bathroom during the fire, but why?

Investigators found a jug of charcoal lighter fluid, nearly empty, on the kitchen table, but could not find a grill anywhere on the premises. They also discovered that Freiburg was having an affair with a divorcee whose ex-husband detested their relationship.

"I better take this one seriously," I quip to Tobin and the detective after digesting the officer's report. Of course, as anyone who comes to visit the Kent County Morgue knows, we take all our cases seriously, but understatement is part of the professional humor that absorbs like a sponge much of the tragedy that pervades the morgue.

The detective voices his hypothesis that Freiburg awoke sometime during the fire and wandered into the bathroom thinking it was a way out of the house, and there he succumbed to the smoke and carbon monoxide that would have clogged his lungs and choked him. At least that's what the officer hopes. No one, especially the detective, wants a homicide today, which will only complicate the case and prevent him from going home to enjoy a sunny Saturday afternoon. And Freiburg, those who knew him reported, smoked and drank heavily and suffered from hypertension and depression.

So, the detective wonders aloud, perhaps the deceased passed out and a lit cigarette started the fire on the loveseat. He knows that many fires begin that way. For this reason, he explains, the toxicology report is very important. A high blood-alcohol level would perhaps make Freiburg unconscious when the smoke alarms sounded and would account for his inability to react.

"The last 'fire victim' we had from Reed City was shot three times in the head," I explain to the officer. The anecdote deflates his hypothesis as if I had plunged a needle into it, and lends an ominous overtone to the impending proceedings. His shoulders slump a little and he looks at the papers on the table in front of him as if searching for some other evidence, some piece that will prove Freiburg's death to be the result of accident or misfortune and not one engineered by an irate ex-husband.

He looks at me as if he discovered something new. "What about the toxicology report?" The detective knows that a blood test taken now, after Freiburg's death, would not provide an accurate blood-alcohol level in the man during the fatal fire because Freiburg lived for a considerable time before dying, and even an injured body continues to metabolize substances while alive. Testing the blood from Freiburg's corpse today in the morgue would not tell us if he had been in the midst of a drunken stupor when the blaze began at his house. What is needed here to determine his blood-alcohol level is a blood sample taken at either of the two hospitals that admitted Freiburg on the fateful evening. I nod, unspoken agreement about the importance of the toxicology results—if they can locate a "viable" sample.

I move down the corridor into the morgue and ask Joel—my twenty-something assistant today—to call the lab and order the victim's admission blood from Thursday July 29 to be confiscated. A few minutes and several phone calls later, Joel reports that the first hospital that admitted Freiburg in Holland ran a toxicology report. The next few minutes are spent trying to pry the results from the grip of hospital officialdom. The nervous detective stands, shifting his weight from one foot to the other, during this pregnant pause.

The detective, Tobin, and the students help themselves to surgical scrubs from the linen cabinet and begin to "suit up" as we await the toxicology report. Once in the morgue, their gaze immediately falls on Freiburg, who occupies the first of the two autopsy tables. His head is tilted back and a thick, crimson red line leads from his nostrils to his eye sockets, where two small pools of blood have formed. His eyelids are closed and bulge from their sockets.

Since Freiburg died in the hospital, his body exhibits the remnants of the hospital staff's desperate and ultimately futile attempts to save his life: most notably, a tunic made of once white, now cream-colored gauze. Last night, hospital personnel applied a coat of a topical antibiotic to his torso, where Freiburg sustained the most damage from the house fire.

These time-consuming efforts to navigate through the maze of hospital bureaucracy and the circuitous path to receiving the toxicology report are frustrating.

"Don't get sick on the weekend," I say to Tobin, who is circling Freiburg's body. A few chuckles sound throughout the room. "On weekends, hospitals are filled with stand-ins and substitutes," I explain. A few minutes later, I receive the results.

"I think you're off the hook," I tell the detective, who listens intently. Freiburg's blood indicates that at the time paramedics delivered him to the local hospital, he had a .24 blood-alcohol level—three times the legal limit for operating an automobile in Michigan. One could reasonably conclude that he had consumed a good deal of alcohol on Thursday—an amount, in fact, that may have rendered him unconscious and oblivious to the smoke detector sirens. His blood also contained the presence of carbon monoxide, the by-product of combustion.

"That makes me feel better." The officer's shoulders relax slightly, the weight of an impending homicide investigation lifted.

With the issue of the toxicology report now settled, the process of Harry Freiburg's autopsy begins with measurements and photographs. As Joel removes the gauze jacket of bandages, the damage left by the fire becomes immediately apparent, but once again the reality contradicts stereotype. Freiburg's corpse doesn't appear overdone, with an over-cooked, blackened appearance as many envision when they think of a fatal burn victim. Rather, the burns peeled away the outside layer of skin from the waist up, leaving a pale, pink color. Like fragments of a smashed vase, shards of the outside layer of skin cling to his body in spots; strings of the greenish gray flesh hang from his waist and armpits, and frame the surface area most affected by the fire. Two rectangles of the now greenish gray skin are anchored by his eyebrows, and two long strips of the original epidermis, now the color of gravel, run across his upper back, anchored by body hair. Flesh hangs from his fingers like strings; while blood for the DNA card is available, the burning has precluded any possibility of lifting a fingerprint. Depending on one's view of such things, tattoos litter or decorate the corpse's chest and arms.

"No burns to the lower extremities," the officer notes as he snaps Polaroid photographs of the victim, his anxiety appearing to grow by the minute. The two students flank the body as they study the victim in silence. With each click, a piece of photographic paper emits from the front of the camera, a bulky ancestor of the Sony Mavica digital camera the autopsy assistants now use; now the Polaroid, once high-tech, seems an anachronism. The detective gently pulls each photo from the camera and places it on the empty autopsy table, where the photographs transform from hazy black to images of the deceased.

Joel, standing on the autopsy table, takes a few photographs from a bird's-eye view with the hospital's digital camera.

"So it looks like we're not going to get that apparatus that allows us to photograph bodies without climbing on the table," I wonder aloud.

"I heard we were," Joel retorts as he clicks a few pictures while the detective watches. The exchange seems humorous with the backdrop of the officer holding his aged camera. Joel photographs each tattoo, which takes a few minutes. The tattoos don't appear faded, which seems odd unless Freiburg just got them in the week before he died. Most tattoos fade with time and take on a muted appearance. All of Freiburg's tattoos appear freshly inked. How is this possible? Did he just decide one night to become a body art aficionado and have a dozen tattoos inked on all at once?

The fire peeled an entire layer of skin from his torso; under the outermost layer, the tattoos wouldn't have faded, and they appear as vivid as the day he acquired them. A tattooed spider crawls across his upper left chest. Does the arachnid crawling over his heart represent an intentional symbolism? A large, ornate skull and crossbones covers most of his left deltoid (shoulder), and a dozen other, smaller designs reside on his arms, forearms, and chest.

"He had a nipple ring," Tobin notes as he points out two holes, one on each side of his left nipple, where at one time in the recent past Freiburg wore a stud.

The corpse also appears bloated, like a balloon ready to pop, giving Freiburg's corpse the appearance of obesity. Gases, Joel explains to Tobin and the students, fill the body cavity. With his index finger, he nudges Freiburg's midsection to illustrate the stiffness caused by the gas. As if to add an exclamation mark, he lightly jabs one of the eye sockets, which are so bloated that they look like they conceal golf balls. The body will deflate, Joel explains, when I make the Y-incision.

After all needed photos have been taken, I begin describing the body into my handheld recorder: "A white male, forty-years-old, 50 to 60 percent body surface burns. . . ." Each tattoo is examined and described; cataloguing Freiburg's various body art takes some time.

Tobin notices a new comic taped to the glass wall above the desk behind the autopsy tables, its crisp white paper a stark contrast to the faded, now off-white paper of the other cartoons on the makeshift bulletin board, which adds a humorous comment to the business conducted in the morgue: a *Far Side* comic in which a bewildered and judging from his facial expression horrified Farmer Brown discovers two heifers studying an "anatomical" diagram of a human body separated into cuts labeled "shoulder chops," "spare ribs," and "throw away." Interestingly, the "throw away" label sits over the outline of the head, a provocative suggestion that we have nothing of value upstairs. The caption reads: "Farmer Brown froze in his tracks; the cows stared wide-eyed back at him. Somewhere off in the distance, a dog barked." The irony presented by the image makes this the perfect "morgue" cartoon.

Joel slides a pile of papers to the side of the desk, and a photograph, another Polaroid, falls to the floor. Tobin picks the photograph up off of the floor, studies its image, and places it on the desk. The photograph shows a man lying on the floor, his legs spread-eagled and his arms stretched straight out from his torso, reminiscent of the famous Da Vinci anatomical sketch of the human body. The man is wearing blue jeans and a short-sleeved, button-down gingham shirt. His face and his arms are jet black, and several tiny bright yellow specks appear on his face.

"What are those yellow things on his face?" Tobin asks Joel, who is keying something into the computer.

"Maggots."

The mere mention of the word conjures a horrific image and triggers the memory of an even more horrific smell. Sometimes, flies find a way into the trashcan and lay their larvae onto organic remains of last night's dinner, usually chicken fat. A few days later, whoever has the dubious job of trash removal will have to deal with the tiny yellow worms.

Joel explains that the photos capture the image of an individual found in a house trailer in the northern reaches of Grand Rapids, *two weeks* after the supposed cause of death. Decomposition had caused his skin to turn to a jet black. Joel assisted in the autopsy conducted yesterday.

The twenty-six-year-old with raven black hair that was gelled into spikes at the top began assisting autopsies three months ago. He "worked his way into the morgue" from the histology laboratory (where tissue slides are prepared). A Grand Valley State University statistics major, Joel likes his job. Does anything bother him about working in the morgue? Like many pathology personnel, he has become somewhat accustomed to the sight of dead bodies and the tragic circumstances that led them to this terminal stop in their lives. Sometimes, though, he explains, the "decomps" still "get under his skin," although yesterday's autopsy didn't bother him.

"I can only imagine the stench," Tobin mutters, studying the photograph.

"Just poke your head into there." Joel points to the refrigerator in which the body resides until the funeral home arrives to collect it. He points to the table holding Harry Freiburg's body; the maggots came into the morgue with the body and a few have taken up residence under the stainless-steel autopsy tables.

Like most, I find the notion of maggots (fly larvae) almost too disgusting to contemplate. Since flies lay their eggs in warm, often decomposing organic material, a hideous stench always accompanies their presence.

For medical examiners, criminologists, and crime scene investigators alike, though, the presence of maggots can provide a vital clue as to when the victim died—an important yet difficult facet of the medical examiner's work. Often in criminal cases, guilt or innocence may hang on isolating the time of death. Alibis and witness testimony may depend on when the victim died. Upon death, the human body changes, and these changes offer an approximate timeline as to the specific point at which death occurred. But what information can maggots and other insects provide the medical examiner? One man, half a world away, can answer this question more thoroughly than anyone. He's a forensic entomologist, an expert on bugs and what evidence they provide, who resides in Honolulu, Hawaii.

BUGS!

Summer temperatures in Michigan come packaged in the cellophane wrapper of humidity, often in the 80 to 90 percent range, which clings to the skin and feels like a warm washcloth. The sweltering heat cooks the black asphalt of driveways and highways, which from a distance results in the appearance of flowing water. But in a few short months, the weather will drastically change. Imagine the scene in *The Wizard of Oz* when the Scarecrow, the Tin Man, and the Lion attempt to rescue Dorothy from the Wicked Witch's castle, and now you have the image of a typical mid-October evening in Michigan, which can often be gray, dark, rainy, and about 45 degrees.

As a light rain taps the roads, the parking structure, and the buildings that form Spectrum Health's Blodgett Campus, half a world away, the weather in Honolulu, Hawaii—the city that Dr. M. Lee Goff, one of the nation's foremost experts in his field, calls home—is sunny and in the mideighties, with a nice island breeze—nature's fan—to keep the atmosphere comfortable (at eight o'clock in Michigan, it is two o'clock in Honolulu).

To abuse a cliché, the forensic community is a small community, and my net of professional acquaintances includes Dr. Goff, who specializes in forensic entomology—the study of insects and the information they can provide about the deceased. Fans of *CSI* or other crime dramas may know that, in certain circumstances, bugs leave vital clues about time of death. Dead bodies draw insects to them like, well, dead bodies. And Mother Nature is predictable, traceable, and therefore can provide the clues necessary to determine just when a person died. Reading these clues requires the trained eye of a specialist.

Enter Dr. Goff, who holds a PhD in entomology, or the study of insects.

What would lead a person to pursue a career studying bugs—a career in forensic entomology?

"A whole series of accidents," Dr. Goff explains.[1] Dr. Goff, an import to Hawaii over forty years ago from Los Angeles, came to the islands, lured from the mainland by the surf. An avid surfer, he still surfs twice weekly (along with about half of the Hawaii state legislature, he adds with a chuckle) and cruises the island in his Harley-Davidson Springer. When he immigrated to Hawaii, Dr. Goff applied for a position at the Bishop Museum, only to discover that the position available was a position in entomology, not marine biology as advertised. His career began with a misprint.

That misprint would lead to a long and distinguished career and national renown in his field of expertise. First came a two-year stint in the

United States Army as an autopsy assistant, or "diener"; a career in academia followed. After twenty-three years as a professor of entomology at the University of Hawaii, Dr. Goff moved to the smaller (enrollment approximately 1,500) Chaminade University in Honolulu and authored *A Fly for the Prosecution: How Insect Evidence Helps Solve Crimes*, which was published by Harvard University Press in 2000. Harvard University Press maintains an online catalogue of its publications. The page containing the synopsis of *A Fly for the Prosecution* also contains an author photo. Straight, silver hair, parted in the middle, and a short, white beard and mustache—imagine a thinner Kenny Rogers in a Hawaiian shirt.

Dr. Goff travels throughout the United States, reading the valuable clues left by insects (he just returned from Boston a few days ago) at crime scenes. And just to make sure that fiction doesn't stray too far from fact, Dr. Goff serves as a consultant for *CSI: Las Vegas*.

According to Dr. Goff, 98 to 99 percent of the time, the forensic entomologist attempts to answer the question: When did this person die? He reviews photographs of crime scenes sent by prosecutors and examines samples taken at crime scenes to determine time of death. While entomologists still do not know what attracts insects to a corpse (some say a "universal death scent")—an enduring mystery of forensic entomology—at death, the human body becomes attractive to insects; in some cases, insects become attracted to bodies about to die.

So how do the insects tell the entomologist when the person died? Within two weeks of death, the life cycles of flies help the entomologist place time of death. Within ten minutes, flies appear, lay eggs, and begin what Dr. Goff calls a "biological clock."[2] When entomologists arrive at the scene, they stop this biological clock, collect the most mature maggots first, and work backward.

Since variables such as temperature affect the life cycle of flies, some regional variation exists: in a tropical climate such as Hawaii, flies are active at night as well as during the day, and the cycle progresses more rapidly than in a temperate climate such as Michigan, where flies are active in the daytime only for most of the year. When the temperature drops below ten degrees Celsius, insect activity generally stops.

If a corpse is found two weeks or later after the time of death, the life cycle of flies can no longer be used to place time of death; in such cases, forensic entomologists turn to a process known as "succession" to place time of death.

"Think of a volcanic island that just came out of the ocean, bare." Dr. Goff offers an analogy. When the island emerges, it is nothing but rock, but eventually, flora grows and covers the rock, making the island habitable for other groups. In this analogy, the volcanic island is the human body, which at death becomes habitable for insect groups that come to the body in waves. Some insect species feed directly on the body, while some feed on the feeders. This process is called "succession." In Hawaii, Dr. Goff has counted 320 distinct insect species that have appeared during succession from the time of death until only a skeleton remains; on the mainland, the number is even greater.[3]

Because "succession" is predictable for a certain geographic area (variables such as weather affect succession), forensic entomologists such as Dr. Goff accumulate data and formulate databases of decomposition studies—elaborate timelines of insect activity on a human body they use to place time of death.

Yet placing the time of death, while the bulk of the forensic entomologist's work, is only one facet of this science—insects can provide the forensic entomologist with a virtual script of the crime. Some insect species live only in fixed geographical locations, and these geographic distributions of insects can indicate where a body died and if the body has been moved. "Some [insects] want to be urban, some want to be rural," Dr. Goff explains.[4] A body containing "urban insects" found in a "rural area" would suggest that the perpetrator moved the body postmortem, perhaps dumping the body in a different location than where the crime occurred.

A "gap in insect development" on a body could also suggest the corpse was moved postmortem. Flies continue to lay eggs constantly; if protected from exposure for a protracted period of time, a "gap" in insect development would occur, and the forensic entomologist would find "two distinct age classes of insects."[5] This situation would occur if, for example, a perpetrator concealed a body in the trunk of a car and dumped it after a period of time; a second group of insects would populate the corpse after it was moved.

One of Dr. Goff's most interesting cases arises from just such a scenario. A woman, missing for thirteen days, is found wrapped up in two layers of blankets. Dr. Goff arrived at the scene on New Year's afternoon to investigate. He could account for ten and a half days of insects on the body, but not the thirteen since the woman first disappeared. He believed that the blanket cocoon around the body kept the insects from her for the two and a half days unaccounted for in the insect record on the body; he wrote a report that the "wrapped body accounted for delay of insect infestation."[6] Everyone, Dr. Goff explains, was satisfied, except the defense attorney for the accused, who believed that the time gap provided reasonable doubt of his client's guilt.

To prove his theory correct, Dr. Goff procured a fifty-pound pig, which forensic entomologists typically use to track the decomposition of human remains. He wrapped the pig in blankets, placed it in his backyard, and observed (which he notes made him somewhat unpopular with his neighbors—and his dog). Two and a half days later, flies managed to penetrate the blankets that, with the ten –and a half days of insect infestation on the victim, equated to the thirteen missing days. Ultimately, this evidence would help convict the victim's estranged husband for first-degree murder.

After the case, the story of the case assumed a life of its own. Dr. Goff wrote about it in the *Journal of Agricultural Entomology*, and the Discovery Channel turned it into a segment for *New Detectives*, and from the resultant exposure, the case appeared, albeit altered, on *CSI: Las Vegas* in the apt-titled segment "Sex, Lives, and Larvae." Dr. Goff finds humorous the discrepancies between the true event and the fictionalized event in the show; one scene has the protagonist sitting in his backyard with a beautiful woman and the decomposing pig. In fact, Dr. Goff notes, the idea of a decomposing, fifty-pound pig and a man observing the insects on it kept people away from him. "Even my dog wasn't as loyal as I thought he should be."[7]

Insects can also tell the forensic entomologist which wounds occurred before and after death. Insects, Dr. Goff explains, go into natural body openings and into wounds inflicted prior to death when blood is still flowing. Wounds inflicted before death will still bleed and attract insects;

wounds inflicted after death will not bleed, and thus not attract insects. The pattern of insects on the body can tell the investigator when the wounds occurred.

Insects can also provide information about the substances in the victim's system at the time of death (although not the amount). Insects store chemicals in their fat bodies, which Dr. Goff calls "their version of our liver"—a process called "bioaccumulation."[8] In skeletal bodies with not enough tissue for toxicological analysis, the forensic entomologist can take insects feeding on a body and use them as a tissue specimen, treating them to determine the presence of drugs or toxins—a subfield of forensic entomology called entomolotoxicology, a name that Dr. Goff wryly suggests may have been born after the consumption of one beer too many.

The forensic entomologist can also obtain human DNA samples from insects; parasitic insects, such as body lice and mosquitoes (that have fed on a suspect), can contain human DNA. In some circumstances, the DNA collected from parasitic insects can help investigators to match victim with suspect, which could occur, for example, if both the victim and the suspect shared a bed and shared "crabs," which would provide a viable source for DNA.

Insects bear witness in cases of child abuse. Some species of flies only lay eggs on live people, so the presence of flies can determine how long since a person has been cleaned or a wound treated with fly larvae (called Myiasis). An investigator might employ this use of forensic entomology to determine the level of neglect of a child or an elderly dependent. Some flies, Dr. Goff adds, are still used to clean wounds in hospitals. "One of my favorite journal articles," Dr. Goff explains, "is a 1930s article in a dental journal that describes the use of maggots in root canal surgeries. Try telling that to your dentist."[9] No, don't.

Did you ever think that insects could be so versatile? Dr. Goff describes yet another forensic use of insects: placing someone at a scene based on an insect bite. In a Southern California homicide case, Dr. Goff placed a suspect at the scene of a crime based on chigger bites; the perpetrator chose to dump his victim's body at the only place containing chiggers for a seventy-five-mile radius, and in so doing sustained several bites. In all his years, Dr. Goff notes with a hint of pride, he has yet to receive a chigger bite, despite working several scenes populated with chiggers!

Michigan is the Great Lakes State, and drowning is a fact of life for investigators in the Midwest. Insects, Dr. Goff explains, are also found on submerged bodies, in marine environments. "Diving beetles will exploit submerged bodies," he explains, but cases of submerged bodies are rare in Hawaii.[10]

This is surprising, since one would think that drowning would occur often in Hawaii, but the presence of another larger creature solves this mystery: sharks—a problem absent in the Great Lakes. In fact, Dr. Goff notes, one of the nation's experts in forensic entomology in an aquatic environment works for Michigan State University—about sixty minutes east of Grand Rapids—which makes sense when one considers the number of drowning victims in the Great Lakes region each year and the absence of carnivorous fish like sharks.

While the rhythmic sound of surf pounds on the sandy beach of the North Shore, waves of raindrops strike the roof shingles, like fingers tapping on the roof, and the wind sends waves of rain against the window. The weather serves as an ominous foreboding of what tomorrow could bring. Tomorrow, once again, if the Grim Reaper comes calling, the Kent County Morgue will receive "customers."

*****

The vacant autopsy table is now covered with developed photos of Freiburg's corpse; in a day or two, the twenty-one-year-old overdose victim will occupy this table. One can imagine the guilt mixed with horror that bereaved parents must experience when they lose a child. A student at one of the local universities, she found some pills and swallowed them. And she suffered from a drug overdose deemed "recreational" as opposed to a "suicidal" drug overdose—an act of unbelievable ignorance from which she would never recover. Her family, perhaps clawing for something positive to emerge from the tragedy, agreed to donate her organs—an organ harvest, which can only occur after death.

For medical-legal purposes, the cessation of brain activity—the result of irreversible brain damage—denotes "death." Hospital personnel conduct several levels of tests to determine the amount of brain activity that occurs. One of the tests involves tickling the cornea; a reaction suggests brain activity, life, in the brain stem. She reacted, thus, while she will never again regain consciousness and crawl off of the hospital bed, she has at least for the time being evaded technical death.

*****

Back to the body that *is* present, stretched out on the autopsy table. On the opposite wall, directly above the table on which Freiburg lies, hangs a sign: "No Food or Drink in the Morgue." Why or how would anyone *want* to eat or drink in this place? Although many who venture into this underworld as observers to human tragedy would welcome the becalming effect of a cocktail, the prohibition makes sense. The image of a cadre of intoxicated pathologists wielding razor-sharp scalpels flashes across the mind's television screen. No, not a good idea. How many errant cuts on cadavers, how many hepatitis or HIV infections from accidental subcutaneous cuts on pathologists would result from this melee?

Perhaps the dead clamor for a drink, nervous about their journey to the afterlife, wherever that proves to be. Another image flashes on Tobin's internal television screen: three corpses, their bodies pale and damaged, attempt to push aside anyone who guards the liquor bottles behind the pane of glass along one of the morgue's walls.

And then the irony, the terrible irony, strikes him. With only two exceptions, all of the deceased discussed in earlier chapters made their way into this fluorescent-lighted underworld because of their obsession with spirits—hard liquor. They drove erratically on a liquid highway. Kevin Gilchrist, who hanged himself in a county jail cell with bedsheets, had a history of alcohol abuse and several drunk-driving convictions. Robert Perry drank one too many (and mixed alcohol with cannibis) and lost consciousness in a bathroom, sustaining what would become a fatal head injury as he fell to the floor. And Freiburg, so intoxicated he couldn't hear and respond to smoke alarms, sustained what would in the end be terminal burn injuries. The overuse and abuse of alcohol seems a common denominator in the tragedies, a theme that the next few visits to the morgue would support.

It takes Joel, the detective, and one of the undergraduate observers to flip Freiburg's corpse over, so the back can be examined for anything that would change the "diagnosis of exclusion," namely, that he died from the nefarious effects of the house fire.

"The entire back is burned," I narrate into the handheld recording device. I continue the narration with a description of the burns. "A distinct line of demarcation extends across the waist separating burned from nonburned skin." Below the waist, where his clothes protected him from the flames, the skin appears pale white, the color one might associate with a marble statue. From the waist up, the fire peeled away the outer sheet of skin leaving a pink tone, the color of a fair-skinned person with sunburn—an odd color for a dead body

"When they're this greasy, they're hard to roll," I note with a playful understatement as my helpers flip Freiburg onto his back. The antibiotic cream applied to his burned skin at the hospital makes the body slippery and difficult to handle. Having accomplished the rolling, Joel takes a breath. "Yuck," he exclaims, as he notices the shards of gray glued to his latex gloves—loose skin the victim shed when they rolled him.

The narrative is concluded with a description of Freiburg's genitals, which have swelled to enormous proportions: "massive edema [swelling] of the genitals." The oversized genitals look like they belong on a statue of Priapus, the Roman god of fertility always depicted with a massive nether-region.

Accompanied by the Who's *Who's Next* on the stereo, Joel makes the Y-incision and the intestines jut through the cut, bloated from the gases that have collected inside Freiburg's body. Joel positions himself and begins to cut through the ribs so he can remove the breastplate and access the chest cavity and the organs inside of it. After viewing several autopsies, it is easy to become accustomed to sights one would never, *could* never become accustomed to, yet the sound of the rib cutters doing their work—the hideous crunching sound of ribs snapping, like the sound of saturated wood fracturing—can anyone ever become accustomed to that cracking sound?

"Is that a fractured sternum?" I ask Joel, as I notice the blood under the breastplate when he removes it. The hospital's blood test had proved that Freiburg consumed a large amount of alcohol the night of his death, and this suggests why he may not have responded to the smoke alarms, but a fractured sternum could point to a different conclusion. I examine the plate—the sternum with the ends of several ribs protruding from its sides and about the size of a small, oblong dinner plate—and conclude that the sternum isn't broken. The blood I had noticed was the result of attempts by emergency personnel to resuscitate Freiburg using CPR. Kevin Gilchrist sustained several fractured ribs in similar circumstances; desperate to save his life, prison personnel conducted CPR, the rigors of which left some damage. Nothing, though, escapes observation in the autopsy.

As Joel begins to excise the heart, lungs, and throat, which he will remove as one large mass, I explain to Tobin and the undergraduates that for a victim who dies in a house fire, the autopsy's chief aim is to determine if the victim died before the fire, which would suggest a death from something other than the effects of the fire, or if the victim died as a result of the fire. If the victim died as a result of the fire, an examination of the lungs and throat should provide the telltale forensic evidence; despite the importance of the respiratory organs, they will conduct a complete and thorough autopsy.

The detective watches, his interest piqued, as the examination of the lungs begins. "You don't have to worry about a hit on the head," I say a few minutes later after completing the examination of the victim's lungs. Tobin shuffles over to the workstation and joins the semicircle formed by the sheriff's officer and the two students. The inside of Freiburg's bronchi (airways) are a deep, crimson red mottled with patches of black. The normal color would be much lighter—a light tan; the red discoloration resulted from smoke inhalation, and the black patches consist of soot from the smoke that Freiburg inhaled. Nothing could please the detective more than this news. The soot in his lungs proves that Freiburg was breathing when the fire ravaged his home; if someone had dispatched him and set the fire to cover up the deed, Freiburg's lungs would not exhibit damage from smoke because he would not have been breathing! The high level of carbon monoxide in the blood is the final piece of the puzzle.

Not a homicide; case closed!

"Makes it easier for you," the detective notes. "Easier for you in the long run." For him, too. No one wants a homicide today; homicides, of course, suggest the insecurity of living in human society and to some degree the frailty of human life, and the discovery of a homicide today would bring with it these unwritten, unspoken sentiments, but it would also bring the unbridled scrutiny of both the police and forensic investigations as well as certain court dates in which pathologist and detective alike would testify.

After discussing the details with those observing, I press the pedal on the floor—the "on" for the work station's recording device—and I begin to narrate those aspects of the autopsy that led me to the conclusion that death was caused by smoke inhalation. The recording—the oral transcript of the internal examination of the victim—will become part of the official autopsy report.

A knock from inside the refrigerator startles the students, who turn their heads abruptly; although they realize that authorized personnel may access the refrigerator from the hospital corridor, imagination takes over and the image of *L'inhumation precipitee* (*The Hasty Burial*), an early nineteenth-century painting by Anton Wiertz, may appear in their mindscapes. The painting depicts an arm protruding from a coffin, as if grasping for air, while the other arm pushes the lid back—the coffin's occupant, the alleged victim of a cholera epidemic, has been buried alive, the accidental victim of an ignorant physician and an overhasty burial.

Before the nineteenth century, physicians had little understanding of coma and frequently declared comatose patients dead, which often meant that they were entombed alive. On more than a few occasions, the "dead" would come alive while inside the coffin. Edgar Allen Poe, the American master of the macabre and the nineteenth century's Stephen King, described the sensation in his short story "Premature Burial": "The unendurable oppression of the lungs—the stifling fumes of the damp earth—the clinging to the death garments—the rigid embrace of the narrow house—the blackness of the absolute Night—the silence like a sea that overwhelms—the unseen but palpable presence of the Conqueror Worm."[11]

The refrigerator door opens, and a small man in a three-piece suit emerges—the representative from a funeral home has come to take one of the refrigerator's residents. His cherry-red complexion provides a sharp contrast to the deep auburn color of his hair and well-trimmed mustache. He announces his intention and, with a curt "thanks," disappears back into the refrigerator.

"No charge," I yell from the workstation across the room. "Especially when taking a stinker." I'm referring to the badly decomposed corpse found two weeks postmortem: the subject of the grisly images captured by the two Polaroids that Tobin accidentally found.

A few minutes later, the door opens a little, and the funeral director's head appears from inside. "Even though it has no tag, we have the right one, don't we?" The obvious what-if scenario looms, and one can imagine a morgue/funeral home mix-up—a macabre "comedy of errors."

The trachea provides a photo-op as evidence about the Harry Freiburg's cause of death. The trachea is placed on a towel-lined tray, the kind one would use in a cafeteria. I slice the funnel-shaped trachea or breathing tube down the center, spread it flat, and place toothpicks along its sides to hold it open and expose its entire inside surface so the camera can capture the forensic evidence inside—the same mottled black spots that appeared in his lungs line Freiburg's trachea and indicate damage from smoke inhalation. One of the students carries the tray into an adjacent room, part of the morgue suite titled "BA: Photography."

"No coronary artery disease," the detective declares as he observes the dissection of Freiburg's heart. "Ironic," he notes, "alcoholics always have healthy hearts, in the autopsies I've seen." The irony is clear: heart disease seems reserved for those who *do not* abuse alcohol. An interesting conclusion, but alcohol use does not guarantee longevity, either. Quite the opposite, if one can draw any conclusions from Robert Perry, and many, many more like him, who stumbled into the morgue because of excessive substance use.

I take a break to sharpen the cutting knife. I slide the blade into the sharpener on a second workstation. The apparatus, which is a wonder, consists of a stone "V" housed inside of a plastic wedge. Made in Finland, its design, which allows the pathologist to sharpen his knife by simply pushing the blade into the V, prevents contact between a pathologist's fingers and a blade covered with blood, and subsequently reduces the risk of an accidental subcutaneous cut and a potential infection with some blood-borne pathogen.

I return to his workstation and begin work on Freiburg's liver as Tobin watches. The golden yellow hue of a liver damaged by alcohol abuse is characterized by some as a pleasant shade; one undergraduate who observed an autopsy described the tone as "quite lovely." Freiburg's liver, though, shows no such signs, the golden color strangely absent. His liver shows no signs of alcoholism.

"So he wasn't an alcoholic?" Tobin asks.

Sometimes, alcoholics and heavy drinkers do not have damaged livers.

Joel calls for help; he is having a hard time removing the testicles, which they will examine for disease such as cancer. We always conduct a complete and thorough autopsy. The discovery of testicular cancer would provide one possible motive for a suicide, should Freiburg's death turn out to be a bizarre suicide attempt. The forensic evidence, though, suggests nothing more than an accidental death.

I turn from the workstation and examine Freiburg's testicles, each the size of a racquetball from swelling, then instructs Joel. "Have a ball." Joel chuckles.

After excising the testicles, Joel begins the process of opening Freiburg's skull. The high-pitched grinding of the Stryker saw cutting through skull fills the room. Joel gently removes Freiburg's brain, places it into a bowl, and hands it to one of the undergraduate students, who delivers it to the workstation. The brain contains nothing out of the ordinary, and the autopsy is completed. The detective, Tobin, and the college students listen intently as I narrate the finding into the microphone. The official cause of death: asphyxia by products of combustion. In other words, Harry Freiburg died from a lack of oxygen to the brain that resulted from inhalation of carbon monoxide caused by the house fire. The clock reads one o'clock; the autopsy took all morning.

With the autopsy completed, Joel dumps the dissected organs into the entrail bag lining the torso cavity; he washes the body and then begins the process of stitching closed the incisions. As Joel prepares Freiburg's body for the funeral home, the detective hypothesizes about what may have caused the fire.

They will look for accelerant such as lighter fluid on the loveseat, which detectives determined as the fire's point of origin. Since the autopsy indicated an accidental death, and since the evidence suggests that Freiburg attempted to flee the stinging flames (which negates the possibility he attempted to commit suicide), he believes that Freiburg accidentally dropped a lit cigarette onto the loveseat. Too intoxicated to respond to the smoke alarms, at some point he came to, but by then smoke had engulfed the house. Smoke choking his lungs and stinging his eyes, rendering him blind, he stumbled through the blaze, in which he sustained the burns while seeking an exit. He entered the bathroom believing he had found an exit, and there he collapsed.

The detective's version of the events on the day Freiburg died, and the damage found in Freiburg's throat and lungs, suggest that he suffered a terrible, painful fate: smoke buried him alive. Edgar Allen Poe's lines from "Premature Burial" capture perhaps what Freiburg experienced in his last few minutes of consciousness: "The unendurable oppression of the lungs," "the stifling fumes, "the rigid embrace of the narrow house," "the blackness of the absolute Night," and "the silence like a sea that overwhelms."[12]

RED SKY IN THE MORNING

Midsummer 2004
Spectrum Health, Blodgett Campus
East Grand Rapids, Michigan

Sailors, aware of the mercurial temperament of the Great Lakes, lived by a rhyme: "Red sky in the morning, sailor's warning; red sky at night, sailor's delight." Most people out and about the city at nine this morning probably didn't notice it, but the sky this morning was red . . . blood red.

Saturday morning in mid-August: a cool fifty-eight degrees and the perfect end to an ugly week in Michigan. On a typical August day, one could feel the heat radiating from the asphalt, but in this unseasonably cool summer, Michiganians have substituted wraps and light coats for bathing suits and T-shirts. Protean Michigan weather aside, two immutable constants remain: Michigan weather will never be constant, and there will always be another summer, which somehow makes the harsh winters less harsh.

This morning, three bodies lie in the morgue awaiting autopsies. Since last night was Friday the thirteenth, now it all makes sense. Bad things happen in threes—they did last night.

101

We have a stinker, I inform Tobin as we walk down the corridor toward the morgue. "Stinker"—some words, through the images associated with them, obtain the power to stun and can strike like an open hand across the cheek. The sting of the blow is caused by an image burned into his mind by a few photographs Tobin accidentally discovered under a sheaf of papers on the morgue table during a previous visit.

This image, captured on two Polaroids, now flashes across his consciousness like a news story scrolling across the stripe at the base of a television screen: the image of a man lying prone on the floor of a house trailer ravaged for two weeks by the forces playing out the show preprogrammed by nature. The Polaroids vividly captured the yellow insect larvae writhing across the man's face. Time, they say, heals all wounds—and given time, nature's cycle would have left nothing but the memory of a man whose life a drug overdose tragically ended too soon.

Nature, it seems, is under the command of no one, and walking down the corridor to the morgue to view an autopsy can make a person feel very insignificant—and for Tobin, afraid of the smell (in retrospect, the very word "decomp" and the less harsh, almost euphemistic description of the victim as a "stinker" trigger a smell that words fail to describe). The thought of finally confronting a victim in the advanced stages of decomposition has stunned Tobin into silence.

After a few moments, his wits return and curiosity about the second victim reemerges like a frightened, reluctant child. "What's the story on the second victim?" he asks.

"Homicide." One word describes the second case. In fact, two homicides occurred last evening. The second, though, will wait in the refrigerator until Monday morning; unless special circumstances arise, such as an accident involving multiple victims, the medical examiner team generally performs just two autopsies on Saturday and none on Sunday.

No book about a medical examiner and forensic pathology would be complete without a discussion of homicide, and when viewing the autopsy of a homicide victim, one witnesses the confluence of fiction and reality. All our lives, television bombards us with images of theatrical violence, theatrical homicides, theatrical corpses, and theatrical medical examiners conducting theatrical medicolegal autopsies. This morning's autopsy will replace those images with the reality of a homicide investigation.

Tobin watches as I punch in the key code to access the morgue (the irony of someone *wanting* to enter the morgue, death junkies aside, still amazes Tobin, although one can understand the necessity of safeguarding the forensic evidence stored within).

Just inside the morgue, Paul Davison, one of the more senior of the county's medical examiner investigators and my long-standing assistant, is preparing for what will be a long morning. Davison began work at the hospital in 1977, and began doing autopsies in 1984. Compared to Davison, my other assistants, Jason and Joel, are relative newcomers; behind the round glasses, his gaze is that of a man who has stories to tell—*volumes* really. I introduce Tobin to the fifty-one-year-old Davison, who at just over six feet two inches with a thin, athletic build and snow-white hair looks like he could double as a retired tennis pro.

"What, if anything, still bothers you about the job?" Tobin asks the same question he posed to the other pathology assistants, aware that he will soon confront the one element of autopsies and the morgue that outsiders find the most revolting: the smell that will enter the morgue when Davison rolls the gurney of the drowning victim into the autopsy room.

After nudging the round glass frames up the bridge of his nose with his index finger, Davison shakes his head. "Nothing," he explains, and it is this immunity that bothers him—a paradoxical answer but one that a person who visits the morgue will immediately understand, because what once proved bothersome no longer does. A glass bottle shard tossed around by the surf will become smooth; likewise, after witnessing the carnage that takes place in the morgue, the senses dull. People can become accustomed to a seismic shift in their reality. They just learn to expect the impact and brace themselves. Their support most often consists of desensitization to the sight of dead bodies.

After a pause, Davison adds that the sight of children in the morgue still bothers him. "They're innocent," he concludes.

"You will want to double up," Davison suggests to Tobin. Davison points to the rack of pale-blue surgical scrubs. For other autopsies, a gown suffices; for a "decomp," he explains, the smell will cling to your hair and your clothes. Tobin searches through the pile of clothes until he finds a shirt, which he pulls over his white, button-down shirt, and pants, which he slips over his black jeans. Next, he slides his arms into a surgical gown that he will wear over the blue hospital garb. Davison twirls his finger in the air—at this unspoken command, Tobin turns around, and Davison ties the strings that fasten the gown in the back.

"Will the smell wash off?" he asks.

Davison smiles and nods. "People will just look at you funny when talking to you." Almost as if following the stage directions of an unwritten script, Paul disappears into the refrigerator to get the first subject just as two deputies enter the morgue: an older man, the detective, dressed in a navy blue suit, and a woman (the evidence technician for the scientific support unit), in the khaki and brown uniform of the Kent County sheriff's department. Without a word to anyone, they move across the morgue to the autopsy table that will hold the "decomp." The fluorescent lights of the morgue reflect off the man's head, which is bordered by a half-moon wedge of auburn hair on the sides and back of his head. The result gives him a greasy appearance. The evidence technician appears to be in her late twenties or early thirties with sandy blonde hair tied into a ponytail. Together, they make an odd couple.

"I'd recommend you all become mouth breathers from this point," Paul announces as he wheels in the gurney containing a blue plastic body bag. Inside the bag are the remains of Patty Fredericks*, a fifty-three-year-old drowning victim. A neighbor found her last evening, floating on her back in a lake just north of Grand Rapids.

Four massive lakes border the two peninsulas that comprise Michigan, earning the state the nickname Great Lakes State. A bird's-eye view of the state would reveal countless inland lakes scraped out of the bedrock when the last glacier receded in the Pleistocene epoch. These lakes dot the landscape like thousands of glistening eyes and provide the setting for those who find themselves drawn to the water for whatever reason. Accidents do happen—a truism that in Michigan often results in drowning victims. If a person frequents a Michigan morgue, sooner or later he or she will witness the autopsy of a drowning victim or a victim submerged in water for some duration. The "sooner" has arrived this morning.

Drowning is one of the more violent processes that lead to death. Instinctively, people hold their breath for as long as possible; but eventually, instinct forces a person to breathe. Only, instead of air, victims of drowning breathe water, inhaling or aspirating draughts into the lungs. The victim fights, struggles, and as a result draws more water into the lungs. The lungs are designed to process air, not water, and since the lungs cannot process the needed oxygen from water, the brain dies.

Yet drowning is a tricky diagnosis for the medical examiner. Two types exist: the aptly named "wet drowning," in which the victim breathes in a large amount of water that fills the lungs, and "dry drowning," in which water in the throat causes a sudden closure of the airway, called a laryngospasm. Most cases fall into the category "wet drowning," but neither type leaves proof of drowning that the medical examiner can readily find. Drowning is a diagnosis made after other causes of death have been excluded. The manner of death may be difficult if not impossible to determine—the suspected drowning could result from an accident, a suicide, or even a homicide.

The difficulty in determining the manner of death in drowning cases lies at the heart of a landmark case: The Oxford Lake Death Penalty Case.

THE OXFORD LAKE DEATH PENALTY CASE

Her body broke through the surface of Oxford Lake, her hands handcuffed behind her back and duct tape covering her eyes and mouth. The sixty pounds of cinder blocks and chain her killer attached to her ankles could not hold her body on the bottom. The accumulation of methane, caused by decomposition, bloated her corpse, floating it to the surface like a balloon. In the end, this miscalculation provided the denouement to the victim's tragedy.

But did she drown? The answer to this question would determine whether the man convicted of her murder would find himself a resident of death row. The murder of Rachel Timmerman is notorious as Michigan's first death penalty case in sixty years; it also illustrates the difficulty drowning can pose for the medical examiner and forensic pathologist and just how difficult it is to determine if a victim drowned or died before entering the water.

If you place your left hand on a table, palm down, you will create a rough map of Michigan's lower peninsula. Along your pinkie finger, or along the northwest coast of Lake Michigan, lies Manistee National Forest—a million-square-acre playground for outdoor enthusiasts. The national park's deciduous forests attract hikers, while kayakers enjoy its miles of winding rivers punctuated by lakes along their serpentine route. One of these lakes is Oxford Lake. It is a place of incredible beauty, except for one tragic moment in June 1997.

One can only imagine Timmerman's final moments on that June night in 1997. The duct tape covering her eyes blinds her; the duct tape covering her mouth muffles her screams. The cold lake water covers her as the cinder blocks pull her to the bottom. She holds her breath, but after a few seconds, her lungs, starving for air, begin to burn. In a desperate but vain attempt to free her body from the chains, she attempts to kick her legs, but the harder she tries, the tighter the chains grip her. She realizes that she will not live to see her twentieth birthday. She is going to die.

And then she inhales, drawing in a deep draft of water through her nostrils and into her lungs, which fill with the turbid water. Her body begins to convulse; she thrashes her arms and legs, but bound with the chain, her body looks like a worm dangling on a hook. After a few seconds, the movement stops.

When Timmerman's body reached the surface of Oxford Lake in July 1997, a month after she and her eleven-month-old daughter, Shannon VerHage, disappeared, suspicion turned to Marvin Gabrion. Timmerman had filed a rape complaint against the forty-eight-year-old Gabrion in 1996. The prosecution's theory posited that Gabrion murdered Timmerman as a way of avoiding rape charges.

This action would lead him to a trial during which he would fight for his life. Michigan does not exercise a death penalty, but the portion of Oxford Lake in which Timmerman was found sits inside of the Manistee National Forest—on federal land. So Marvin Gabrion would face a jury in a federal court. If the prosecution, led by United States attorney Tim VerHey, could prove that Gabrion murdered Timmerman on federal land, inside Manistee National Forest, Gabrion could receive the death penalty for his alleged crime.

Investigators found convincing evidence that tied Gabrion to the victim. After Timmerman filed the rape complaint against Gabrion, she told friends that she was afraid for her life. Witnesses stated that they saw Timmerman with Gabrion by Oxford Lake just before she disappeared. He owned cinder blocks of the same type used to anchor Timmerman's body, and investigators found keys in Gabrion's house that unlocked the locks used to fasten the chains.

But did Timmerman die inside Manistee National Forest? Because the trial took place in a federal court, jurors could only convict Gabrion if they believed Timmerman died on land or water that falls under federal jurisdiction. Therefore, the cause of death became the key point of contention in the trial. If Timmerman drowned, she would have died on federal land because the portion of the lake in which her body surfaced belongs to the Manistee National Forest and is overseen by the federal government. If she didn't drown, she could have been murdered somewhere else and dumped into Oxford Lake. Since drowning leaves no forensic evidence, in cases of suspected drowning, forensic pathologists conduct an "autopsy of exclusion"— the autopsy, in other words, becomes a vehicle to rule out other possibilities. If the autopsy results in evidence to contradict the conclusion that the victim drowned, such as severe skull fractures, which would indicate the victim sustained a fatal head injury, the forensic pathologist will rule out drowning.

Even without contradictory evidence, though, the forensic pathologist must consider other possibilities. When questioned by Gabrion's defense attorney during the trial, I admitted that while drowning was the most likely cause of Timmerman's death, I could not dismiss the possibility that she was strangled or suffocated on state property. Strangulation, though, usually leaves tangible evidence, such as fractured neck bones, bruised or torn skin, and tiny hemorrhages or broken blood vessels called petechial hemorrhages around the throat, inside the throat structures, and in the eyes. Still, if the perpetrator had placed a towel around Timmerman's neck and choked her, the petechial hemorrhages might not occur. Even though I found no such hemorrhages on Timmerman's body, I could not rule out the possibility of a death by strangulation.

Paul Mitchell, Gabrion's chief defense attorney, argued that if Timmerman drowned at the bottom of Oxford Lake, she would have breathed in some of the mud that lines its bottom. And no mud was found in her lungs, throat, or nasal passages.

Prosecutor VerHey countered with a powerful argument. If Timmerman was already dead when thrown into Lake Oxford, why the duct tape over her mouth and the handcuffs on her wrists? The killer would have used the tape to silence her, but a dead body cannot scream. The killer would have used the handcuffs to restrain her, but a corpse cannot resist.

An alternative explanation exists: her killer taped Timmerman's mouth shut and, as a result, she asphyxiated, either by her killer's design or by accident. In such a scenario, the perpetrator would still be guilty of first-degree homicide, but if Rachel Timmerman died in any way other than drowning, she could have died on Michigan land, not federal property. Her killer would face life in prison rather than the death penalty.

Gabrion took the stand; in testimony, he placed the blame for Timmerman's death on a number of other individuals: two other men who also disappeared, state police, and even members of Timmerman's family. During his testimony, he also claimed that he once worked for the CIA.[1]

Gabrion's testimony failed to produce a reasonable doubt and could not overcome VerHey's formidable argument; jurors deliberated for fewer than five hours just six days after the trial began. Gabrion sat calmly and listened as the jury read the verdict: guilty.[2]

During the sentencing phase, Gabrion's defense team argued that the defendant's history of violence resulted from a combination of drug use and physical trauma suffered from motorcycle and car accidents. Their arguments proved ultimately unconvincing. Nearly three weeks after its first verdict, the jury in the sentencing phase became the first jury in Michigan since 1937 to order a death sentence.

Pending a chain of appeals, Marvin Gabrion will die for the murder of Rachel Timmerman. Though a suspect in the disappearances of four others presumed dead, he will face the ultimate punishment for his involvement in the murder of the Newaygo teenager.

The story of Marvin Gabrion is hardly complete, however. An assistant US attorney discovered documents which indicate that, while the federal government owns the Manistee National Forest, it may not possess legal jurisdiction over what occurs there. The US Sixth Circuit Court of Appeals sent the case to the US District Court in Grand Rapids.

After hearing arguments, in late August 2006, US District Court judge Robert Holmes Bell ruled that the federal government did not overstep its boundaries, literally, in trying Marvin Gabrion for a murder committed in its jurisdiction. Gabrion will remain on death row, although the case will likely return to the US Court of Appeals and possibly the US Supreme Court. Gabrion, it appears, will have a long wait before meeting the executioner.

Yet the question of execution is a question beginning with "if," not "when." If at any step in the process Gabrion succeeds in his appeal to convince a judge or judges that he was tried in the wrong court, his death sentence *and* conviction would be vacated. He would walk away from death row in Terre Haute, Indiana, a free man, if only long enough for prosecutors to ready their case for retrial in a state court. If convicted of first-degree murder in a state court, he would face an automatic sentence of life in prison without the possibility of parole, but he would *not* face the death penalty. Another trial would also bring a chance of acquittal.

A tragic postscript: Shannon VerHage has never been found. Despite a $5,000 reward, no information about her whereabouts has surfaced.

*****

In the case of Patty Fredericks, drowning is the diagnosis of exclusion, so during the autopsy we will look for injury or disease—anything that will be a more compelling cause than drowning. We will attempt to exclude any other cause of death. The "possibilities" revolve around two central questions: Did Patty Fredericks die before or after she entered the water, and of what did she die? If no evidence of another cause of death is found during the autopsy, drowning becomes the diagnosis. And once again, context provides vital information. The report explains that the neighbor who discovered Fredericks's body found her legs entangled in a rope attached to a dock, which suggests that if she did drown, her death was most likely an accident. The final few minutes of her life may have occurred like this. In a drunken stupor, she wandered to the end of the dock, where her feet became entangled in a rope. She slipped, fell into the lake, and could not free herself from the rope and drowned.

The report also suggests another possibility. Fredericks took clinical doses of oxycodone—an extremely powerful painkiller—and the report contains the phrase "Hx of EtOH abuse." In other words, she had a history (Hx) of alcohol (EtOH) abuse. The circumstantial evidence suggests that Fredericks may have stumbled onto the dock in a narcotic and alcohol-induced stupor, passed out, fell into the lake, and drowned. Or she may have taken an overdose of narcotics, died, then fell into the water, where her body floated to the surface a few days later. The report also contains a minor mystery. It states that the "right side" of Fredericks's face is missing, and that her body was found in a state of moderate decomposition. Why would half of her face be missing?

The answer lies in the dynamics of what law enforcement personnel call "the floater." A dead body, whether caused by drowning or some other manner of death, sinks to the bottom of the lake, the heavier upper torso leaning toward the lakebed, posed like a whale during whale song, the head and hands dragging along the bottom. It was during this phase that Patty Fredericks lost the right side of her face, as crustaceans and turtles, indigenous in freshwater lakes of the Midwest, dined on her flesh.

Soon after death, with the body hovering on or near the lakebed, it begins to decompose. The decomposition process results in a buildup of gases within the body; the gases buoy the corpse, and it gradually begins its ascent toward the surface. Water temperature greatly influences the length of time it takes the body to reach the surface. Frigid water slows the process of decomposition; in fact, had Fredericks fallen through a sheet of ice on a Michigan lake in January, months could have passed before her body returned to the surface. In the warmer summer months, the process takes much less time, and within a few days, Fredericks's body popped through the surface becoming what police refer to as a "floater" and medical personnel call a "decomp" and I call a "stinker."

No superlative exists to describe the stench that fills the morgue when

Paul unzips the body bag. The sickening-sweet odor floods the morgue like a tidal bore, enveloping everything and everyone in the room. The smell, like an invisible hand, shoves Tobin to the doorway—"upwind" considering the ventilation design of the morgue. He races toward the table containing a brown glass jar. He opens the bottle of wintergreen Lorann oil, holds a Kleenex over its mouth, and shakes. He dabs the Kleenex over his mask, and the pleasing odor of wintergreen for a moment permeates the corner of the autopsy room. By the table containing various autopsy paraphernalia, such as packages of cotton swabs, sits the stereo. The background music Paul has chosen for the first autopsy today features the distinctively raspy vocals of Rod Stewart crooning about Maggie May: "*Wake up Maggie, I think I've got something to say to you. . . .*"

The female deputy moves around Fredericks's body snapping photographs, seemingly unaffected, even oblivious to the stench. Tobin watches the others in the room from the corner, amazed at their resistance to the noxious odor that by now has filled the room, hovering in the atmosphere like an invisible cloud. How do they do it? How do they approach the body? Do they have enough control to breathe only through their mouths? Do they imagine clothespins over their nostrils? The female deputy and her partner are marvels to Tobin; they stand over the body, unmasked, and do their jobs. Tobin is the only one in the morgue who has dipped into the bottle of Lorann oil.

Paul cuts off the blue denim dress and the white panties that she wore on the final day of her life to reveal the rotund physique of the five foot one, one hundred and fifty pound Fredericks, who now looks nine months pregnant—the gases trapped inside her torso and saturating her tissues have created an extremely bloated appearance. Her skin is a mixture of dull, pale blue and pink, creating a marbled appearance streaked with dirt from the lake. Decomposition mixed with the immersion in the water has left the skin loose (except on her midsection, where the bloating has caused the skin to stretch like the skin of a balloon); shards of skin dangle from her feet and the skin on her torso is flaked and peeling. Gray-green weeds are woven through her toes. Half of her face has vanished, as has her right ear, leaving the bluish white skull exposed and the eye socket empty, vacant, dark, deserted. Her blonde hair, matted with clumps of dirt and weeds, dangles over the exposed skull.

Breathe through your mouth, only your mouth, Tobin looks to be reminding himself, but instinct takes over and he takes in a deep breath through his nose. He begins to gag, and races to the bottle of Lorann oil, drenches another tissue, and holds it over his mask. He manages not to vomit as the bottle of Lorann oil works like a fountain of youth.

"What did you find?" Tobin asks in a voice muffled by the wintergreen-drenched tissue he holds tightly against his mask.

"We've got a fat maggot," I note. Sometimes, the maggots enter the morgue with the bodies.

"Don't talk about yourself that way," Paul retorts. His mock scolding brings a smile from the Kent County deputies and, like a scalpel cutting through the thickness in the air, eliminates some of the tension in the room.

Circling the body, I note important forensic details into my handheld recorder, including several scars on the victim's wrists—evidence of her troubled past. A few minutes later the external examination is finished. The autopsy unfolds without conversation between the pathology personnel and the Kent County deputies; devoid of the usual banter, the atmosphere becomes very businesslike.

"Watch this. You'll find this interesting," Paul calls over to Tobin, who has taken refuge behind the steel table containing the wintergreen oil.

In one hand, Paul holds a yellow disposable lighter and in the other a large needle with a flared end like a funnel—one that looks like the type used to inflate a tire or a basketball. It's a twelve-gauge veterinary needle. He inserts the sharp end of the needle deep into Fredericks's midsection, just below the sternum and deep enough to penetrate the skin, fat, and muscle. Then he flicks the lighter, holding the flame next to the flared end of the needle. Nothing happens.

This process, Paul explains, will release and burn the methane that has collected inside the body, alleviating much of the stench; the needle provides an avenue for the gas to escape the body cavity, and the flame incinerates the gas. Once in contact with the flame, he explains, the methane creates a flare and an imposing sight—the morgue's best effort to create fireworks. The smell remains.

An older man in his seventies and wearing a suit and tie enters the morgue. His attire makes him appear like one of the cadre of funeral directors who visit the morgue to claim victims for burial. As he passes he smiles; the plastic nametag pinned to his lapel identifies him as "J. Connolly, Medical Examiner." Like Davison, Connolly is a death scene investigator, one of the dozen or so employees dispatched to investigate crime scenes. Tobin watches in stunned silence as Connolly walks into the morgue and straight to the table holding Patty Fredericks. No mask, and, more impressively, no wintergreen oil. He circles the table once, carefully studying the drowning victim, then turns and leaves the morgue.

As Paul makes the Y-incision, the smell actually intensifies and spills to the other corner of the morgue where Tobin has attempted to take refuge from it, hunkered behind the steel table like a soldier in a foxhole.

"Sugar, sugar . . ." Rod Stewart's "Da Ya Think I'm Sexy?" emanates from the stereo along the wall behind him as Paul snaps through Fredericks's ribs and removes her breastplate.

He dips another tissue and dabs his facemask, which now must reek of wintergreen, but nonetheless, the stench of decomposition penetrates the barrier. He tosses the tissue onto the steel table; next to him, a skeleton is poised on a stand placed against the load-bearing column where the corridor meets the morgue. The skeleton, therefore, literally greets those entering the morgue; it is the first thing they see. Positioned behind the pillar, the skeleton has its back turned to the business of the morgue, which now seems like an advantageous spot. Behind the skeleton, Rod Steward provides the vocals that are ironic and oddly appropriate: *Some guys have all the luck.*

Another female officer in plainclothes—which today means a pair of faded blue jeans, a blouse, and a forty-caliber pistol (which seems to be the weapon of choice among local law enforcement) strapped to her waist—enters the morgue. A detective from a neighboring county, she has come to attend the autopsy of the homicide victim, who waits, zipped inside a white plastic bag on the table in front of me. With the detective is her partner for the day—a medicolegal death scene investigator with raven-black hair. In black slacks and high heels, her appearance presents a stark contrast to the detective. They scan the scene and, perhaps repelled by the stench, disappear into the conference room at the other end of the corridor leading to the morgue.

One can envision the scenario of Patty Fredericks's demise; it's a common story in cases of drowning victims and those found dead in Michigan's numerous lakes and rivers. The night she died, Fredericks may have consumed a large amount of alcohol. A few cocktails mixed with the powerful painkillers (she had a history of Oxycontin [oxycodone] abuse) she took may have assisted in creating her blackout and would indicate how and why she drowned. In a stupor, she fell into the lake and drowned. Her history—repeated Driving Under the Influence (DUI) convictions—suggests that she periodically doused her troubles in alcohol. A toxicology screen of her blood, though, would not provide definitive evidence in this case.

After death, bacteria growing in the deceased body often produce large amounts of ethyl alcohol, the presence of which would render the tests inaccurate. And the body continues to process substances like alcohol until the heart stops, so, for example, a postmortem blood sample from an accident victim who lived for a few days on life support before dying would not yield an accurate picture of the substances she took at the time of the accident. Remember Harry Freiburg from chapter 3? A blood sample taken postmortem could not have established if he had consumed enough alcohol to render him unconscious during the house fire, where he died. But the hospital that admitted Freiburg took a blood sample and ran a toxicology screen, producing an accurate blood-alcohol level. No such sample exists for Patty Fredericks, whose body wasn't found until several days after her death. If she did travel to the morgue riding on the liquid highway, she certainly would not be the first or the last, as the morgue's glass cabinet filled with liquor bottles illustrates. Each of these bottles has a story to tell, most about alcoholics who sustained fatal injuries during falls but ironically managed to protect the sacred nectar of their addiction.

Somehow, Tobin pushes away the smell and drifts toward the workstation where the dissection of the lungs has begun. They bear the "scarlet letter" of a longtime smoker: large, charcoal-black blotches. Meanwhile, the smell in the morgue does not get any better when Paul slices through the intestines, adding yet another sour element to the pungent odor of decomposition.

Breathe through your mouth, Tobin reminds himself, *breathe through your mouth. BREATHE THROUGH YOUR MOUTH!*

No don't . . .

TOO LATE.

Back to the wintergreen oil and the table and the skeleton against the pillar, who now appears to be grinning.

"She's a smoker," I note to Tobin, who has returned and positioned himself next to me. The interior of Fredericks's lungs bears the telltale signs that result from years of smoking—normally tiny microscopic holes (air spaces or alveoli) dot the lungs, but lung damage in chronic smokers is manifested by breakdown of the walls of the alveoli, making holes (known as bullae) that are visible to the naked eye. The size of pinpoints (about one millimeter), the holes look like dozens of tiny canker sores.

Next, her liver is examined. I hand Tobin a long, tube-shaped plastic bag and ask him to stick his hand into the bag. He inserts his hand into the bag, which seems to envelope his hand and entire forearm. I ask him to open his palm and stick out his hand; into his open palm, I place a slice of Patty Fredericks's liver. With his other hand, Tobin peels the bag toward his hand, effectively reversing it and encasing the liver without contact with his gloved hand. The liver will travel down the corridor to the histology lab where technicians will conduct tests to determine the amount of alcohol and the narcotics it contains, providing a clear picture of what the deceased consumed in the hours leading to her death and possible drowning or overdose.

The autopsy continues and, with the exception of the lung damage, uncovers nothing out of the ordinary. On to the last step in the process: the excision and examination of Fredericks's skull and brain. Paul Davison places a bowl under her head, which is propped up by a white piece of plastic called a head block.

The Stryker saw makes its familiar and very distinctive sound, like a high-pitched drill. Tobin watches from across the room as Davison works the saw across the skull, creating two converging lines that meet on both sides of her head. Davison also makes a notch in the calvarium so it will stay in place later when he sews together the incised scalp. As Davison works the Stryker, Fredericks's head moves from side to side, like she disagrees with the procedure—a macabre sight.

After removing the calvarium, the woman's brain spills into the bowl placed at the base of her head. Unlike the stiff, off-white brains removed from "fresh" corpses, hers is purplish brown and semiliquid from decomposition—so soft that it oozes from the opening in her skull.

While Fredericks's brain is sliced into cross sections (or to use the medical jargon "bread-loafed" in order to study it), Davison sprinkles a gray sandy substance in her chest cavity. The plastic container, about the size of a peanut butter jar, contains "Safe Embalming Powder"—the paraformaldehyde in the embalming powder, he explains, will help to mask the odor of decomposition.

One point of procedure remains for the Kent County deputies: they must collect fingerprints from the deceased, which usually consists of both thumbprints and one other finger. After applying ink to the fingertip, they roll the inked finger over a small white sticker that looks like an office tab. They stick the tabs to a plastic sheet for their records.

But on bodies submerged in tepid water for a protracted period of time, skin loosens, which will make the normally routine task of fingerprinting somewhat difficult and more complicated. They try over and over again to lift a thumbprint. The loose skin moves each time they roll the thumb across the paper, smearing and obscuring the print. Paul watches, smiling, as the deputies grumble, their complaints inaudible but the tone of their voices indicating their frustration.

Paul mentions that sometimes, when the condition of the "decomp" renders a print difficult, medical examiner personnel will actually remove the outer layer of skin from the thumb and place it over something solid. His expression and the sheer absurdity of the idea strikes Tobin as oddly amusing, and the image of Larry, Moe, and Curly in a morgue conducting an autopsy brings a smile to his face. Paul, one can deduce from his smile, must be joking.

While the deputies struggle with the right thumb, Paul bends over

Fredericks's left hand. The scalpel rises as Paul's elbow moves. He's doing something with her hand or possibly her arm; from the corner of the morgue, it is difficult for Tobin to see what he is doing.

The deputies manage to lift the print from the victim's right thumb after several attempts. The female deputy doesn't look pleased, as she moves to the other side of the table to take the left thumbprint—that is until she sees what Davison has just done, and a smile spreads across her face.

Tobin can't believe what he's seeing, so despite the smell, he moves over to the table where the female deputy is applying ink to Davison's left gloved hand. The deputy stands next to Paul as she rolls the white sticker tab across his left thumb. Tobin stares in amazement: Davison is wearing the skin of Patty Fredericks's left thumb, complete with her thumbnail, over his left thumb like a glove. The skin of the woman's left thumb looks too small and too feminine for his hands, and looks odd on the outside of his glove!

While the examination of the internal organs is completed, Davison sprinkles more embalming powder on an empty gurney lined with a black plastic body bag that will hold Patty Fredericks's body at the conclusion of the autopsy. The mysterious embalming powder will help mask the smell—a silent "goodwill" gesture to the funeral home employees (like the washing of blood from the skin) who will handle Fredericks after she leaves the morgue.

Lasting just about an hour, this is one of the faster autopsies Tobin has viewed. Paul explains that this often happens with "stinkers." The stench is traumatizing; while it doesn't appear to bother the death investigators, the speed of the autopsy suggests otherwise. The stench may have led to a more rapid autopsy, but not a less thorough one. The fifty-one-year-old Davison, who began conducting autopsies in 1984, seems immune to the smell and the many other macabre sights frequently found in the morgue.

With her autopsy complete, Patty Fredericks does not receive a post-mortem clean bill of health. She suffered from emphysema, and her history suggests a constant battle with substance use, but the autopsy uncovered nothing to exclude the supposition that she drowned or overdosed on drugs, alcohol, or a combination of the two.

Pending an ugly surprise, she drowned or she overdosed. An ugly surprise in this case might consist of a toxicology screen that indicates she ingested a poison, such as cyanide, which would suggest that someone might have murdered her by adulterating her drink of choice with a toxic agent.

But no such ugly surprise would ultimately appear; according to the toxicology report, her liver held an amount of narcotics and alcohol that proved fatal. Fredericks was locked into a tug-of-war; the combined pull of prescription painkillers and alcohol ultimately won. In a substance-induced stupor, she wandered onto the dock by her home and fell into a state of unconsciousness from which she would never awake. She over-dosed and her body plunged into the lake.

The (live) bodies that filled the morgue only a few minutes ago vanish as quickly as they arrived, perhaps driven from the room by the smell or the fact that they don't want to be in the morgue on a Saturday (or any day).

Tobin pulls off his mask and places it on the table next to the com-puter; two strings loop around the ears, pulling the mask close to the face. Pinching the strip that runs across the bridge of the nose brings the mask even closer to the face, preventing the potential inhalation of "bad" or infected air. After an hour or longer, though, the strings pull at the back of the ears and become uncomfortable, but compared to the potential problems of not wearing the mask, the discomfort is little more than an annoyance. If wearing the mask during an autopsy is a mosquito bite, then not wearing the mask is a snakebite, and the unmasked observer faces many risks (see "Risks," chapter 1).

Tobin takes a much-needed breather then joins me inside the confer-ence room, where the tall blonde with the forty-caliber pistol strapped to her belt and the raven-haired woman in the black slacks and high heels await my arrival. A large oval table occupies much of the room's floor space; a large office enclosure, a photocopy machine, and a large file cab-inet occupy the little remaining space. While a small room, smaller than an average bedroom, the furniture gives the room a cramped feel, unlike the more spacious morgue. The low ceiling and the cinder-block walls add to the claustrophobic feeling, and the absence of any natural light in this room (the entire morgue is devoid of sunlight) combined with the blue hue of the fluorescent lighting creates an eerie effect, like the sensation of standing inside a bomb shelter.

Three skulls sit on top of the office enclosure—a human skull and two canine skulls. The canine skulls provide useful models for matching canine bite marks. Across the room, behind glass doors of a cabinet attached to the wall, a line of bullets of various calibers shine like teeth.

"In shorts?" "Raven" asks as I enter the conference room, surprised at my choice of attire: beige shorts that reach midthigh, a grey T-shirt bearing the logo of Beckwith's Gym (a local Mecca for hard-core weight lifters), and tennis shoes.

I begin the introductions to Tobin, who has wandered into the conference room and slumped into one of the chairs around the table. I nod at the blonde with the pistol: "Venus, Venus Dyke." She smiles. "Raven" smiles. They look like two kids watching the effects of a practical joke they engineered. Someone once said that the truth is stranger than fiction; if a novelist created a name like Venus Dyke, suspension of belief would disappear.

"Really," Tobin says, his tone slow and deliberate, careful not to offend.

"Really," she says, and the two women chuckle like kids at a lunch table. Dyke is a detective in Ottawa County—the county bordering Kent to the west; miles of yellow sand dunes and beaches form Ottawa County's border to the east, and picturesque lakeside cities with names like Grand Haven, Holland, and Saugatuck dot the coast. With bright yellow hair and an athletic build, she is a few inches taller than Tobin.

"And Wavelet Thompson." Thompson, the raven-haired woman in the black slacks, logged many hours in morgues as a pathology assistant before she became the death investigator for Ottawa County. Her slighter build and ink-dark hair with an auburn tinge makes her the physical opposite of her partner. She hands Tobin her business card.

It is easy for those with limited experience in the morgue and the criminal underworld to be a little intimidated by the two investigators, yet unlike the nameless Kent County detectives who cast a few awkward glances at Tobin while he observed them taking Fredericks's fingerprints, these two seem not to mind; perhaps they even welcome his presence.

After the introductions, the two investigators begin their briefing. To investigators, a homicide represents a certain degree of intrigue. For a person not involved in the law enforcement community, the notion of an interesting homicide may seem odd at best, bordering on perverse. After several trips to the underworld, though, a person can appreciate the curiosity they perhaps feel this morning.

Yet devotees of both crime fiction and nonfiction read or watch from the safety of their living-room couches. In order to visit the morgue to watch a real case unfold on Saturday, as Tobin and several others have, someone must actually die Friday night. For those like Thompson who visit the deceased often, suicide and heart attack victims must become mundane, albeit tragic, stories. With homicides, the "medicolegal" investigator plays a crucial role in reading the clues provided by the crime scene and the deceased to ensure that justice will conquer the insidious forces that lead to homicide.

Of course, with intrigue comes scrutiny, as defense lawyers love to pounce on errors committed by investigators.

Thompson would have waited some time for a homicide; Ottawa County, dominated by conservative Christians, boasts one of the lowest violent crime rates in the state, averaging just two homicides per year. In a few minutes, we will meet the victim of one of them.

Dyke and Thompson begin the briefing, and describe the unfolding of their investigation into Richard Sullivan's untimely demise.

Friday the thirteenth, last night, would indeed prove unlucky for fifty-five-year-old Richard Sullivan. At 6:15 PM, his lifetime partner and room-mate would discover Sullivan's body lying on the floor of their Saugatuck home. Chicago police arrested three men in Sullivan's car in an area called "The Bricks," in South Chicago. Officers tracked down the trio after purchases had been made with Sullivan's credit card. Of the three, two claim that the man driving Sullivan's car picked them up while they were hitchhiking to Chicago.

"Of course," I add, "because if present at the scene of the crime, they would be charged as accessories, which carries the same penalty as murder."

Yet the house was not ransacked, like one would expect with a robbery.

Dyke, though, suspects ("a gut feeling" as she describes it) that the crime was not sexually motivated, although Davison will conduct a rape kit on the deceased; if he was raped, the kit would preserve DNA that could potentially pair the killer with the victim.

With their briefing completed, the investigators move into the autopsy room where Paul Davison has prepared Sullivan for autopsy by removing the victim's clothes. Sullivan's appearance on the autopsy table leaves no doubt as to the horror of his final moments of life.

With a 35 mm camera, Venus Dyke snaps photographs of Sullivan (which the prosecution will later use in court—see "The Last Chapter," chapter 13), whose face and chest is a deep purple color; he was found facedown, so gravity pulled the blood toward his face, creating the purple and bloated appearance. His eyelids are closed, but the eyes bulge in their sockets and look like golf balls just under the surface of the skin. A portion of his pale-red tongue protrudes, clamped between his teeth.

The ugliness of the physical injuries Sullivan sustained sharply contrasts with the evidence that in life Sullivan took pride in his appearance. He wore his blond hair short, spiked, almost shaved; he kept his white sideburns neatly trimmed, and from the look of his left hand, he kept his fingernails manicured. A white plastic bag covers his right hand, placed by investigators to preserve any evidence, such as small pieces of skin that may have become embedded under the fingernails in a struggle. The skin pieces would yield DNA that, like the rape kit, could help prosecutors link the perpetrator to the victim.

Sullivan knew his fate and, powerless to prevent it, he succumbed to a death that was neither quick nor painless. Given that Sullivan obviously suffered greatly before his death, the alleged robbery motive seems an incredible reason for his demise; the violence that characterized his death seems excessive for a mere theft. No, Sullivan could not have died over a stolen Pontiac and a few credit cards.

Venus Dyke continues her photographic record of the deceased. A running shoe, the left one, dangles from the left side of his neck, its lace wrapped around Sullivan like a necklace—except the shoelace is embedded in the skin of his throat. The killer created a garrote, wrapping the shoelace around his neck from behind, and twisting until Sullivan died of asphyxiation.

Sullivan's body rests on his wrists, which are bound with the shoelace from his other shoe; detectives found the "lace-less" right shoe at the scene. Unlike the shoelace noose around his neck, the shoestring binding Sullivan's hands is loose—a curious fact that raises the specter of sexual asphyxia (see "The Rough Sex Case" below). Handcuffs found at the residence added to the suspicion that Sullivan's death may have occurred as a "misadventure" between two lovers engaged in bondage or "rough sex." The injuries, though, contradict the injuries consistent with an accidental death from a sex act gone bad. According to his life partner, Sullivan did not participate in bondage, and the trio arrested in Chicago in Sullivan's car supported the possibility that theft motivated this crime.

"Rough sex" or bondage, though, has on occasion provided clientele for the Kent County morgue, but a death that results from a sex act gone awry always raises an important and difficult-to-answer question: Was it an accident or was it murder?

THE ROUGH SEX CASE

The case of *The People of the State of Michigan v. Brian Anthony Briggs* was a case of he-said, she-couldn't say, as the decedent, Ann Marie Briggs, died during an alleged session of sex gone awry—a misadventure that would send her husband in front of a three-judge panel in a bench trial on a second-degree homicide charge. In the end, her body would do the talking. The case turned on the forensic evidence uncovered during the autopsy and illustrates the fine line between homicidal asphyxiation and accidental asphyxiation resulting from a sex act.

Thirty-year-old Ann Marie Briggs was found lying on the living-room floor of her home. Her husband, Brian, informed the authorities that they had engaged in a sex act that included strangulation; some people experience a heightened sense of euphoria that results from a decrease in blood oxygen during sexual activity, which often leads to unconsciousness. Taken too far, an accidental death could result, which the defendant claimed occurred on that fateful night at the Briggs home; he therefore admitted to strangling his wife, but contended that her death resulted from an accident and nothing more.[3]

The autopsy provided the proof that Ann Marie Briggs was indeed strangled, and at first the proof seemed to corroborate Briggs's version of the events. I found the tiny pinprick-sized broken blood vessels called petechiae (or petechial hemorrhages) in her eyes and face—telltale signs of asphyxiation—but not necessarily evidence of homicide. These broken blood vessels can result from the application of force on the throat, by a person's hands, for instance, for fifteen to thirty seconds or longer.

For a death by strangulation to occur, three to four minutes of neck pressure would have to be applied. During the trial, I outlined the process: during the first sixty to ninety seconds, the victim would remain conscious and struggle to free herself from the asphyxia. After ninety seconds, the victim would have lost consciousness. After three minutes without oxygen, brain damage and death result. The broken blood vessels on Ann Marie's face, eyes, and neck could have resulted from just fifteen to thirty seconds of pressure on her neck; therefore, the strangulation done as part of a sex act could result in these hemorrhages.

Under Michigan law (*People v. Goecke*), four conditions must exist for a defendant to be found guilty of second-degree homicide: "(1) a death, (2) caused by an act of the defendant, (3) with malice, and (4) without justification or excuse."[4] The question became, then, how did the forensic evidence suggest that Briggs, the defendant, acted out of malice, defined by Michigan law as "the intent to kill, the intent to cause great bodily harm, or the intent to do an act in wanton and willful disregard of the likelihood that the natural tendency of such behavior to cause death or great bodily harm"?[5] It wasn't the petechiae, which could have resulted from their sex game gone awry. Without the presence of malice, the jury could not convict Briggs of homicide.

My main reason for ruling homicide was the injury to her neck, which was more extensive than would be found in consensual sex.

But the autopsy also uncovered additional, damning evidence that supported this finding of homicide. The examination uncovered petechiae on her shoulders and upper chest—a rare occurrence in a case of consensual, manual strangulation (such as a sexual use of asphyxia). For blood vessels to pop in these areas, a greater force must exist, such as the force of several hundred pounds that would result if someone became trapped under a car after a tire jack slipped, or if a man leaned on a woman, pushing his weight on her with all of his force. The bruises on Ann

Marie's upper arms and an abrasion on the back of her left elbow provided further evidence that allows me to envision Ann Marie's final moments of life: someone grabbed her arms and forced her to the carpet, against which she scraped the back of her left elbow. Since the scrape bled, she had to have sustained the injury prior to her death.

This evidence was damning indeed because it undermined the husband's claim that Ann Marie's death resulted from an erotic act that had gone too far. In a sexual act involving asphyxia, since the aim is sexual pleasure not homicide, the person strangling would stop after his partner lost consciousness. Had Brian Briggs ceased the strangulation when his wife lost consciousness, had Ann Marie Briggs's body exhibited only broken blood vessels in her face, eyes, and throat, then her death could have resulted from a sex act turned tragedy—an accident.

As I outlined in my testimony, however, Ann Marie would have lost consciousness after ninety seconds of pressure. If the broken blood vessels on her shoulders and chest could only occur from someone forcing his weight on her, the three judges concluded that after Ann Marie lost consciousness, after several minutes of pressure, the defendant continued to apply pressure for a while, perhaps as long as several minutes. Strangling someone after that person has lost consciousness amounts to homicide, not overzealous sex play. This proves the intent to kill. In short, the defendant acted out of malice.

The three judges found the presence of malice, and after the nine-day bench trial, they found Brian Briggs guilty of second-degree murder and sentenced him to between seventeen and sixty years in prison.

During the appeal to the Michigan Court of Appeals, Briggs's lawyer argued that the hemorrhages on Ann Marie's shoulders and arms do not prove that he exerted force against her neck lasting the two to three minutes necessary to kill her. And during my testimony, I did not state that two or three minutes of force were necessary to create the broken blood vessels on her shoulders and chest.

The appellate court, though, found that the circumstantial evidence (the bruising to her arms and the scrape on her left elbow), coupled with my testimony that during a sex act involving asphyxia the passive partner does not struggle enough to be injured, when viewed together, indicates the presence of malice. In short, despite the fact that the broken blood vessels covering Ann Marie's shoulders and upper chest did not prove that Briggs strangled his wife for minutes after she lost consciousness, the circumstantial evidence provided enough proof to support the argument that Mr. Briggs acted out of malice. Michigan case law provides that judges can find the presence of malice if they can infer from the evidence that the defendant "intentionally set in motion a force likely to cause death or great bodily harm."[6] While the hemorrhages alone did not prove this, the judges properly inferred from the other forensic evidence (the bruising and the scrape) that Briggs acted out of malice. They upheld the lower court's ruling.

Brian Briggs is serving a sentence for second-degree homicide.

In the end, Ann Marie Briggs had the loudest voice, and the court heard her.

*****

I examine the superficial wounds on Richard Sullivan's body, all the while noting the slightest detail into my handheld recording device as Dyke documents the evidence with her camera, and Thompson feverishly records every detail onto a legal pad. Every injury is noted—a meticulous, painstaking, and time-consuming process necessary in a homicide investigation. Before I begin to catalogue the injuries, Thompson asks me to look for any evidence that the killer smothered Sullivan with a pillow; she suspects that the perpetrator smothered Sullivan before garroting him. An examination of the body, though, suggests that Sullivan was conscious as the killer twisted the shoelace tighter and tighter.

Among the many bruises and scrapes over Sullivan's body, a scuff appears on his left shoulder and another above his right eyebrow. In addition, both knees are scuffed, which is consistent with the killer forcing Sullivan onto his knees before strangling him. Another minor abrasion is found on the back of Sullivan's heel. Every detail is noted. Richard Sullivan suffered, and the longer the catalogue of injuries becomes, the more hideous the crime appears, and the hotter the temperature in the autopsy room seems to grow. An Eric Clapton blues tune plays in the background like a hushed conversation, a choice of music that seems to cool the atmosphere in the room.

Paul Davison and I roll the body onto its side to examine Sullivan's backside for injuries. Here we discover streaks of feces covering his buttocks and upper thighs. Upon death the sphincter muscles relax, often resulting in the expulsion of feces. Or perhaps he defecated in panic when he realized, at the moment just before everything faded to black, that he was dying.

With the superficial features noted and photographically catalogued, Paul cuts the shoelace around Sullivan's neck, removes the shoe, and places it on the vacant autopsy table that thirty minutes ago held Patty Fredericks. With the shoe removed, the damage done by the shoestring garrote becomes evident—a white groove pressed into the now-purple skin of Sullivan's neck. The deep purple offers a stark contrast with the white groove, a juxtaposition that seems to scream "murder."

I pry open Sullivan's jaws to examine the inside of his mouth, in which appear tiny red dots that cover the lining of his mouth like bright red pinpricks—those pinpoint hemorrhages that have come to be the "signature" evidence of strangulation. A quick glance at the clock reveals that thirty minutes have passed and the Y-incision has yet to be made. While procedure dominates the business of the morgue, homicide investigations require fastidious adherence to procedure and an obsessive attention to detail. Nothing goes unnoticed or unstudied, because what is discovered during the autopsy is evidence that will contribute to the prosecution of Sullivan's murderer. In the weeks and months that follow that fateful Friday the thirteenth in mid-August, I will testify at both the preliminary hearing and the trial of the alleged killer. The forensic evidence collected today will vividly re-create for the jurors Sullivan's last moments. And every piece of evidence counts.

Next, Davison conducts the rape kit on Richard Sullivan, which consists of cotton swabs and heavy cardboard stock folders, the size of three-by-five-inch index cards, lined with plastic sheets. Davison dips the tips of several cotton swabs into a jar of alcohol, sterilizing them. Next, he conducts the "rectal" by inserting the ends of the swabs into Sullivan's rectum. He withdraws the swabs, now light brown in color, and one at a time rubs each against the glass slide encased in the heavy cardboard folder. He then lays the folder, open, onto the vacant autopsy table. Paul then dips another swab into the jar of alcohol and runs its tip across a white streak, "white mucoid material" he calls it, on Sullivan's left thigh. He "swabs" the lining of the mouth (oral sex would leave evidence here) and the tip of the penis; DNA found here would indicate when and with whom Sullivan had had sex on the day he died.

After half an hour of noting injuries and taking DNA samples, Paul Davison makes the Y-incision, snaps through the ribs around the sternum, and begins to remove the internal organs, placing each in the bowls now situated between Sullivan's legs.

The evidence collected now covers the vacant, stainless-steel autopsy table. On the table, the DNA folders look like small children's board books, but these books will tell investigators the "story" of Sullivan's murder: Did consensual sex between the victim and the perpetrator precede the murder? Or did the murderer also rape? Did Sullivan manage to scratch his attacker, "trapping" skin underneath his fingernails?

The autopsy will leave no proverbial stone unturned, but in most autopsies the apparent manner of death dictates that the medical examiner focus the examination on one or more "regions" of the body: in the case of a strangulation death, the throat structures may contain vital forensic evidence. The twisting of the shoelace garrote would leave evidence on the inside of Sullivan's body as well as the outside.

Davison removes Sullivan's entire throat structure as one intact mass, which consists of a group of throat muscles, the tongue, and the hyoid bone. Tobin watches as Paul moves the blade of his scalpel back and forth under Sullivan's neck to remove the tongue.

The examination of the long, rectangular mass that consists of the throat structures begins. Out of the body, the tongue flattens and appears an oversized, huge, grotesque, tough pink-purple mass. I dissect through the structures, noting the deep red and purple hemorrhaging throughout the tissues—the damage caused by the squeeze of the shoelace around Sullivan's neck. I pause while Venus Dyke snaps a few photographs of the inside of Sullivan's fatal injuries.

The neck structures are placed on a towel-lined plastic tray, the type used in a college cafeteria, and given to Paul, who takes the tray into an adjoining room to photograph the neck structures. A few minutes later, the photography complete, Davison returns with the tray, and the examination continues as he adds to the mass of evidence by taking Sullivan's fingerprints.

"We have another photo opportunity here," I call to Venus Dyke, who moves toward the workstation where more damage is discovered: a fracture in one of the horns (called cornua) of the thyroid cartilage. This fracture suggests that in addition to a ligature strangulation, Sullivan was manually strangled.

After she snaps a few photographs, the autopsy proceeds. Each organ is carefully examined with samples placed in the pink cassettes and in the stock jar labeled with Sullivan's case number. One can imagine the impending court scene, with a stern-faced prosecutor in a three-piece suit delivering his opening statement to a shocked and horrified jury. What does he say? He might be discussing one final piece of evidence the autopsy uncovers: unlike many of the other victims who enter the morgue, Sullivan enjoyed perfect health. No evidence of illness, disease, or injury other than that caused by the murderer is discovered. Sullivan's clean bill of health underlines his vicious and senseless murder. The prosecutor would likely inform the jury that had the perpetrator not ended his life, Richard Sullivan would have lived a long, healthy existence.

"Just to make sure, you *are* calling this a homicide?" Thompson asks.

"Oh yes," I respond. The forensic evidence indicates that Sullivan did not die as the result of an accident or misadventure during a session of rough sex.

"Do you want to run an HIV test on him?" Davison asks.

After a few seconds, I agree.

"Does an immunization exist for HIV?" Tobin asks me as I raise my arm and place the back of my palm under the blue triangle at the base of the workstation's top shelf—an electric eye to start and stop the flow of water. Lines of cold water run across the table, washing the blood and detritus "down river." The specter of HIV adds another level of danger to the autopsy proceedings. To avoid HIV, the pathology personnel are careful, very careful.

"Condoms," I reply, and Tobin chuckles.

One can appreciate the humor that for a few seconds diverts our attention from the tragic ending of Richard Sullivan, if only *for a few seconds*. A glance back at the remains of this poor man on the table, now literally just the shell of a human, underlines the fact that the sky was red last night . . . the color of blood.

*****

In the days that follow the autopsy, the *Grand Rapids Press* runs a series of articles about the Sullivan case as it evolves from investigation to arrest and then to prosecution. The investigation hinges on the discovery of the perpetrator's potential motive. Why did this poor man die? This question would reappear like a ghost, haunting investigators for some time after that Saturday in the morgue. Over the next few weeks, the case would unravel, puzzle piece by puzzle piece, to form a picture—an ugly portrait—of the circumstances that led to Richard Sullivan's murder.

The news articles are replete with testimonials from neighbors shocked by the violent homicide they cannot believe occurred in their neighborhood; the victim kept to himself, and his neighbors knew *of* him more than they knew him—a fact that deepens the mystery of his slaying. Nonetheless, his neighbors in the quiet hamlet of Saugatuck are shocked by the murder of a man well liked by everyone.

Everyone, that is, except his alleged killer, whose visage appears in an article two weeks later.[7] The day after Richard Sullivan's autopsy, Ottawa County prosecutors issued a murder warrant for the chief suspect. In the photograph, the alleged killer peers at the floor, seemingly emotionless. The deep lines and contours of his face give him a "hard appearance"; small eyes set deep under a jutting brow ridge and a large, spade-shaped nose give him a sinister appearance.

Chicago police arrested the suspect along with two other people after they attempted to use Sullivan's credit cards at a department store. A store clerk became suspicious and called the police, who found the perpetrator in Sullivan's car. According to the arrest warrant, they (the trio) planned on using the stolen credit cards to charge items, return the charged items for cash, and use the cash to purchase drugs. While in custody in Illinois, the alleged perpetrator made a partial confession, telling his side of the story of what occurred on that fateful Friday the thirteenth (his lawyer is challenging the legality of this confession, however, on the grounds that the suspect requested, but police denied, legal representation).

The alleged perpetrator's story is a he-said, he-said account. According to the suspect's account of the crime, Sullivan invited him back to his home under the pretense of offering him a job. Once at the residence, in the living room Sullivan asked him about his sexual preferences, and the suspect informed him that he was not a homosexual.

Following this rejection, the alleged perpetrator stated to police that Sullivan left the living room and the suspect found him twenty minutes later, naked, in the bedroom. After Sullivan allegedly made a suggestive comment, the suspect became enraged and attacked him. He admitted to placing Sullivan in a headlock, where he lost consciousness, and binding his hands behind his back with a shoelace, but denied strangling Sullivan with a second shoelace. Someone did, though. The suspect also admitted to stealing various items and attempting to make the crime scene appear as a robbery by leaving the scene disheveled.

Sullivan offered his version of the story as well, although the only speaking he could do would emanate from the damage left on and in his body. As I testified at the preliminary hearing, the injuries to Sullivan's body suggest that he struggled after his hands were bound with the first shoelace. The injuries are consistent with a scenario in which Sullivan was strangled with someone's hands, regained consciousness, and was strangled a second time with the lace from the running shoe found partially embedded in the skin of his neck. The mute testimony offered by Sullivan's body confirms the suspect's version—the "partial confession" (he denies the actual murder)—of the crime that Sullivan was choked twice. (I will detail how the forensic evidence indicates this finding during the subsequent trial—see "The Last Chapter," chapter 13.)

The suspect, who has a history of misdemeanors including three assault charges, faces a life sentence. The notion of a "life sentence" provides a bitter irony, one difficult to swallow: the suspect faces a sentence of *life*, albeit a confined life . . . but life nonetheless.

SKELETONS IN THE CLOSET

Late Summer 2004
Spectrum Health, Blodgett Campus
East Grand Rapids, Michigan

For these two, the party will end in the parking lot. The security light mounted on a pole leaves the setting and the details obscured in darkness. From a distance, they appear as shadows, as black outlines, like Shadow Dancers, but their frenetic, jerky movements indicate the degree of animosity in their dance.

Another reveler, who watched the ugly scene unfold in the apartment a few minutes earlier, followed them to the parking lot and now watches the shapes from a distance. She sees something, a flash of silver, like a bolt of lightning; one appears to strike the other in the chest a few times—an odd place to punch a person—and the other, the larger of the two, slumps forward, his shoulders drooping, then falls to the ground where he lays, motionless.

Meanwhile, a few hundred miles to the south, a man is preparing his bed for the night. . . .

The high-school intern looks nervous as she sits in the lounge chair in Spectrum East's main lobby. Chairs, couches, and bar stools around tall, circular tables litter the entrance hall—the hospital does its best to make people comfortable. The hands of the clock point to 8:20, five minutes later than the time arranged to meet for this morning's autopsies. She fishes through the pockets of her black slacks and finds a single wintergreen Life Saver mint wrapped in a cellophane square; even unwrapped, the wintergreen scent is strong. Wintergreen is usually associated with trees, bathroom deodorizers, and breath mints. The autopsy of an "advanced decomp" changes the association to something more negative and less desirable. Just ask Tobin.

She sits, legs crossed, looking at something on the screen of her cell phone. She looks up at the clock for an instant, smiles, and returns to her cell phone musings. She wiggles her foot; the spastic twitching makes her foot appear to assume a personality of its own. The gesture—nervous energy released into the air—is typical for a teenager and belies her age, although she looks much older than sixteen.

She is tall, about five feet nine, with straight, raven-black hair that reaches the middle of her back. Physically, Anna is still a fawn with long, gangly legs, yet one day soon she will become an elegant, graceful doe.

Today, though, she will mature years ahead of schedule. Years of television images of the deceased, theatrical autopsies, and theatrical violence will be sliced away with a scalpel. The door to the morgue should carry a warning sign that reads, "Beware: enter at your own risk; this room will change you forever." When one crosses the river Styx and enters the world beyond—the underworld—if fortunate enough to escape again to the side of the living, one cannot forget the images of the tortured, tormented souls on the other side. Anna will soon make the journey across.

Anna, a City High School junior who must complete a semester-long internship to graduate, awaits her first experience in the Kent County Morgue; by the time she has finished her five-hour-a-week internship, her experiences will fill volumes. She will live through a season of *Law & Order*, only this time it's for real. Many observers—students, interns, and interested laypeople—have sat in the same chair, nervously awaiting their first foray into the morgue and the beginning of their journey into the underworld of the medical examiner and forensic pathology. Tobin sits next to her, now seasoned after observing several autopsies. Four months earlier, he sat where she does now.

"Are you nervous?" Tobin asks.

She shakes her head. "My parents are more nervous than I am." Is this bravado just a façade? In moments she will meet two victims: a man murdered with a butterfly knife and a man who converted his car into a gas chamber and subsequently a crypt.

The clock on the lobby wall reads eight forty-five. Just beyond the wall, through the window, the trees in the courtyard beyond captivate attention. The trees offer a lovely panoply of color made more vivid by the dull backdrop of burnished brown steel siding. They also provide a welcome reminder of the cycles that pervade nature and human existence. While some leave this world through the portal of the morgue, others arrive at Spectrum East's campus maternity wing. The rays of the sun on a cloudless day have begun to creep into the courtyard, creating eerie shadows and an image that reminds me of a forest at dusk. It's a cool sixty-four degrees this morning with a warm eighty-degree high antici-pated and a possible thunderstorm.

I arrive around nine o'clock. With a smile as a cheerful "Come on, kids," I lead the way down the stairwell to the hospital's basement level.

Inside the morgue, with Anna and Tobin in tow, I greet the two FBI agents who accompanied the murder victim. In the autopsy room, Paul Davison is prepping to the Tex-Mex music of Los Lobos, the bouncy Latin rhythm filling the room. The music is a welcome diversion, although one would expect something more consistent for the occasion, such as Karl Orff's heavy medieval chants.

The Grim Reaper had a busy Friday night, it appears, dragging five individuals from their earthly existence and filling the refrigerator with their corpses bundled in white sheets. With only two autopsies on tap this Saturday, Monday will be a busy day in the morgue.

In the conference room, Anna and Tobin, seated at one end of the oval table, listen intently as FBI agents Dick Johnson* and Bob Saunders* provide details on the murder victim—a twenty-two-year-old Native American man murdered on a reservation in Michigan's upper peninsula; the location of the crime accounts for the involvement of the FBI.

Both agents came in casual dress to the morgue. Saunders is in khakis and a polo shirt. His straight dark brown hair shines under the fluorescent lights, and with large, round-rimmed glasses, he looks more like a lawyer or an accountant. Johnson is also wearing khakis. A crisp white T-shirt, absent one single wrinkle, tucked into the khakis, complements his trim, streamlined athletic build, like that of a swimmer. Johnson sports a head of cropped blond hair, like a crew cut overgrown, and a forty-caliber gun in a holster strapped to his belt. The similarities between the two agents drown the cosmetic differences; approximately the same height and with the same build, they look like fraternal twins. They seem somewhat nervous, but who can blame them? The morgue, any morgue for that matter, can be daunting to the uninitiated, and the federal agents don't usually handle homicides in Michigan.

Six hours may seem like a long way to go for an autopsy, but the jurisdiction of the Kent County medical examiner includes several other counties throughout the state that do not have access to a forensic pathologist, and this victim, Jeffrey Easton*, needs the services of a forensic pathologist because he exited the world far before his time—and his death did not need to happen. If justice prevails in this case, it would do so armed with my scalpel. The slain Mr. Easton awaits on the stainless-steel autopsy table in the adjacent room.

The details are sketchy. Last night, Easton attended a party during which an argument ensued between his friend and him. Easton had become involved with his friend's girlfriend, and as "drunks and babies tell the truth," the affair was exposed during the party. After a few punches, the two men were separated, only to finish their fight in the parking lot. An eyewitness who saw the incident from a distance reported seeing the perpetrator strike Easton several times in the chest, which caused Easton to slump and fall to the ground.

The alleged perpetrator, now in custody, claims self-defense—a common excuse given in homicide cases. Of course, the self-defense plea fails when considering that Easton was unarmed and sustained four knife wounds, which proved fatal. He died last night at a hospital in Michigan's upper peninsula. Still, killers rarely stumble on the facts when invoking a self-defense plea.

Tobin, the two FBI agents, Anna, and I proceed down the hallway to the morgue—an odd procession of physician, law enforcement agents, teacher, and high school student. When they enter the room, Anna and the two agents look at the unclothed body in silence.

"I guess you can rule out starvation," Tobin quips as he first sees Easton's nude body stretched out on the autopsy table. Easton's midsection appears bloated, like the skin over his midsection is concealing a pillow. Tobin's deadpan humor produces a muffled chuckle from the agents and provides an appropriate and welcomed icebreaker, as does the rhythmic Latin beat of Los Lobos playing in the background. One word reverberates: *decompression*—the word I often use to describe this moment when the uninitiated cross over into his world, the world of forensic pathology. At this moment when she comes face to face with a victim, Anna has begun her decompression.

Anna and the agents search through the linen cabinet for gowns while Easton lies on the autopsy table nearest the corridor leading into the autopsy room. Easton, at five feet ten inches tall and 282 pounds, was a rotund man. Hairs like whiskers cover his head, which he had shaved in the not-too-distant past, and tattoos cover his arms, with a large crucifix occupying his entire left deltoid and a tattooed flame encircling his left forearm. Another cross adorns his right shoulder, and the name "Harley," in old English script, runs vertically down the inside of his right forearm. Small white metal rings, one in each nipple, glisten in the light as do the earrings in each ear—dime-sized white metal rings, each with a gun-metal-gray ball in its center. Like many other corpses that appear in the morgue, the combination of blood and gravity (lividity) has created a bruised appearance to his back.

Like many others that enter the morgue, Easton bears the brand of hospital personnel who last night in vain attempted to save his life: a few square white EKG pads used in an attempt to "kick-start" his heart and a giant chest tube protruding from his left side about six inches to the side of his left nipple, disappearing into the skin covering his upper rib cage, inserted to drain blood in his chest cavity caused by the four stab wounds on his torso and hip. Through the transparent plastic, drops of deep crimson, almost black, blood sit trapped inside of the tube.

Easton's blood-drenched clothing and personal effects sit on a long steel hospital gurney, covered with a white sheet, resting along one wall of the morgue. Two Polaroids of the death instrument, a blood-spattered knife, sit on another table next to the gurney. The knife—the murder weapon that took Easton's life—is called a butterfly knife, and is available at any surplus or martial arts shop; the bifurcated green-metal knife handle, like a Japanese fan, parts and folds over to encase the four-inch blade when not in use.

Several stab wounds perforate Easton's chest; three of them look like dime-sized circles with slits at their centers. They look much too small to have been inflicted by the butterfly knife in the Polaroid. They look like the products of a thin, narrow blade like a stiletto or an Exacto knife. The fourth wound, in his upper left side, is an inch-long slit that looks like the product of the butterfly knife.

Easton sustained three wounds to the chest—one directly under the sternum and two on either side of the rib cage—with the fourth on the left upper thigh just below the hip. The table behind Easton contains his clothes, saturated with sticky, partially dried, coagulated blood; it is hard to believe that the four wounds would be enough to create the damage that would lead to the amount of blood on Easton's clothes, let alone kill a man. Even his white high-top tennis shoes are stained with the dull crimson of dried blood.

I begin describing Easton's body and the circumstances of his murder into my recorder when a knock on the refrigerator door brings two technicians, both women wearing white pants and flower-print shirts, wheeling into the morgue a large white machine that looks like a miniature Zamboni (the machine used to smooth the surface of an ice rink). They wheel the machine—a mobile x-ray unit—next to Easton's body.

"What's that thing?" Tobin asks.

The procedure for stabbing victims requires x-rays to determine if a portion of the blade broke off and became lodged inside the wound. I warn everyone to stand back a few feet as the technicians ready the machine. In the time it takes Tobin to jot a few notes on a legal pad, the two technicians have finished and are wheeling the equipment back through the refrigerator door (the refrigerator has a large access door on the other side that leads into the hospital corridor beyond). A few minutes later, Paul Davison hands me the x-ray of Easton's chest; it is free of any metallic objects.

Next, Easton's teeth are examined. I pull his lips apart to find two rows of coffee-brown, decaying teeth. Tobin peers into Easton's mouth and marvels at the sight of the jagged, rotting stumps. The description of the body continues with the cataloguing of each tattoo and body piercing.

A few minutes later, at my direction, Tobin searches a wall unit containing diagrams of various body positions. He removes a sheet titled "Thoracic abdominal, male, and anterior and posterior views"—a standard form produced by the American Society of Clinical Pathologists, whose logo, the letters ASCP circumscribed, appears in the upper-left corner of the page. The diagram shows the anterior and posterior of a male torso from the neck to the top of the buttocks. On it, I will sketch the placement of the four stab wounds, one of which sealed Easton's fate. Davison, though, points out that he already filled out a similar diagram before he arrived.

Agent Saunders snaps pictures with a 35 mm camera as each injury that resulted from the fight is meticulously described and catalogued for the official report: scrapes on Easton's face, the result of punches or from falling to the ground; inside the left ankle, a faded, blue tattooed "W" that appears barely visible at first glance.

Tobin notices the tattoo. "I would have missed that one," he remarks.

"Since it's sideways," I suggest, "it's a jail tattoo."

Paul Davison takes measurements, such as the victim's height, and dictates the numbers to Anna, who notes the measurements on the autopsy report, as a silent sentinel watches. He watches all of the autopsies conducted and provides a macabre greeting to anyone who ventures into this room; the plaster cast skeleton next to the pillar at the entrance to the morgue is the first image seen by anyone who enters the room, and it can be a daunting reminder of the business that takes place here. A door behind him leads to the refrigerator, inside of which lie five bodies wrapped in white sheets, like giant cocoons, on the shelves.

Someone with a healthy sense of humor taped a new comic to the glass window looking into the refrigerator. The comic contains the image of a cross-eyed boy and the caption "God put me on earth to accomplish a certain number of things. Right now, I am so far behind, I will never die." The caption would make any man with a "honey do" list smile. Did Jeffrey Easton feel the same way? Did he feel the weight of a "honey do" list pushing down on his shoulders? One thing is certain: he must have possessed an unwritten list containing dozens of things he wanted to accomplish but never will.

After the measurements, I initiate the process of examining and investigating the stab wounds, which begins with a determination of each wound's "clock position." The FBI agents listen intently as I explain to Anna and Tobin the mechanics of "clock position," which is a metaphor adopted by medical examiners specifically to describe knife wounds. The elastic fibers in skin deform the wound, causing it to stretch, elongate, and pull back around the wound, forming the pale pink circles—the "clock"— that appear around three of the four knife penetrations. The stab wounds are evident inside the reddish interior of the circles, appearing as slits, which, to return to the metaphor of the clock, represent the "hands" or the original wounds; the ends of the stab wound point to two different "clock positions." One end of a stab wound on Easton's chest points to ten o'clock; the other end points to four o'clock, yielding a "clock position" of 10:4.

The red tissue inside the circles is muscle; when a knife blade penetrates muscle, the muscle "grabs" the blade, literally squeezing it. Inserting a knife thus always meets less resistance than removing it, a fact that explains why the slits appear smaller than they should given the width of the knife that caused the injuries.

I study the first wound—wound number one—and call out its "clock position" to Anna, who notes the information on the autopsy report. We will meticulously report the details of each stab wound because, in such homicides, part of the medical examiner's job is to determine which wound proved fatal.

Knives most often have a dull end and a sharp end, I explain to Anna, who watches, fascinated with this explanation. I point to wound number three, just to the left of Easton's left nipple. Inside the circle formed by the retracted skin—the "clock face"—is the mark left where the knife penetrated the deep reddish orange muscle; the two edges of the butterfly knife that killed Easton, the "dull end" and the "sharp" end, form a wedge-shaped slit in the reddish orange muscle.

"Here, we can see where the knife twisted in the wound." Anna and Tobin listen intently. I point to wound number four, the knife wound in Easton's upper left thigh. Inside the "clock face," a wider, less pronounced slit indicates that the perpetrator twisted the knife handle while the blade was embedded in his victim's thigh.

Davison produces and hands me a probe—a long thin blade that looks like a car's dipstick only thinner and sharper—with which I will determine the path of the knife blade as it penetrated Easton's body and the depth of each penetration. First, wound one, in Easton's upper right rib cage, is probed by inserting the probe as far as it will go. I read the estimate to Anna, who notes the numbers on the autopsy report.

"Something has to have done something here or he wouldn't be dead," I explain to Tobin and Anna upon examination of wound two, the wound just under Easton's sternum. With a pair of scissors, I widen the hole slightly and push my pinky finger inside the wound. This wound likely struck the heart.

On to wounds three and four, which I widen with the scissors first, then probe with first my finger and then the metal probe.

"This takes some time," Tobin notes, surprised by the meticulousness with which each wound is probed, sketched, and described for the official autopsy report.

"It's the same with gunshot victims," I explain. "We describe each bullet wound." The legal system requires painstaking procedure for homicide victims because the evidence collected must withstand scrutiny in court; a significant portion of medicolegal autopsies of homicide victims, as a result, consists of describing and investigating wounds and other evidence, such as the victim's clothing worn during the crime. In this context, the medical examiner becomes as much a detective as Hercule Poirot or Sherlock Holmes or any police investigator, real or fictitious. In this regard, to a certain degree one can find a confluence of fiction and reality, not unlike the medical examiner's fictional counterparts on television.

And if anything is missed, as unlikely as this might be, Agents

Saunders and Johnson are snapping enough photographs with their 35 mm camera that they could assemble a veritable "photo journal" of the proceedings.

The wound to Easton's upper left thigh appears very deep. I slide the probe into the wound and discover that the butterfly knife penetrated five inches into the hip, which suggests the possibility that the blade could have nicked the femoral artery—a vast superconductor of blood that runs down the upper, inside thigh. Severing the femoral artery could lead to a fatal loss of blood in minutes. A glance at Easton's clothes stretched out on the gurney in the corner of the morgue—drenched with blood—verifies a staggering loss of blood.

"Five inches deep," I note to Anna, who expresses surprise that morgue protocol requires measurements in inches rather than centimeters, but measurements taken in inches are easier to understand by juries. The prosecutor will most likely show the jury the murder weapon—the butterfly knife—and when the prosecutor tells them that Easton's killer sank the knife blade five inches into Easton's upper thigh, they will realize that this means he sank the knife blade to the hilt—a vivid depiction of the crime's ferocity. Generally, a juror can make an association with a measurement in inches; five inches, the juror may realize, is roughly the length of a water glass. A measurement in centimeters would have no such effect on a populace raised on the English standard of measurement.

Finished describing and investigating the wounds, I begin the process of cataloguing the victim's clothes and personal effects at the time of the crime, which include a cellular phone and a pack of Camel cigarettes, both spattered with Easton's blood. The last shirt the twenty-two-year-old victim wore—a blue T-shirt with the logo of a local bar and grill—is covered with streaks of still-wet, coagulating blood that looks like finger paint. While I describe each item to Anna, who inventories them on the official report, I study the T-shirt very carefully, probing the holes caused by the knife wounds, identifying the holes, and matching the evidence on the clothes with that on the body. It takes a few minutes, but I'm able to identify holes in the shirt that correspond with stab wounds one, two, and three.

Next, I fish through Easton's jean shorts and find two Baggies filled with what I'll describe on the official report as "a green leafy material." Although I suspect the substance is marijuana, I cannot report it as such on the official report until a chemical test verifies it.

As the cataloguing of Easton's possessions is concluding, Paul Davison begins prepping the body for the autopsy. As he pulls out the chest tube, blood drips from the hole. It is hard to imagine after viewing Easton's blood-drenched clothing, but Easton will continue to "bleed." As Paul and I push him onto his side to examine his posterior for possible wounds, blood pours from his mouth and runs across his face, forming two thick red lines across each cheek. By far, this autopsy is "bloodier" than any of the others discussed so far.

"What will you look for?" Tobin asks.

During the autopsy, I will look for the fatal wound, the depth of the wounds, and any other natural disease. Obviously, the knife wounds killed Easton, but if I find some natural disease, I could warn relatives who may also be afflicted with the same predisposition for the disease.

I ask Tobin to move Easton's head to an upright position and hold it so I can examine both sides and note any injuries that may be found. His facial expression suggests that he finds the task somewhat disconcerting. No one enters the morgue without becoming somewhat involved in the autopsy proceedings. Observers become active participants and cross over the invisible line separating the observer from the subject, the journalist from the story, and become part of the proceeding, part of the story.

Easton's head is cold and heavy, like a bowling ball, and his brow is furrowed as Tobin holds the head in place while I note various facial wounds, bruises, and contusions—evidence that suggests the deceased engaged in a frenzied fight last night. The FBI agents snap a few photographs. While we conclude this final aspect of the superficial detail, Paul Davison readies the next phase by placing a large stainless-steel bowl between Easton's legs. Now, he is "ready to open."

While conducting most autopsies, the pathology assistant (Davison on this day), and I form a tag team; Davison removes the organs and places them in bowls from which I retrieve them, weigh them, dissect and examine each—revealing medical details the presence of which not even the deceased was often aware. Today, though, the nature of this victim's demise—homicide—will slow down the process, and both Paul Davison and I will remain at the autopsy table during the removal of the organs, because the organs must be examined in situ (in their natural position) to determine what if any damage the knife wounds caused.

It is vitally important to this morning's autopsy that I discover without doubt which wound proved fatal. With a scalpel, Davison draws two fine, bright red lines down each shoulder to a point above Easton's sternum, where they meet to form a wide "V"; from the point where the two lines meet, he continues the line to Easton's waist. Davison's wrist does not waver as he makes the incision; the razor-sharp scalpel cuts through the skin and underlying fat without pause, without effort, and without sound.

The incision creates three flaps; with a few slices to separate the layer of skin and underlying fat from muscle and bone, Davison flips up the "V" created at the top of the incision, which obscures Easton's face, hiding his eyes from the macabre proceedings and the sight of his own interior. A few more slices, and the two flaps along the side slink to the sides, allowing a cross-sectional view of the dermis and the underlying fat—a bright, golden color—which in Easton's case is an astounding two and a half inches thick.

The Y-incision reveals damage unnoticed during the probing of the wound: a circular hole in the upper left rib cage the size of a quarter not found when the hole was explored with the probe, the scissors, and my fingers. Here, the knife wound to the side of the left nipple penetrated the rib cage and may have pierced the heart—a wound that could have proved fatal. This evidence contradicts my original hypothesis that the wound under the sternum began the process that killed Easton.

People, given the right conditions, can become accustomed to things they never believed they could, but no matter how many autopsies one witnesses, it is difficult to become accustomed to the sound of cracking, wet wood caused by rib cutters snapping through ribs. Many observers cringe each time they hear an autopsy assistant pull together the long handles of the branch snapper, severing each rib, as Davison now does as he cuts through each rib on both sides of the sternum to form a "breastplate" that he will remove to access the organs underneath the protective rib cage. In the background, the two FBI agents watch the proceedings, like mute silhouettes on the wall, and the bouncy rhythm of Los Lobos's Latin beat fills the room, but not loud enough to drown out the cracking of the rib cutters in action.

With the breastplate removed, Davison places a long, thin steel stem connected to a brown tube into the cavity and turns on a pump. If having never seen the victim of a stabbing death before, one may assume that blood from the various wounds filled the chest cavity. Before he can proceed, Davison needs to remove the blood. After a few minutes, he turns off the pump and holds up a large glass jar, about the size of a small fat pitcher, containing about an inch of crimson fluid.

"Two hundred and fifty milliliters," Davison calls out.

"Why would the amount of blood in the chest cavity matter?" Tobin asks, puzzled by the importance of this statistic.

The blood is drained from the pericardial sac, Paul explains. The pericardial sac, part of the heart, can only handle so much fluid at one time. A sufficiently large accumulation of fluid in the pericardial sac will prevent the heart from beating. Congestive heart failure is the gradual accumulation of fluid until the heart fails. When the heart sustains an injury that causes bleeding, such as a stab wound, this buildup is massive and occurs within seconds, as blood floods into the pericardial sac. As a result, compression of the heart occurs, which when caused by the accumulation of blood or other fluid is called tamponade. The heart shuts down and death occurs. The normal amount of fluid in the pericardial sac, Davison explains, is 10 to 15 milliliters; Davison pumped 250 milliliters from Easton's pericardial sac.

So, in last night's fight, Easton sustained four knife wounds, one or two of which pierced his heart, which caused a flood of blood into the pericardial sac. His compressed heart stopped beating, and he died. Within minutes of the fatal wound, he slumped to the ground, an eyewitness stated to the police who initially investigated. Easton, his body laid open by a massive incision running the length of his torso, embodies the fragile nature of human life, an image that slaps the casual observer like an open hand across the face.

Paul Davison and I delve through the shades of red and deep purple that are the heart and lungs, looking for the fatal wound. The surfaces of the organs indicate that the wound to the side of the left nipple pierced the edge of the lung and the left ventricle of the heart. I reach into the chest cavity and probe the path of the wound under the sternum, which is three and a half inches long—the wound penetrated the heart, causing significant damage. As first suspected, this wound proved fatal, leading to the compression of the heart that killed Jeffrey Easton.

On the dissecting table, Easton's heart is the size of two fists with yellow fat covering much of its surface. With a scalpel, I make a series of cuts along the path of the arteries to probe for potential blockages. The process, though, is superfluous for a twenty-two-year-old. But a complete and thorough autopsy involves an examination of the coronary arteries, because if the victim is at risk for heart disease, family members who may face similar risks can be notified.

Halfway through the autopsy, the smooth vocals of Elvis Costello replace the bouncy beat of Los Lobos. I look back at the two FBI agents, who are both huddled over the instruction book for their camera, and chuckle. With the homicide, they're out of their usual jurisdiction. They seem mystified as to how to deal with the clothes spread out across the gurney in the corner of the morgue, which is evidence in a homicide investigation. Davison has set up a few heat lamps on tripods in an attempt to dry the still-wet blood covering the clothes, which the agents will then carry from the morgue in the same paper shopping bags in which the clothes came and deposit them in a central, evidence archive in Grand Rapids.

"In the land of the blind," I proclaim, "the one-eyed man is king." Anna chuckles, as do the FBI agents. Ironically, the statement applies to the agents; unaccustomed to working murder cases (which usually fall under the purview of state law enforcement agencies), the agents are figuratively blind, feeling their way through this homicide investigation.

As I slice into two halves the kidneys (which resemble beans only four inches from top to the bottom), I explain to Anna that a few unlucky individuals suffer from kidney stones.

"Would they be readily apparent?" Tobin asks, interested.

Tobin leans closer as I point to a small cavity, about the size of a quarter, where the stones could move around. "This guy is not stoned," I quip and Tobin laughs, as we are reminded of the two Baggies of a "green leafy substance" in Easton's pocket.

Next, I examine the reddish white, half-dollar-sized testicles. I slide my index finger under a few sinews and pull—if they're "stringy or elastic," I explain, "the patient is thought to be fertile." Anna is learning valuable anatomy lessons today, becoming acclimated to the inside of the human body. She stands, hands folded behind her back, and listens intently. If he lived longer, Mr. Easton could have become a father, but fate had other plans.

As the examination of Jeffrey Easton's internal organs nears completion, the FBI agents take a set of fingerprints using a pad of ink and a roller. I place the back of my hand under the top edge of the workstation, under four colored triangles that are heat activated. Jets of water gently stream across the table, removing the detritus. With the wave of a hand under the desired triangle, the medical examiner can supply hot water, cold water, rinse, and disposal. With the wave of my hand, the table is clean and ready for the next autopsy.

The FBI agents, finished with the chore of collecting fingerprints, ask for names of observers for their official report. "I'm not sure I want them to know my name," Tobin jokes. Agent Johnson jots down his name on the report.

"They probably already do," Paul chides, smiling. Agent Johnson inks Paul's name next.

Anna and Tobin retreat to the conference room of the morgue suite to snack on some bagels Anna brought. As they leave the room, they come face to face with the skeleton dangling next to the support pillar.

The skeleton is useful to the medical examiner; if he or his team needs a reference for an unidentified bone, they match the bone with one on the skeleton. The skeleton, unlike those that occupy the biology section of many museums, is just a cast.

"You can't find a real one, now," Davison explains to Anna and Tobin as he wheels the second subject into the morgue from the refrigerator. A cast skeleton runs about five hundred dollars, so one can only imagine the cost of an original, perhaps available only at some clandestine auction the focus of which is a number of "antique" anatomical skeletons. Original skeletons often came from India, Davison continues, from bodies that washed up on river deltas after they were dumped as part of a funeral rite.

A knock on the outer door of the morgue suite brings a priest who has come to provide the last rites to one of the deceased residing in the adjacent refrigerator. The tall, thin, older man disappears into the refrigerator; inside the refrigerator, he stands next to a body wrapped in a bedsheet and reads the last rites, his muted speech inaudible over the hum of the refrigerator. Bodies cocooned in bedsheets line the refrigerator, so how did the priest know what body to bless? The morgue is overrun (an odd word choice in this context) by bodies whose owners met their fate last night, including a civil engineer who was run over by a truck on the work site. The civil engineer's death will likely provide the impetus for civil litigation involving a significant sum in damages, so many eyes will watch the outcome of this autopsy.

After about a thirty-minute break, the second autopsy of the morning begins. The FBI agents gather Jeffrey Easton's clothing in the brown paper grocery bags in which they brought it and depart.

Paul Davison changes the music, and a good portion of this autopsy will be accompanied by the music of Great Big Sea, a Celtic folk band. A strumming guitar floats through the morgue as Tobin and Anna study the corpse lying on the second autopsy table. Unlike the other victims described in earlier chapters, this man's body is contorted—his torso is prone, but his legs are drawn up and to the side in a semifetal position. He arrives in the morgue in the same clothes he wore on his "deathbed": blue hospital scrubs and a white T-shirt.

At six feet three inches tall, Pete Kuipers* was a tall yet thin man— his hip bones protrude through the blue hospital scrubs; the cheekbones jut through the skin, giving his face a sunken, skeletal appearance. The light brown color of his mustache offers a contrast to his deep, auburn hair, which is streaked with gray. His mouth hangs agape; his eyes are closed. Most of the victims who enter the morgue come with their eyes closed, Paul Davison notes as he cuts away the deceased's clothing. Very seldom do corpses come into the morgue with their eyes open, he explains.

Fifty-six-year-old Pete Kuipers went to bed around midnight in the guest bed, which he sometimes did. He placed pillows in the bed to make it appear occupied, to prevent his wife, who may look in on him during the night, from discovering his preconceived plan. Sometime during the night, she did check on Kuipers and discovered his ruse, but by then it was too late—he had completed his final act in the garage, where she found him, deceased, jackknifed on the concrete floor. He had committed suicide.

Davison found the front seat of the car made into a makeshift bed, a garden hose channeling noxious fumes from the tailpipe into the car, and keys in the ignition locked into the "on" position. Oddly, Davison explains, the wife found Kuipers's body outside of the car—a curious discrepancy. The carbon monoxide may have left Kuipers disoriented and nauseous and he left the car. Another possibility exists, one that goes unmentioned this morning but hangs in the air like an invisible yet perceptible humidity: someone murdered Kuipers and altered the scene to make it appear to be a suicide attempt. It is an extremely unlikely scenario though, because Kuipers left a suicide note that cited failing health and suggested his wife would be better off without him.

And he may have been right. Kuipers suffered from bipolar disorder, a chemical imbalance that causes alternating swings between deep depression and intense mania. Six months ago, he tried to kill his wife with a .22-caliber pistol that he then planned to use on himself in a botched attempt to end both of their lives. Although not a religious man, according to his wife, Kuipers had formulated a supernatural explanation for the pains that wracked his aging body: he believed that demons haunted him.

With the clothes now off Kuipers's body, the examination begins, and key forensic details are recorded. Even a glance would prove sufficient to notice the large purple abrasion at the base of Kuipers's spine—a scuff about the size of a sticky note. More scrapes appear under the left arm. Sometimes with carbon monoxide poisoning, the victim experiences convulsions, which perhaps led to these wounds. And the wife did find Kuipers sprawled out on the concrete floor of their garage.

When the examination is finished and all the relevant details noted for the official autopsy report, Davison attempts to straighten Kuipers's legs to facilitate the taking of blood from the femoral artery in his groin. The body is stiff and makes an eerie creaking sound as Davison forces the legs to bend so he can take the requisite blood sample, the contents of which will travel to the toxicology lab. A toxicology screen of the victim's blood will determine the amount of carbon monoxide ingested, while the autopsy will serve to exclude any other possibilities. The discovery of a massive skull fracture, for example, would call into question the determination of death by suicide. The amount of bruising on Kuipers's body is somewhat bothersome, but it is not uncommon in such suicides.

"See the cherry red color?" Paul Davison asks Tobin, pointing to the muscle under the chest revealed by the Y-incision. "The color is caused by the carbon monoxide in the blood." The color red of the muscle is so vivid that it seems to almost glow. Davison's description of the color, cherry red, is a good one.

A few minutes later, the dissection of Kuipers's heart has begun. As I slice through the red heart muscle, Anna watches the proceedings intently. With one autopsy behind her, the second will appear less shocking—the next one a little less shocking, the next one a little less. Each autopsy observed numbs the soul a bit to the point where the blood and cutting no longer shock, although the tragedy of the victims remains. It is the tragedy that intoxicates some observers. An autopsy is like the ultimate gaper's block. The sight of human suffering becomes somehow entrancing, perhaps because a thin, invisible line often separates the living from the dead; the driver who slows to see a victim wrenched from a car crushed like a tin can could the next day suffer the same fate. This thought horrifies, yet its horror fascinates. It is a dark form of voyeurism, narcissism by proxy (a self-obsession with one's own mortality through a proxy, in this case a victim).

Paul chuckles as he notes the lyrics of the satiric Great Big Sea song in the background: "I'll hang myself if I get married again." "Steve's theme song," he chides.

"This patient has atherosclerosis," I explain to Anna, who is standing behind my left shoulder, watching me make a series of cuts across the coronary arteries. Atherosclerosis occurs when the lumen coronary arteries narrow and decrease the flow of blood—the result of a buildup of fatty deposits called "plaque." Unlike those in twenty-two-year-old Jeffrey Easton, the off-white walls of the coronary arteries in Pete Kuipers's heart have thickened, hardened, calcified. Looking at a cross section of one of the occluded arteries is like looking at the cross section of a noodle, only it isn't soft but stiff—the scalpel makes a snapping sound as I cut through them.

If Kuipers had had a heart attack, the normally brown-colored heart muscle would be white in the affected area. The investigation indicates that while Kuipers didn't suffer from a heart attack, the blockage in his arteries suggests that he may have experienced a heart attack or a stroke in his near future had he lived longer.

Kuipers also suffered from emphysema, as an examination of the lungs would reveal. His organs are forming a picture of poor health created by damaging lifestyle choices. Charcoal black blotches, "anthracotic" pigment due to deposition of carbon particles from cigarette smoking, cover the outside skin of his lungs (the visceral pleura). The inside of the lung tissue is dotted with bullae, or holes in the lung walls from years of smoke damage. The lungs function much like a filter; tiny alveoli, all three hundred million of them in each lung, stretch and expand with each breath of air, passing the oxygen in air into the bloodstream. With each exhalation, the alveoli contract, sending the remainder in the form of carbon dioxide out of the body. Emphysema destroys alveoli and causes the surviving ones to lose their elasticity; upon inhalation, they overexpand and never fully contract, trapping air. Consequently, breathing becomes progressively harder.

Smoking causes the majority of emphysema cases. Inhalation of smoke destroys the delicate hairs called cilia that cover the bronchial passages and block bacteria, fungi, and other harmful substances from entering the lungs. Without the protective cilia, germs invade the lungs and cause pneumonia. At first, Kuipers would have experienced trouble catching his breath after physical activity. Eventually, walking up a flight of stairs would have left him gasping for breath. A persistent and ever-present cough or hack would have accompanied him everywhere he went. He would have felt a constant exhaustion (due to the lack of oxygen sent to his blood) and experienced a loss of appetite and subsequent loss of weight.

"Hey, this guy's missing something," Paul calls from across the room; the bad health report continues. As he continued to remove the organs, he discovered that Kuipers lacked a left kidney. Pete Kuipers, it appears, suffered from a number of physical ailments and in his later years lived a life tinged by discomfort and even pain, which in conjunction with his bipolarism, provides a motive for his suicide.

Inside the one kidney present, I discover cysts—deep brown-colored, circular patches about the size of a pencil eraser head. These lesions would have eventually killed Kuipers, had he not trumped Mother Nature in his "car bed."

Kuipers's kidneys also harbor a secret: tiny metallic clamps, gray in color after years in his kidneys, around the renal artery—evidence that at one time he had surgery.

"That's a neat device," Tobin states as he watches me jab the scalpel blade into a box the size of a cigar box labeled BLADEX on one of the shelves on the workstation. He watches, spellbound by the robot; as the handle of the scalpel rotates, the light turns green, and I remove the scalpel fitted with a new blade. The used blade drops into a biohazard container located just below the apparatus. Such robotic, laborsaving devices prevent the risk of subcutaneous infection that could result from the manual changing of blades during an autopsy. Preoccupied and perhaps tired medical examiners and pathology personnel pulling the ultrasharp blades from the knives and replacing them with sharper blades amid blood-streaked gloves—one slip of the hand and a cut results.

The autopsy resulted in nothing that would overturn the "diagnosis of exclusion." In fact, quite the contrary: the autopsy revealed a list of ailments that together would have made Kuipers's final few years uncomfortable at best. The autopsy uncovered Pete Kuipers's demons.

With the autopsy concluded, Anna and Tobin remove their masks and protective shields and throw them into the biohazard waste bin. Next, they untie their gowns and toss them into a container for dirty linen. They pull the covers from their shoes and toss them into the biohazard container. They peel off the gloves last, ensuring that their bare hands do not touch any garment that could have accumulated blood droplets. Tobin moves into the corridor toward a bathroom where he will wash his hands. Davison remains in the autopsy room, where, with a spool of white string and a large needle, he has begun to stitch closed the Y-incision.

The skeleton against the pillar is the first and last image seen when entering and exiting the autopsy suite. It also offers a comment about many victims who enter the morgue, most of whom harbor figurative skeletons in their closets. Pete Kuipers's skeletons consisted of "demons" he believed plagued him. Medically, his skeletons resulted from lifestyle choices.

Jeffrey Easton's skeleton consisted of an affair with his friend's girlfriend.

In the morgue, under the study of the medical examiner, these skeletons venture out of the closet and into the fluorescent light.

ACCIDENTS

Midfall 2004
Spectrum Health, Blodgett Campus
East Grand Rapids, Michigan

The rains began just before the sun went down, around five in the early evening. What was first a light shower of flickering white lines grew into solid ropes that lashed the trees, the grass, roof shingles, and asphalt. The pillowlike nimbus clouds covered the moon, smothering the moonlight and soaking the night with teardrops of rain. Shadows cast by streetlights and headlights danced through the darkness. This was the kind of night where the cold soaks through one's clothes into his soul . . . the kind of night one wants to shelter in the warmth inside of bars, movie theaters, and homes . . . the kind of night where the beams of car head-lights bounce through the opaque atmosphere and off of the glistening asphalt of roads and highways like wayward searchlights . . . the kind of night in which it is very hard to see . . . the kind of night in which acci-dents happen . . . and last night two people died, their bodies waiting in the morgue, human debris left from two accidents. These two victims died too young, their life's stories ending prematurely, but they aren't the youngest to enter the Kent County Morgue.

THE SHORTEST CHAPTER

Was Xavyor French a person? Although it may seem like a strange question, this was the question at the heart of the *People v. Marty Alan French*—the case that followed a tragic accident that occurred on the night of January 3, 2001.

In Michigan, winter can last from November through March, and residents love to complain about unpredictable weather changes. Frigid temperatures combined with precipitation in a variety of forms that may include rain, hail, sleet, freezing rain, ice, and snow make travel an adventure. These conditions can also make travel hazardous, as Marty Allen French and his girlfriend, Kara Hanford, would discover on that fateful night in January.

Unable to stop because the car's brakes locked, French's car collided with a train traveling thirty-eight miles per hour. The impact struck the passenger side of the car and threw Hanford, who was nine months pregnant, through the passenger-side window. Paramedics rushed her to Spectrum Hospital, Butterworth Campus, where physicians discovered that her placenta had separated from the uterus, ceasing the blood flow and leaving her fetus without a source of oxygen. An emergency caesarian section followed, and Xavyor French entered the world, only to be placed on life support. Four days later, on January 7, 2001, Xavyor French was pronounced dead of hypoxic encephalopathy, or brain damage caused by a lack of oxygen that resulted from the cessation of blood flow. An autopsy was performed on Xavyor.

Marty French operated the car that night despite a suspended license, and soon after the death of his unborn son, he found himself facing a felony charge of negligent homicide. But did Marty French cause the death of anyone? In other words, was Xavyor French, under Michigan law, a "person"?

At the time of the incident that led to Xavyor's death, a similar court case set the standard for the legal definition of "life." Six years earlier, a motorist struck the car of a woman who was six and a half months pregnant at the time. An emergency caesarian section followed, and physicians recorded that the baby took two or three breaths and had a heart rate of 100 before being placed on life support. Two and a half hours later, the respirator was removed and the baby subsequently died.

This case, *People v. Selwa*, provided the precedent and the definition of life used in the French case: the baby constitutes a "life" if following the baby's "extraction from the mother, there is lacking an irreversible cessation of respiratory and circulatory functions or brain functions."[1] In other words, some medically certifiable evidence must exist that the baby is alive at birth. If alive at birth, the baby qualifies as a "person" under Michigan's negligent homicide statute. In the *Selwa* case, the existence of breaths and a heart rate indicated that the baby was alive after "extraction."[2]

So did Xavyor qualify as a legal " person" according to this standard, thus allowing the state of Michigan to prosecute Marty French for his wrongful death? The prosecution called just one expert medical witness at the preliminary hearing: me. In testimony, I indicated that, in my expert opinion, Xavyor French lived for four days after the emergency C-section. However, the prosecution did not call another expert witness, such as an attending physician, to testify about recorded evidence of "life," such as a heart rate or the existence of Xavyor's Apgar scores.

At one minute and again at five minutes after delivery, an infant undergoes a series of five tests, collectively called Apgar tests. Each test measures a different function: alertness, response to pain, heart rate, and respiration. The infant can score from zero to two on each test, yielding a potential score of zero to ten. A double zero would indicate little to no brain activity and would suggest that under the definition of life set by *The People v. Selwa*, Xavyor didn't qualify as a "person" in the legal sense of the term.

So what occurred in the interval between the emergency caesarian section and the pronouncement of death? Without specific examples, such as a recorded heart rate or Apgar scores, no proof of life existed. And if by law Xavyor didn't qualify as a "person," the defendant, Marty French, could not be held accountable for causing the "death of another."

During the preliminary examination, the district court found that the prosecution established reasonable cause to support a negligent homicide charge, but the circuit court, on appeal, ruled that the district court had erred in this finding. The prosecution appealed the case to Michigan's

Court of Appeals, whose members agreed with the circuit court (with one dissenting opinion) that at the preliminary hearing, the prosecution did not produce evidence that Xavyor qualified as a "person" under the terms set by the *Selwa* decision.

Between the incident that occurred on January 3, 2001, and the Court of Appeal's decision on December 4, 2003, Michigan passed a law, MCL 750.90a, which attaches criminal consequences to intentional acts that result in the death of an embryo or fetus. No longer do cases in Michigan hinge on the definition of "person" and "life." The timing of this law, though, prevented the Court of Appeals from applying it to the French case.

If the tragic collision that led to Xavyor's death would occur tomorrow, he would die as a "person."

Ironically, Michigan's Court of Appeals, in its opinion, refers to Xavyor by his name and not by the generic, clinical term "fetus."

*****

The rain has brought autumn, which has appeared a few weeks late this year. Autumn in Michigan is a beautiful woman, the type whose visage one never tires of, yet the type who turns your lust against you with her cold, impersonal demeanor; with a chill-to-the-bone, she can cool the hottest of blood and leave a coldness that lasts for days. The drive down Plymouth Road to Spectrum Health's Blodgett Campus in East Grand Rapids offers a tapestry of colors—a watercolor of red, yellow, and orange hues, and the grass curtain surrounding the hospital has become a yellow carpet of fallen leaves.

Nine fifteen arrives, and I find Tobin waiting, a legal pad under his arm, in the hospital lobby.

"How did the chess match go?" he asks. My online chess match was scheduled for an early 7:00 AM start, but by 8:30, my Russian opponent had bested me.

"At least it's over."

"Where can I get a jacket like that?" Tobin has noticed the navy vinyl jacket with "Kent County Medical Examiner" on the back in bright yellow capital letters.

"You have to be a medical examiner."

Tobin shakes his head. "Couldn't handle the blood."

We briskly make our way to the basement level and the morgue, where Raymond Gale* awaits the last examination he will ever receive from a doctor. Gale, a kid of nineteen, attempted to cross the busiest thoroughfare in the city when a car struck him. He did not attempt his crossing at an intersection but instead darted into the middle of the street toward the movie theater on the other side, where he was late meeting some friends.

By his body police found a pair of battered headphones and a CD player that Gale may have been wearing when the mishap occurred. They also found two AA batteries in the pocket of his blue jeans, perhaps emergency spares. He didn't see the car coming—an easy mistake in last night's rain—and the headphones suggest he didn't hear it, either. The pair of headphones sits on a table in the corner; the sight of the player sits as a reminder that Gale represents thousands of other kids his age, who move about life wearing a pair of earphones connected to a CD player they carry—the music the aural symbol of a particular stage of their lives. Gale died before his CD ended, both literally and metaphorically.

So here is just a kid who wanted to cross the street, traveling to the movie theater when his fate struck him. He is lying on the autopsy table nearest the corridor when we arrive. Behind him on the second table, the second victim—a drug overdose from Charlevoix County (in northern Michigan)—awaits his turn.

Inside the autopsy room, Jason Chatman has begun the process of collecting evidence by taking Gale's fingerprints. Crosby, Stills, Nash, and Young (their greatest hits) will provide the soundtrack to this autopsy—the acoustic rhythms coming from the stereo provide a soothing, becalming rhythm, but the sight of the young man on the slab in front of me suggests something more dour, something from the genre of the Blues. Chatman obtains the fingerprints by dousing each digit with black powder and rolling each over a white sticker, like a file folder tab. He then places each sticker onto a white plastic sheet.

Tobin circles the body, in a sense getting to know the victim—if only superficially. At six feet one and 171 pounds, Gale's physique provides a visual foil to the man on the other autopsy table, who outweighs his morgue neighbor by a 120 pounds and whose ivory skin, mottled with the purple blotches caused by lividity patterns, contrasts with the chocolate tone of Gale's skin. Half closed lids reveal the whites of his eyes; upon closer examination, Gale's left iris, a nickel-sized brown dot, becomes visible. To paraphrase the famous quote, if the eyes are the windows to the person within, the occupant of this house vacated last evening amid an assault of icy raindrops. Two silver-dollar-sized EKG pads—one on both sides of his upper chest—shine under the morgue lights, and his teeth still clutch the white plastic bite guard emergency workers inserted to prevent him from biting his tongue during their efforts to resuscitate him . . . efforts that would prove futile. Their patient left before he arrived.

"Why the EKG?" Tobin asks, puzzled by the attempts to resuscitate a victim who appeared to have died instantly.

Everyone arriving to the hospital receives an EKG, Jason explains. Between the words of his statement, one can see the letters that form the word *futility*.

"Fatal car accident" conjures the image of a body battered, hammered into a bloody pulp. But not always. The exterior of Gale's body contains evidence of just one injury, although more insidious ones must exist below the surface because the superficial wound did not kill him: his lower right leg contains a massive hole, the size of a baseball, where something struck him with enormous force to split the skin and snap the shin bone, or tibia. Strands of bright red muscle tissue protrude from the hole. Inside the hole, one can see the fractured bone—bright white, the color of a polished tooth. The wound appears painful, and the sight of the gash would make anyone who has banged a shin flinch; one can only imagine what Gale must have felt, *if* he felt anything at all. As the autopsy would uncover later this morning, Gale never felt the injury. He never had time for the pain.

The morgue is quiet this morning—an ironic statement—with only Tobin, Jason Chatman, and me in attendance. One new, curious item appears taped to the glass windows that separate the morgue from the refrigerator: a photograph of the marquee from the First Baptist Church, which reads

Behold! For I come quickly!
Preacher: Stephen D. Cohle

Tobin notices the sign and chuckles. "A preacher with the same name as you!"

"That's Paul's sense of humor," I explain. Paul Davison created the billboard using a Web site (churchsigngenerator.com). "Dr. Cohle's 'sermon'" about timeliness and brevity is Davison's ribbing of my sense of time; I love to teach, and students who have visited the morgue to learn a bit about forensics would understand the joke and appreciate the humor in Davison's cryptic message. They will testify that one autopsy can turn into an all-morning affair.

"We're going to get you involved," I tell Tobin with a wry smile as I dress for this morning's work. The statement seems to have frozen him in time, the only movement being his Adam's apple, which rises slowly, disappears, and then descends in a GULP!

He shivers at the thought of handling a razor-sharp scalpel and can envision tomorrow's headline: "Teacher-turned-pathology assistant succumbs to a rare virus acquired during a visit to the morgue."

After adding the customary two layers—a plastic bib and a surgical gown—to my morning outfit of a T-shirt and hospital scrubs, I begin recording the description of Gale's injuries. This morning, we will maintain a brisk pace, because when I leave the morgue today, my son David and I will travel north to Mount Pleasant's Soaring Eagle Casino and Resort—this year's host of the state's medical examiner's convention, referred to by the ironic acronym MAME (Michigan Association of Medical Examiners). Tomorrow morning, I will travel to Padua, Italy, for a conference on cardiovascular pathology—one of my key interests.

The open fracture on Gale's lower right leg is the probable point of impact. The wound likely occurred when the car's bumper struck. An injury on the lower leg just above the ankle suggests that the car was braking when it struck him, which makes sense. When braking, momentum would cause the front end of the car to dip.

The various abrasions that cover Gale's body are catalogued for the record. When investigating an accidental death, the medical examiner assumes the role of medical detective, yet this morning I will look for evidence much different than that sought in a homicide investigation to answer a number of questions:

What killed Raymond Gale? Unless something shocking surfaces, like the presence of cyanide in Gale's blood, the answer lies in the accident report on the desk in the corner.

What injuries did Gale suffer? The autopsy will define the victim's injuries—evidence that could play a role in a potential civil suit or criminal prosecution that will result from this tragic accident. If the autopsy uncovers evidence that Gale had remained conscious and in pain for a sustained period after the car struck him, the civil penalties could rise. And of course, a toxicology report revealing a substantial amount of a substance could potentially mitigate the driver's responsibility.

The next phase of the examination would create one of the eeriest moments one can experience in the morgue. I roll Gale onto his side so Jason can take pictures of the injuries on his back; I place my hand on Gale's right hip and grab his right wrist and pull him onto his side. And the faint, muffled sound of a groan is heard, not from Jason or me or Tobin, but from Gale's body! The victim groaned! A soft, hoarse moan, like the sound a person might make during sleep. Somewhere between a purr and a moan, but quite distinctive.

Behind the plastic shield of his mask, Tobin's mouth hangs agape, like he has just seen, or rather heard, a ghost. One could hear the knock of his jaw striking the floor.

It's a humorous image.

I chuckle as I hold Gale's arm and Jason collects the photographic evidence. "That happens," I explain, as I assure Tobin that he has not just heard a ghost and that the hospital did not make a horrific mistake; Gale is really dead. "It's just air escaping from the lungs." The air passed through Gale's throat, so the groan occurred with his voice! A voice from beyond the grave, so to speak.

Tobin retreats, slumping onto the office chair by the desk to catch his breath, as I sketch with red ink Gale's injuries onto a line drawing of the anterior and posterior views of a male figure. After a few minutes, the red dots and scratches cover the diagram.

Since Jason stepped out of the morgue, I ask Tobin to assist in the next phase of the examination. His Adam's apple assumes a life of its own, and again it rises slowly, disappears, and reappears as a large knot at the front of his throat as he lets out another GULP!

Tobin's job will be to help roll Gale back onto his side and hold him in place while I explore a bruise on Gale's lower-right back, a wound I suspect as a point of impact. When a large, heavy object such as a car traveling thirty to forty miles an hour strikes a human, the fat underlying the point of impact often liquefies from the crushing effect of the car.

As I direct, Tobin reaches across Gale's body and places his right hand on Gale's right hip. Through the thin latex gloves, the skin feels ice cold. He grabs Gale's right wrist with his left hand and pulls. The victim is heavier than he expected, and his grip begins to slip, so to strengthen his position, he leans back, allowing his weight to balance the victim's. Like raindrops, drops of blood fall from Gale's left ear and strike the steel table. Tap. Tap. Tap. Blood emerges from his mouth, forming a crimson river that runs down his cheek, creating a small pool on the table.

I slice into the bruise with the scalpel; under the skin, I find partially liquefied fat—evidence of a glancing blow, but not the evidence for massive blunt force that I suspected the bruise concealed. The car first struck Gale on another part of his body, most likely on his right shin, which now appears more mangled than before. When Tobin rolled Gale onto his side, Gale's torso and legs moved, but his right lower leg didn't, leaving the horrific image of a lower leg twisted at a right angle, exposing the bright white shin bone that now partially protrudes through the gaping hole left by the car's bumper.

I nod and Tobin slowly rolls Gale onto his back. Dirt, blood, and hairs from Gale's arm cover his gloves. Tobin moves quickly toward the disposal bin for biohazardous waste, where the pathology personnel dump perishable items that contain potentially harmful spots of blood and other hazardous material—he wants to remove the soiled gloves as fast as he can and replace them with new ones, but he's not yet done with his role in this morning's procedures.

"Let's roll the second victim," I suggest. While we wait for Jason to return, and to save time, I will begin the examination of the second victim's back; this person weighs over a hundred pounds more than Gale. And Tobin thought Gale was hard to roll!

This time Tobin knows the drill, and he's prepared. I'm sure that he's just hoping that this time the victim won't groan.

Tobin widens his stance to create a more stable base, and on cue he pulls on the victim's wrist and leans back—way back. No rain of blood drops this time. Just one very big guy whose appetite for alcohol surpassed his body's limits and whose torso and face are covered with giant purple blotches.

"Tobin, based on the pattern of lividity, can you tell in what position he died?"

"Facedown." He's learning.

By this time, Jason has returned. With his scalpel, he makes the Y-incision in Raymond Gale's torso.

"He's very thin," Tobin notes as he watches Jason snap through Gale's ribs with the rib cutter. A pencil thin layer of yellow fat lies sandwiched between his skin and red muscle tissue. The thickness of this subcutaneous fat will be noted in the official autopsy report: for heavier victims, two or more inches; for Gale, less than half an inch. Unlike the drug overdose victim or many others who enter the morgue on a gurney, whose midsection rises toward the ceiling like a pink and purple mound (the shape is reminiscent of a landfill), Gale is fit—just a kid and his music.

Jason fills the steel bowls with organs and places them on the workstation, and the autopsy continues with the internal examination of Gale's organs. Before dissection, each organ is weighed in a scale suspended from the ceiling and the organ weights noted on the white board.

When students observe autopsies, I often assign each a job—my way of creating an experiential lesson. One job consists of writing the organ weights on the white board. This morning Tobin is given that chore.

Streaks of dried blood cover the white pen barrel of the blue dry erase marker.

"Use a paper towel." I point to a box of paper towels on the upper shelf of the workstation. "That will protect you from any hepatitis viruses on the pen barrel." Even something as seemingly innocuous as the dried blood on a marker in the morgue could carry a potentially hazardous virus.

"His lungs contain bruising," I explain to Tobin, who is standing next to me.

Gale's lungs contain a significant amount of bruising—dark purple patches on the outer surface skin of the lungs. Two mechanisms could have caused this bruising: blunt-force trauma to the chest or aspiration of blood.

"See the gouge?" I ask Tobin, who leans closer to examine the damage the collision caused to Gale's lungs. The gouge in the lungs indicates that Raymond Gale sustained rib fractures. The presence of the dime-shaped puncture suggests that some terrific force to his chest caused a fractured rib which jabbed one of his lungs.

The lung bruises could also have resulted from a second factor that might seem surprising: skull fractures, which cause bleeding inside the skull during which sinuses drain blood into the throat. The victim will either spit out blood or inhale it, and thus the blood often flows into the lungs, causing the bruised, discolored patches.

Skinnier victims are easier to autopsy than heavier ones; the absence of larger amounts of fatty tissue that would exist with heavier victims leaves fewer obstacles while dissecting. Gale's heart is the size of a softball with less yellow fatty tissue than would exist with someone weighing considerably more.

While I dissect Gale's heart, Jason begins the process of removing the one organ that remains inside of the victim's body: his brain. Jason makes an incision across the top of Gale's head and tugs the scalp and face forward to reveal the top of his skull.

Jason snaps a few digital photographs of Gale's skull, which looks like a cracked nutshell, several large fractures having created a crisscross pattern or a waffled appearance. Remember how a tiny hairline fracture in the back of Robert Perry's skull caused a chain reaction that killed him (see "Contrasts," chapter 2)—a fact that underlines the massive head injuries Gale sustained.

"Looks like he took a massive hit," Tobin remarks as he studies the fragmented skull.

"He got humpty-dumptyfied," I remark as I examine the damage. Indeed, all the king's horses and all the king's men couldn't put this skull back together again. The Stryker saw sits on a shelf under the table below Gale's head. No need for the saw here.

Jason peels off the pieces, which look like pieces of a coconut shell. They come off with little effort and a cracking, sucking sound. As Jason removes the pieces of Gale's skull, the brain becomes visible; unlike the usual off-white color, Gale's brain is crimson, mottled with hemorrhaging from being flooded with blood. Jason does use the bone saw, with its oscillating blade in the shape of a fan (the Stryker attached to the other autopsy table contains a circular blade that looks like a large, wafer-thin silver dollar), to remove a piece of the skull toward the back of Gale's head, creating an opening just large enough to remove the brain.

Unlike Robert Perry, who died when the grains of his "golden hour" ran out, Gale did not die when his brain stem swelled into the foramen magnum. Gale didn't have an hour; he didn't have a minute.

"So he died when his brain swelled?" Tobin asks.

"No time to swell," I explain. "He took a huge whack, basically." I point to the tiny red dots, red pinpricks that represent hemorrhaging around the blood vessels in Gale's brain. The brainstem contains nerve centers that control bodily functions. In this case, the brain sustained damage to these nerve centers—the accident destroyed the control center of Gale's brain, equivalent to smashing a computer's hard drive against the sidewalk.

Gale died instantly.

The extent of the damage to the skull indicates he died on impact. He most probably never knew what hit him. Yet the damage to Gale's skull would not have resulted from an impact with the street or a sidewalk; his head must have struck something harder, perhaps something with an edge. Maybe the force of the impact threw him onto the car's hood, where his head struck the top edge of the windshield.

"How will you manage to put the head back together?" Tobin asks, wondering how Jason will put this smashed skull together again at the end of the autopsy.

"A couple of stitches in the scalp. It'll hold," Jason responds. Routine.

He places the skull fragments in the skull and packs it with a quantity of cotton to absorb any remaining blood, and with the coarse string from a large spool and a large-sized needle that looks like a knitting needle,

Jason closes the skull. Gale's head, though, appears misshapen, an unnatural ridge appearing under Gale's left eyebrow as a portion of the broken skull underneath is pushing against the skin of his forehead. Gale's appearance at the funeral will be left to the art of the mortician, or his coffin will remain closed at the visitation. Forty-five minutes after it began, Raymond Gale's autopsy is sewn up: he died as a result of massive head trauma.

*****

Jason briskly moves to the table holding the remains of James Valerio*, found by his brother with his face embedded in his living-room carpet. Valerio maintained a résumé of alcohol abuse; the official report that accompanied the body to the morgue states that he had a "history of ethanol abuse," and investigators found in the pocket of his blue jeans a marijuana cigarette, suggesting that he may have mixed intoxicants on the evening he died. I will order a toxicology screen on his blood, which in a week will indicate what he consumed and in what quantities on the night of his death. Blood does not lie. (Or does it? This question will be examined in "Bad Medicine," chapter 12.)

Wild tangles of wavy brunette hair spill over Valerio's rotund face and give him a windblown appearance. He wore a neatly trimmed, bushy brown mustache intertwined with strands of white, like bright white thread. His tongue is clamped between his teeth and partially protruding.

Jason begins the Y-incision, and the skin flaps sag to either side revealing a thick, dirty-yellow layer of fat. Doc notes 3" on the white board.

In the background, the fast Latin rhythm of the Gypsy Kings emanates from the stereo—the fast, bouncy rhythm is livelier than the sullen acoustic guitar that characterized the Crosby, Stills, Nash, and Young selections of earlier in the day. The Latin beat is a closer fit to the brisk pace of today's autopsies. As Jason opens Valerio's chest cavity with the rib cutters, the fact that skinny subjects make easier autopsy subjects becomes clear, as under the breastplate Valerio's intestines lie in a mound.

Fat complicates autopsies by creating more barriers in the examination of the heart and other vital organs; thus, Valerio will be an uncooperative patient, but not the heaviest patient that could enter the morgue. It could be worse. Much worse.

In our weight-conscious society, where, by the way, a great many people are significantly overweight, clinical definitions of obesity exist. Visitors to the morgue will spy a half sheet of paper taped on the wall describing the various levels of obesity:

Obesity: Methods of Definition

1. Relative Weight
    *   = body weight/"desirable weight"
    *   desirable weight defined as midpoint value recommended for "medium frame person" on standard height / weight tables.
2. Body Mass Index
    *   = body weight (kg) / height (m)^2
    *   Normal = 20–25

Obese =	RW >120% or BMI > 27.5
Mild Obesity =	RW >120–140% or BMI 27.5–30
Moderate Obesity =	RW >140–200% or BMI 30–40
Severe "morbid" Obesity =	RW >200% or BMI > 40

According to the official report that accompanied Valerio from Charlevoix County, he weighed 292 lbs. (132.5 kg) at a height of 73½ inches (186.7cm). Simple arithmetic produces a body mass index of 37.97; Valerio was "moderately obese" based on the definitions provided by the Kent County Morgue wall.

A strong, sour stench spills into the room as Jason removes the length of Valerio's intestines and places them into a large bowl situated between the decedent's feet. The intestines overfill the bowl; they look like pale yellow-pink bratwurst. The smell intensifies as Jason, using scissors, opens and examines the intestines in the sink basin at the end of the autopsy table. The odor is so intense, in fact, that it fills the room.

Not unlike the stench of a "decomp," this powerful odor affects the uninitiated in several different ways. Some breathe through their mouths and avoid the noxious smell. Some race to the bottle of wintergreen oil to dab some on the outside of their masks. Days later, they discover that they have developed an odd psychosomatic aversion to wintergreen mints. The mere smell of wintergreen makes them nauseous. Others retreat to the end of the corridor, rip off their masks, and suck in deep draughts of air, like they are dying of thirst and have just stumbled upon fresh water. A few draughts later, they loop the elastic strings of the mask over their ears and return to the morgue.

Back in the autopsy room, Jason has completed the odious task of examining the intestines, and the examination of Valerio's internal organs is under way. Acute drug overdose, including ethanol or alcohol abuse, leaves no trace, no evidence in the internal organs, except for rare occasions when I find pill fragments in the victim's stomach. Thus, the autopsy serves once again to exclude any other possibilities other than drugs and alcohol, to determine if anything else such as natural disease or unseen injuries may have caused or contributed to Valerio's death. Since he was found dead—his death not witnessed—the autopsy must leave no forensic stone unturned. His case history suggests the possibility of an overdose, but he could have been stoned in another way: someone could have struck him in the head, causing a lethal injury. The autopsy will determine what led to Valerio's death.

"How does an overdose kill a person?" Tobin asks.

With "uppers" (e.g., stimulants such as cocaine and amphetamines), an overdose will cause the heart to fibrillate, or to quiver, which prevents it from pumping effectively and delivering sufficient blood to sustain life. Without the pump functioning, blood flow ceases; since blood carries oxygen to the brain, a broken pump signals the death knell of the brain. "Downers" (e.g., narcotics and other depressant drugs) and alcohol slow breathing until it stops so that no oxygen travels to the brain, the brain stem shuts down, and all bodily functions cease. And, as one realizes after a few visits to the morgue, the brain stem is boss.

A brisk thirty-five minutes later, the examination is finished; Valerio suffered from diverticulosis—an "out-pouching" of the intestine lining caused in part by a lack of fiber in the diet. The "out-pouching," called a diverticulum, can become infected and rupture, which could cause death. This condition, though, did not contribute to Valerio's death, making the toxicology report the key element of this autopsy. The report will indicate if he ingested an amount of some substance that would have killed him. From the morgue, the vials of blood will travel down the hall to the toxicology lab. A few days later, the report revealed that Valerio's blood contained a cocktail of alcohol and hydrocodone—a prescription painkiller. This dangerous combination stopped his breathing.

Jason wraps up the autopsy by scrubbing Valerio's body with soap. In the background, the upbeat rhythm of the Gypsy Kings bounces from the morgue walls; the refrain of the song "Viento del Arena" provides an ironic overtone to the business of the morgue: "*Vive, Vive*" (Live, Live) . . . but does the refrain apply more to the people who visit or work in the morgue or to them, the victims?

15 SECONDS

Midfall 2004
Spectrum Health, Blodgett Campus
East Grand Rapids, Michigan

Dark oak Victorian armchairs sit on the office floor like aged colleagues. Curios—relics from famous cases—litter the room. On
the matching desk, a large jar contains three bullets found in the stomach
of a ninety-two-year-old heart attack victim who lived with constant pain
because he didn't want doctors to discover his mob roots in Chicago of
the 1930s. Next to the jar is a rust-encrusted railroad spike—the weapon
used by the city's most infamous serial killer. On an adjacent shelf rests
the dirty white skull of a woman who died from complications of drilling
a hole in the top of her skull; the top of the skull contains a neat, dime-
sized hole. She claimed that a hole strategically placed in the skull would
relieve her life's pressures. It did, just not in the way she expected.

The real medical examiner's cinematic and literary parallels might
work in an office that fits this description; this is the vision of a medical
examiner's office that years of television and film have created in the
minds of viewers. The reality, as Tobin has come to see, is much different,
and much more interesting.

Michigan, indeed, is a state of extremes. This afternoon, west Michigan enjoyed an unseasonably warm sixty-five degrees, but tonight nature will bring a cold front led by a storm of rain mixed with sleet. Through the Venetian blinds of my office on the third floor of Spectrum Health's Blodgett Campus Hospital, a muted gray hue—nature's cheese-cloth—covers everything.

No bodies today, so after a leisurely lunch, Friday afternoon will consist of tying up loose ends, finishing paperwork, and making calls in the third-floor office. For Tobin, this Friday afternoon will include a tour through a unique museum of tattoos, tattoos that entered the morgue on victims.

While I spend most of my time beneath ground in the morgue, three floors below, solving forensic mysteries posed by an infinite variety of victims, I maintain an office as well. Behind the plastic plate titled "Forensic Pathologist, Dr. Stephen D. Cohle," the office has over time become a repository for the paperwork generated by the medical examiner's responsibilities. The office, about the size of a small, one-car garage, is spacious, but the massive U-shaped desk unit occupying most of the floor space creates a claustrophobic sense of cramping.

Two large bookcases, crammed with books, cover one entire wall of the office from floor nearly to ceiling. These shelves contain titles one would associate with a medical examiner, such as *Gunshot Wounds*, *The Pathology of Trauma*, *Wound Ballistics*, and Casarett and Doull's *Toxicology* among hundreds of other books, including works on forensic entomology, or the study of insects in forensic contexts (see "Bugs!" chapter 3), and toxicology. A second scan reveals an anomaly: the vivid orange and blue dust jacket of *Roadkill*, a murder mystery by Kinky Friedman, one of my favorite authors.

Five wooden boxes fill an entire shelf of the bookcase; each box contains thin steel shelves. The shelves house tiny glass slices, each about the size of a stick of gum with a computer-generated identity label across the top. Each slide contains a vibrant magenta blot, which is a quarter-sized piece of tissue stained with hematoxylin (a blue stain) and eosin (a red stain), which differentiate the various cells and tissues. These ultrathin, translucent slices of tissue are stained to show various components of cells. During each autopsy, tissue samples are collected and placed in pink cassettes. From the morgue, the cassettes travel to the histology lab, where technicians create the slides.

The samples may provide key evidence in an investigation. For example, let's say that someone—a young person—is killed in a car crash of indeterminate cause. One of the questions the medical examiner must answer is, what caused the accident? Perhaps the driver suffered a fatal cardiac arrhythmia and lost control of the vehicle. Yet some diseases such as viral myocarditis (a viral infection of the heart muscle) can cause such an arrhythmia even in a heart that appears normal to the naked eye. Since the microscope can find things the naked eye cannot, the slides may provide vital forensic evidence.

Tobin once asked how he could obtain a jacket with "Kent County Medical Examiner" across the back in yellow letters. Now, as he scans the walls, he can see how I obtained my jacket; my professional credentials hang on the wall opposite the bookshelves above four beige file cabinets. They chronicle my career and the road to the post of forensic pathologist and chief medical examiner of Kent County.

Omnibus et Singulis; Quibus Curae Sunt Literae et Mores; Hae Literae datae sung quae testificentur; Stephen David Cohle; Magnum Cum Laude (William Jewell Collegii, May 1972)

The Curators of the University of Missouri, To all whom it may concern, Greeting; Be it known that the Curators, having been advised by the Faculty that, Stephen David Cohle, A.B., has completed the course of Study required of candidates for the degree of Doctor of Medicine (14 May 1977)

The Texas State Board of Medical Examiners Hereby Authorizes and Licenses Stephen David Cohle, M.D., to practice Medicine in the State of Texas (27 August 1978)

The American Board of Pathology Hereby certifies that Stephen D. Cohle, M.D., has pursued an accepted course of graduate study and clinical work and has demonstrated proficiency to the satisfaction of the Board of Trustees . . . Anatomic and Clinical Pathology (29 May 1981)

Baylor College of Medicine; Affiliated Hospitals Residency Program, Houston, Texas. Stephen David Cohle, M.D., has served satisfactorily as Chief Resident, 12 months from 1980 to 1981 (30 June 1981)

Baylor College of Medicine; Affiliated Hospitals Residency Program, Houston, Texas. Stephen David Cohle, M.D., has satisfactorily completed the educational requirements of the program in Pathology, 48 months from 1977 to 1981 (30 June 1981)

The University of Texas Southwestern Medical School Department of Pathology. This certificate is presented to Stephen D. Cohle, M.D., in recognition of accomplishments and contributions made during a 1-year Fellowship, Forensic Pathology (30 June 1982)

The American Board of Pathology Hereby certifies that Stephen D. Cohle, M.D., has pursued an accepted course of graduate study and clinical work and has demonstrated proficiency to the satisfaction of the Board of Trustees . . . Forensic Pathology (31 May 1982)

Tobin points to a picture frame standing on top of one of the file cabinets and smiles at the humorous image it contains. "A circa-seventies Steve Cohle," he remarks. The photograph contains a humorous image of me, sporting checkered pants and large mutton chops, pointing a gun at the head of a wide-eyed man sitting at a desk—a bit of gallows humor between pathologists in Dallas, where I first began my career as a pathologist.

The office also contains a glimpse of my personality: the large tub of whey protein perched on top of the shelves of the desk enclosure symbolizes an avid interest in competitive weightlifting. Next to the protein, a chess set, which symbolizes a love of chess and online chess matches. Below these reminders that life exists beyond the walls of the hospital, the U-shaped desk appears the survivor of a tornado that blew papers, medical journals, and various other ephemera across its surface.

Once again, the reality does not fit the stereotype; except for the tissue specimens, the office does not contain mementos of major cases, unlike the parallels of the real medical examiner's fictional counterparts. The visitor to this office will not be greeted by the jawbone of a cannibal killer, or a blood-streaked full-metal jacket dug from the body of a murder victim, or the false eye of . . . but it does contain the "Museum of Tattoos."

THE MUSEUM OF TATTOOS

A rose-colored three-ring binder houses hundreds of slides that comprise the Kent County Morgue's museum of human tattoos. Each page contains twenty slides, each an example of body art that ranges from the pedestrian (a Pink Panther strolling across a shoulder blade) to the sublime (a Geisha girl under a bended palm tree that covers an entire forearm) to the bizarre (see below for highlights, or lowlights depending on the reader's perspective).

Tobin opens the cover of the binder, removing slides and holding them up in the light. "Unbelievable. Un-be-lieve-a-ble," he remarks after studying a few slides.

"The crap people do to themselves never ceases to amaze me," I respond, as the pages of the rose-colored binder prove that there is no limit to how people use their bodies to convey messages, even bizarre, tawdry, and crude ones.

- One slide contains the image of a woman's nether region; five roses form a tattoo belt across her lower waist, and dangling just above her pubic hair, "Carl's Pussy" leaves little doubt as to whom in life she loved.
- Ouch! A male viewer might flinch at the image of a tattoo on a man's penis (the name of a lover scrolled vertically). Another (another!) reads "USDA GRADE A CHOICE," and on still another member (!) a black widow spider sits at the base of the shaft.
- A comic figure sitting on a man's front right thigh giggles and points to one o'clock, the exact position of the wearer's genitalia.
- A dull-blue, homemade tattooed fist adorns a suicide victim's thigh, the middle finger extended in a gesture immediately recognized by anyone who has traveled an American highway. Ultimately, its wearer "flipped off" the world and shot himself in the head.

- The Grim Reaper's skeletal head protrudes from a vibrant blue robe on a tattoo covering the back of a man's arm. The figure holds a bloodstained sickle above his head. The owner of this tattoo would meet the Grim Reaper when he committed suicide by using a garden hose to channel the carbon monoxide from the exhaust pipe into his car.

  "This guy is popular," Tobin notes. The Grim Reaper, in various poses, appears often among those who take their own lives.

  "I see a lot of Grim Reaper tattoos on risk takers, those who drive one hundred miles an hour down the highway," I explain, "as well as on suicide victims."

  Another tattoo seems to add an exclamation point to this statement: a Grim Reaper on a motorcycle above the slogan "DEATH IS CERTAIN, LIFE IS NOT." Another Reaper accompanies the phrase "DEATH CALLS."

- The massive image of a bikini-clad woman, her legs spread in a very provocative pose, virtually covers the entire chest of a man.
- "Fuck the Police" in pale blue: an unsubtle message adorns the chest of a convict from a maximum-security penitentiary in southern Michigan who died when he fell from a third-tier balcony. State police, who investigate crimes in prisons, were in charge of the case. Of course, no one saw anything, but somehow the victim sustained a stab wound, a nonfatal wound, between his shoulder blades that likely led to his thirty-foot fall. In other words, someone helped him off that ledge.
- Another angry one: the slide shows the pink inside of a man's lip, which contains the pale blue words "Fuck You." One wonders, given the location of the tattoo, who he intended to see the message!
- A tattoo that covered the entire right buttock of its owner presents a humorous irony. The tattoo contains a pair of lips, in vibrant red color, encircled by the sentence "GIVE ME HEAD / 'TIL I'M DEAD." The victim shot himself in the head, though, so ultimately he didn't get his wish.
- More penis tattoos (!), all placed vertically down the shaft. Two

with names, and another with the slogan "SIT ON IT" stretched out down the entire length of the owner's penis.

- Another slide captures the image of a homicide victim (gunshot wound to the head and chest), his sleepy eyes open yet focused on nothing, the inner inhabitant long since gone from the body. As if to presage the sad end to his story, a stream of tattoo tears runs from the corner of his right eye down his cheek.
- "Another popular guy," Tobin remarks as he hands me a slide. "I've seen a number of those," I respond as I hold up the slide and notice the image of the Tasmanian Devil, a popular tattoo subject among those who eventually find their way into the morgue.

*****

After a few hours, Tobin's afternoon visit to my office comes to an end, as does the workweek. All over the Grand Rapids metropolitan area, people flee their places of employment for a two-day furlough of R and R, but the medical examiner's workweek extends into Saturday, if someone dies tonight.

Outside Blodgett, a few people run across the street to the parking ramp to flee a brisk wind that grabs like a firm grip on the lapel. A gray blanket has begun to cover the sky from the west: a storm is coming.

*****

Every parent faces his child's "terrible-twos," but after this morning, the phrase will take on a new and ghastly meaning. . . .

At eight thirty, the sun has begun its rise from the east, creating an eerie orange glow outside of the hospital's lobby. As the storm passes, the clear, icy skies of a cold front follow—a harbinger of winter's encroachment. In the adjacent courtyard, the naked branches of a tree reach toward the sky like outstretched arms.

The hospital is very quiet this morning, almost sleeping. A victim, the one case to solve this morning, awaits on the floor below. One hospital patron walks past, her arms full of gift bags in various colors—presents for someone, but who? Perhaps the gifts are for her husband hospitalized for a bypass surgery, or for her child who fell off a swing set at the neighborhood park—a terrifying thought. One thing is for sure: they aren't for whomever waits below.

Tobin arrives at eight thirty sharp, our agreed-upon time, and I arrive at ten to nine, twenty minutes after the anticipated start time for this morning's case. Tobin is all smiles as he waits in his usual attire of button-down shirt, black jeans, and tennis shoes. He does not know the specifics of this morning's case; if he did, he wouldn't be smiling.

We quickly move through the vacant lobby, throwing a "good morning" to the elderly receptionist. For Tobin, anticipation builds with each step toward the morgue as two questions captivate him: What mystery will he confront this morning? What tragedy will unfold before his eyes?

I punch my code into the keypad and enter my professional realm. Once inside, we move down the corridor and into the autopsy room, where Paul Davison awaits in his usual hospital garb; he has removed today's subject from the refrigerator: a child.

The sight stops Tobin, who stares, silent, at the boy lying on the autopsy table. The boy is roughly the same age and size as his oldest daughter. That fact could not have escaped him, and his inner monologue is screaming so loud one can almost hear it: A child! A child! A child! This is a sight for which even detectives with ice water in their veins can never prepare themselves, can never steel their nerves.

One wants to look away, to ignore the frigid reality that last evening a child perished, but like a powerful magnet, the boy keeps pulling the attention of all present back to the table on which he rests.

Innocent. Innocent. Innocent. The word reverberates, the echo of something Paul Davison said when asked if anything still bothered him about his work as a death investigator. "Children," he responded. "The innocent. . . . The helpless. . . ."

Paul is not alone in his aversion to child victims. One Kent County police officer, whose occupation occasionally brought him into the underworld of the morgue, described the spectacle of a child on the autopsy table in familiar terms: "Seeing the autopsy of a child . . . one never for-

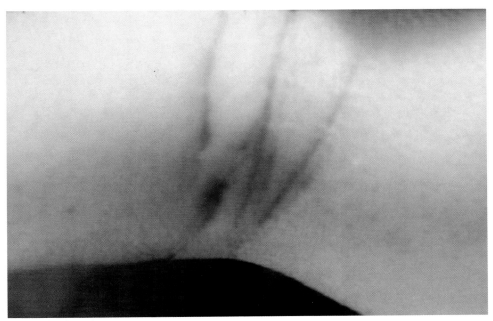

Marks on a wrist caused by the rope used to bind a murder victim.

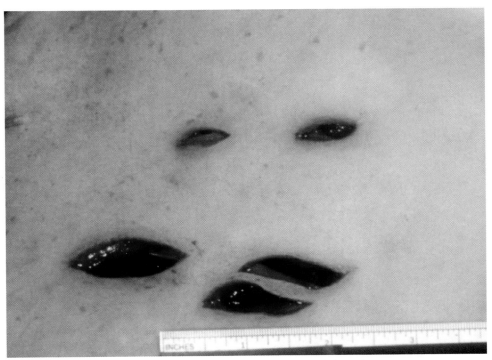

Stab wounds in the back of a murder victim with bound wrists.

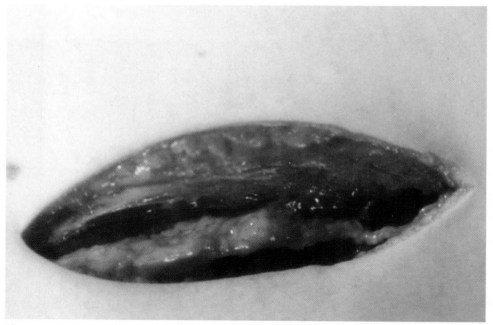

An example of a double-edged (both edges sharp) stab wound. (This is the first in a series of five photos that detail evidence which can indicate the type of knife used in a stabbing. For an explanation of stab wounds and "clock position," see chapter 5, "Skeletons in the Closet.")

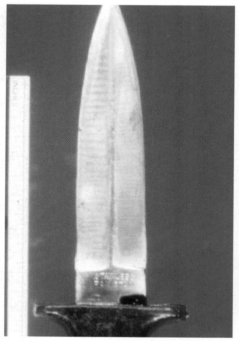

The double-edged survival knife used to cause the stab wound in the picture above.

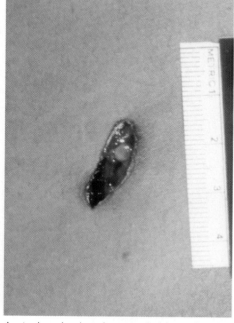

A single-edged stab wound. Note the dull end on the top and the sharp (tapered) end on the bottom.

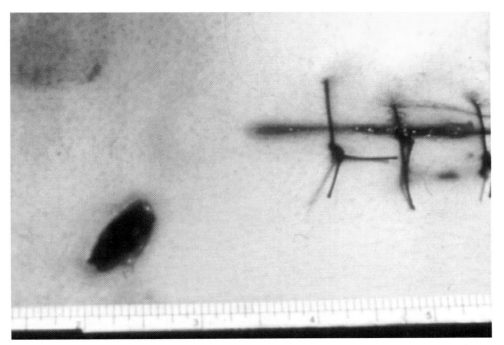

A stab wound on a victim's chest; it is difficult to determine whether it was caused by a single- or a double-edged weapon.

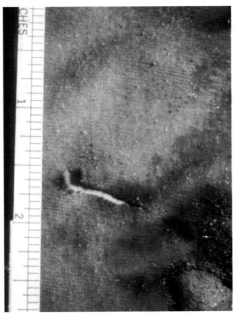

The shirt of the victim with the stab wound in the photo above, showing the shape of the blade and indicating that the blade was twisted after insertion into the body.

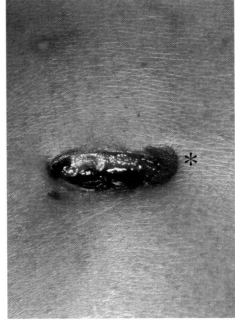

A single-edged stab wound with a patterned abrasion (*marked* *) caused by the hilt of the weapon at the superior edge.

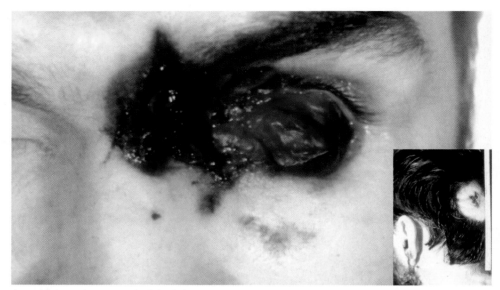

A suicidal gunshot wound of the left eye. Note the abundant black soot around the entry wound. *Inset:* The exit wound in the back of the head. Note how the hair had to be shaved around the wound to identify the wound characteristics. (This is the first in a sequence of five photographs that detail a mystery created by a jacketed bullet and another example of how such bullets can be deceiving and trick even law enforcement. "The Hand of God," in chapter 11, covers another case in which a jacketed bullet would lead to a false impression about cause of death.)

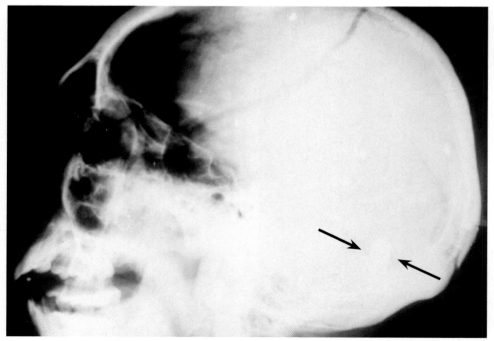

An x-ray of the skull from the individual in the photo above, showing bullet fragments in the brain. How can this be? There was an entry and an exit wound.

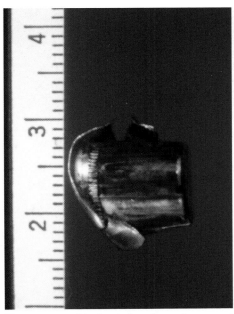 

The recovered bullet jacket from the wound in the case illustrated on the previous page. Explanation: the lead core exited the head but the bullet jacket was retained.

An unfired bullet cut in half. Note the powder in the lower half of the bullet and the lead core partially surrounded by copper in the jacketed upper portion of the bullet.

Two examples of jacketed bullets (*left and middle*) and one nonjacketed bullet (*right*). Note the copper jackets on the left and middle bullets.

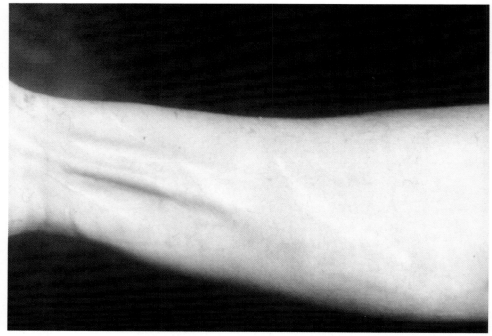

The forearm of a suicide victim showing multiple healed wrist scars. Suicide victims often leave such evidence of past attempts. (See chapter 4, "Red Sky in the Morning.")

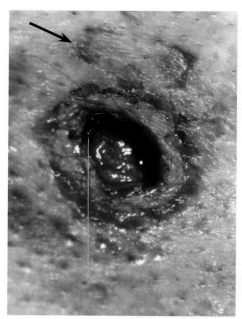

A contact gunshot wound of the chest showing a pattern of the bullet muzzle circumferentially around the wound and a site abrasion along the upper margin of the wound.

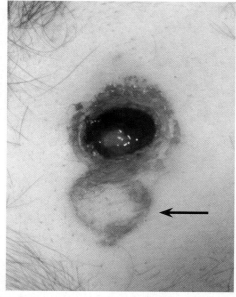

A patterned muzzle abrasion on a victim's chest. Note the figure eight. The top half of the "eight" is the actual gunshot wound while the bottom half is from the circular structure immediately beneath the barrel.

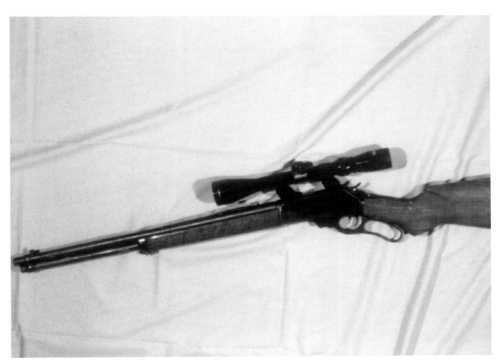

A photograph of the 30-30 rifle used to inflict the wound in the previous photograph.

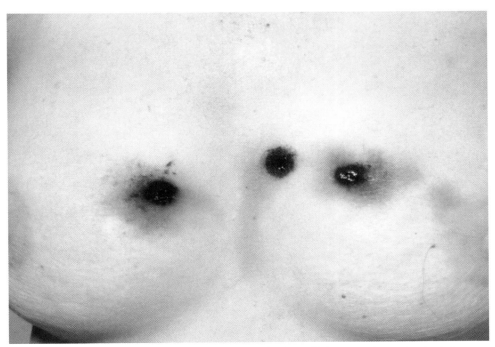

Three contact suicidal gunshot wounds on a victim's chest. If they are determined, victims can inflict multiple wounds as long as the first wound is not incapacitating.

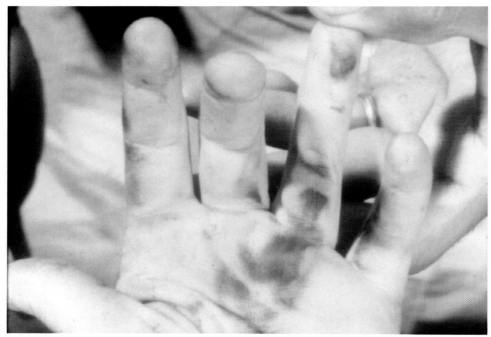

Soot on the left hand of a suicide victim. This is the hand that steadied the weapon against the head. (For more explanation about soot and gunshots, see "The Hand of God," in chapter 11.)

A young man after a shootout with police. The victim's face is at the top of the illustration. Note the portion of the entry wound in his right temple (*marked* *). The question was whether this individual shot himself or if police shot him in the head. (This is the first of four photographs that illustrate the clues which differentiate between suicide and homicide. See "The Hand of God," in chapter 11.)

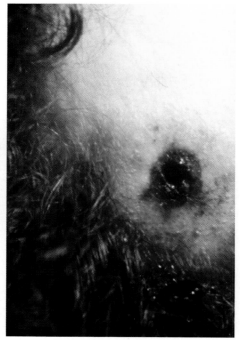

A contact wound with soot in the right temple. Note the hair was shaved to expose the wound.

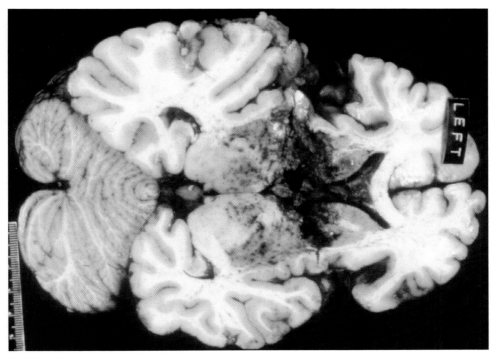

A section of brain (CT plane) showing the bullet path extending across the frontal lobes.

A close-up photograph of the bullet recovered from the victim's head showing pieces of the victim's hair (*arrow*) and bone (*marked* *). A comparison of this bullet with one test fired from the victim's revolver showed identical markings, which supported the conclusion that the victim shot himself.

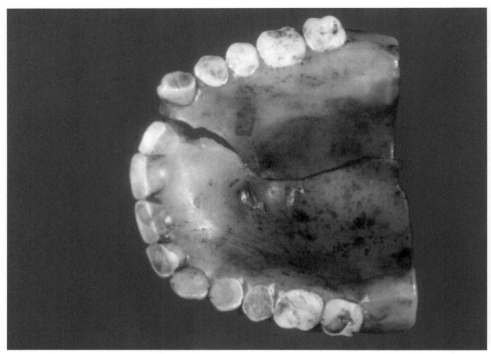

The cracked dentures with abundant soot from an individual who shot himself in the mouth.

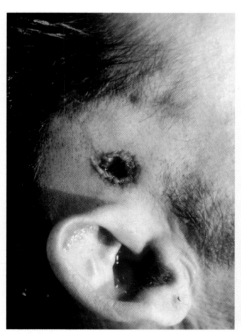

A patterned contact wound of the right temple. Note the suggested octagonal-shaped abrasion around the entry wound.

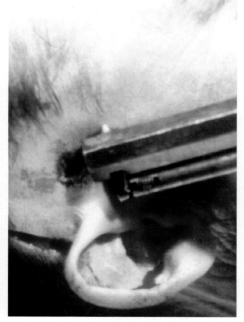

The weapon used to inflict the injury in the previous photograph. This is a black powder pistol with an octagonal barrel.

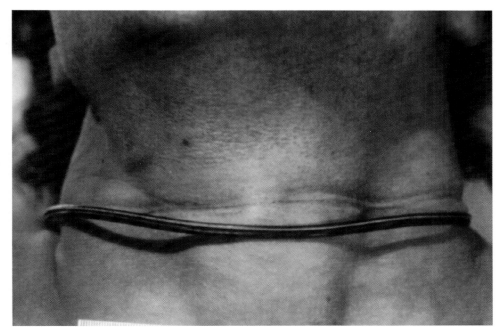

A hanging victim with a ligature and a patterned abrasion around the neck consistent with the ligature. This is the type of damage that can result from a hanging suicide (see chapter 11, "Endings"), but not all hanging suicide victims exhibit such ligature marks (see chapter 2, "Contrasts").

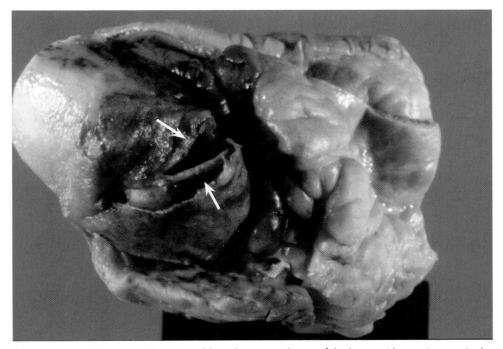

A young man with an aortic dissection. Note the external view of the heart with a gaping tear in the aorta (*between the arrows*) showing a split within the wall of the aorta caused by dissecting blood.

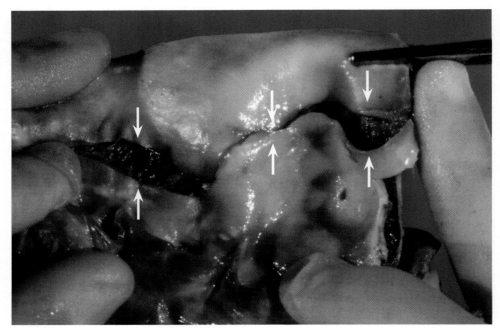

A photograph of the opened laceration (tear) in the lining of the aorta through which blood entered the aortic wall. There was a rupture through the outer wall of the aorta with exsanguination (massive fatal hemorrhage).

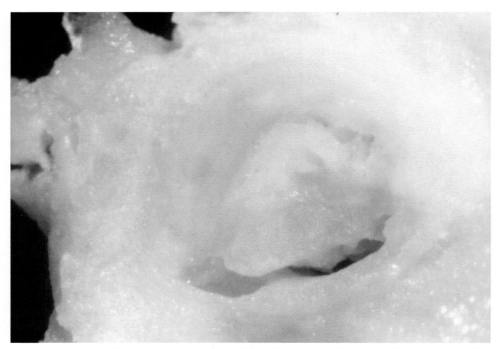

A coronary artery with severe narrowing by yellow atheromatous (cholesterol-laden) plaque. (See chapter 1, "Decompression"; chapter 9, "Broken Hearts"; and chapter 10, "Of Zebras and Horses.")

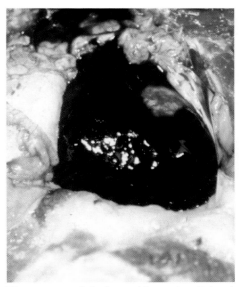

The sac around the heart (the pericardial sac) filled with blood from a ruptured myocardial infarct. When this sac fills rapidly, as it might from a stab wound (see chapter 5, "Skeletons in the Closet"), the heart becomes compressed by the blood and cannot pump effectively.

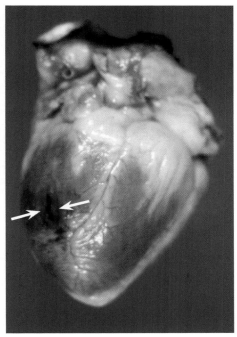

A photograph of a heart with a slit-like rupture (*between the arrows*) along the left margin.

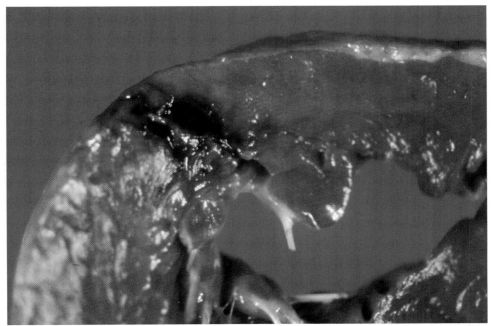

A cross section of a heart showing the rupture track from inside to outside. The heart muscle around this hemorrhagic track was infarcted (dead). (For an explanation of infarcts, see chapter 1, "Decompression," and chapter 9, "Broken Hearts.")

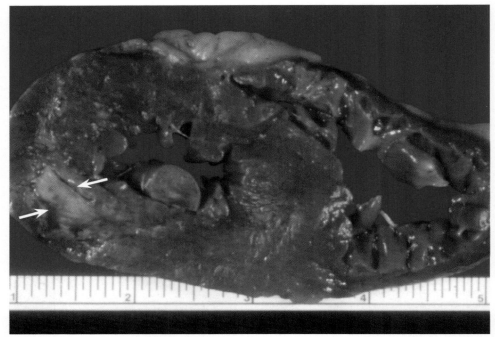

A cross section of a heart with a nonruptured recent infarct. This is the lower left side of the left ventricle (*arrows show the infarct*).

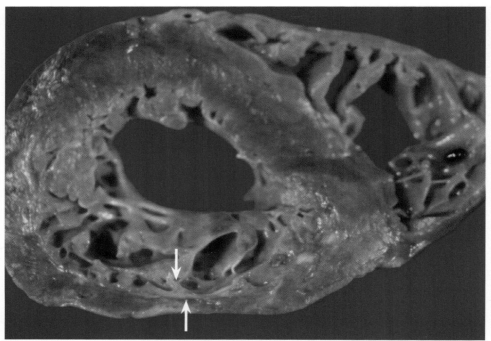

An example of an old infarct with marked thinning of the posterior wall of the left ventricle (*arrows are on either side of the infarct*).

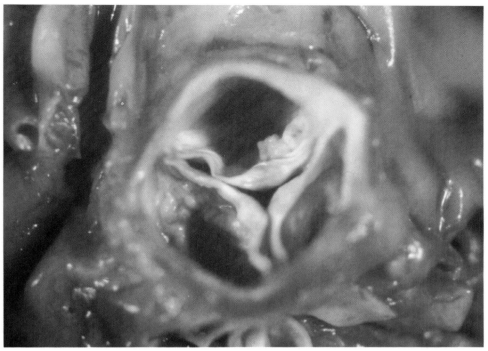

A close-up view of a normal aortic valve with three cusps.

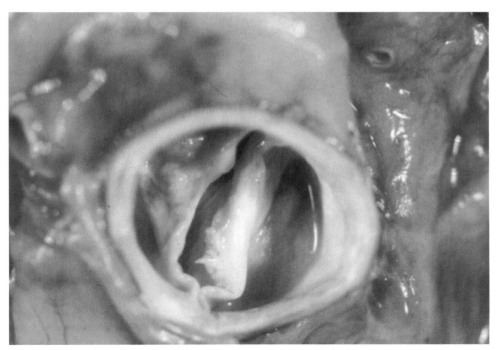

An abnormal aortic valve with two cusps. These cusps became calcified, causing stenosis (narrowing) of the aorta and sudden death.

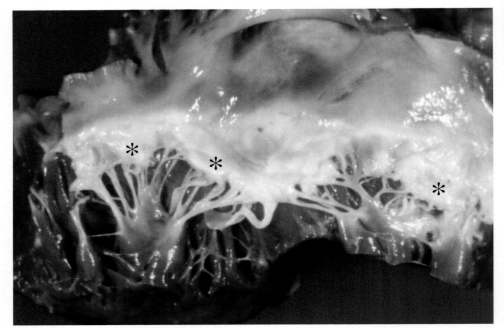

A view of myxomatous degeneration of a mitral valve (also known as a floppy mitral valve). These thickened valve leaflets (*marked* *) can be associated with sudden unexpected death. (See chapter 9, "Broken Hearts.")

The collection of liquor bottles that arrived in the morgue with victims, many of whom sustained fatal head injuries while the bottles remained intact. The bottles represent one common thread that ties together many of the stories in this book. (See chapter 1, "Decompression.")

gets . . . it remains in the back of your mind. Some images, like watching a child of similar age playing at the park, cause the subconscious to vomit up the memory of the autopsy. The image never goes away; it lingers like the burning and taste of bile in the back of the throat."

A few months ago, another young officer who entered the morgue on police business may have felt a similar emotion. It is a scene in the drama of the morgue that is often repeated.

The short scene begins with the image of a young police officer in his midthirties who accompanied the victim who hanged himself in his jail cell (see "Contrasts," chapter 2). When Paul Davison makes the Y-incision that marks the cutting phase of the autopsy procedure, the officer retreats into the morgue corridor.

"Don't like the sight of blood?" Paul asks.

The officer shakes his head and explains that he once observed the autopsy of a child. . . .

Tobin circles the table and studies the boy lying naked there. The boy's head is cocked to the side, his eyes closed; his copper-brown hair is cropped short, and a large incision runs from his upper chest to his abdomen, knitted closed with large, black stitching, the result of an organ harvest. His liver and kidneys will save another child . . . they cannot help him.

Various medical paraphernalia accompany his body; an orange catheter tube protrudes from his penis, and a white plastic bite guard sits inside his mouth, which hangs agape as if he is asleep. No image on earth is as peaceful as the sight of a child asleep. At one time or another, every father tiptoes into his child's bedroom at night to catch a glimpse of his child sleeping, tucked up into a fetal position, her arms encircling her plush "dolly" that was once vibrant pink but now faded after three years of use. She is peace itself, the mere sight of which erases the clutter accumulated by adult life. While the sight of a child stretched out on a morgue table would affect anyone with a beating heart, the experience of parenthood will bring a person closer to this boy's tragedy.

One can study innumerable tragedies as a student, read Aristotle's theories of tragedy, or perhaps analyze a few Shakespeare plays like *Romeo and Juliet* or *Macbeth* in high school or college, but this moment more than any simulated tragedy illustrates the notion of *pathos*. What must the boy's father and mother feel at this moment, after losing a child? I couldn't help feeling that it must be like a very painful kidney stone rolling around in the heart. Despite the presence of others in the morgue this morning, conversation is hushed, like people conversing in a church.

There are two visitors in the room today. A short, blonde woman in her late twenties, wearing blue jeans and a navy blue turtleneck blouse, introduces herself as the assistant prosecuting attorney for the eastern Michigan county in which this boy died. In their brief conversation, she reveals that she has just received notice that she successfully passed the bar; this will be the first autopsy she witnesses. Accompanying her in the brown and beige uniform typical of the Michigan sheriff's deputies is a deputy sheriff, whose twenty-plus years of experience provide an ironic juxtaposition to his partner's inexperience.

Anyone entering this place for the first time arrives shielded by a bubble containing years of illusions fabricated by youthful naiveté and television "reality." But experiencing the morgue is like running through a corridor of people all of whom are throwing darts at you. Few leave unscathed, and no one leaves with his or her bubble intact. The young prosecuting attorney will leave indelibly changed by what she will see this morning. So will Tobin. Everyone present will.

And then the rookie assistant prosecuting attorney throws a dart of her own that sticks in the heart when she briefly details the case. Thursday afternoon, by his own admission, the boy's father slapped the child in the back of the head and shook him vigorously. At two years old, this boy is beyond the age at which shaking would likely result in death. In fact, I explain to those present, who have formed a circle around the table on which the victim lies, some doubt exists in the medical community as to whether a child can sustain a fatal injury from shaking without suffering a concurrent injury, such as a blunt-force impact to the head. Research conducted in the eighties suggests shaking can only kill a child if combined with an impact.

Since this research was published, two groups have formed around the issue. One group consists of physicians who believe that shaking can lead to death only if accompanied by another head injury. The other group is dominated by pediatricians who maintain that a mere shaking can lead to death—the "shaken baby syndrome," or SBS.

"So the father must have done something other than shake the boy?" Tobin, who listened intently to my explanation about SBS, asks.

"The bottom line," I respond, "is that he killed the kid. You don't want to get caught up in semantics."

While the two visitors disappear down the corridor for a cup of coffee, I peruse the particulars of the case as Tobin looks over my shoulder. No need for them to rush—they will have time, because the official report runs several pages of typed, single-spaced text and narrates a tragic, pathetic tale of two-year-old Aaron Michael Edwards's* final day. This is a serpentine story, the direction of which changes several times, and is told by a snake.

As I read the report, a fast acoustic rhythm, an Irish folk pub sound provided courtesy of Leon Russell's *Retrospective*—the music Paul Davison has selected for this autopsy—breaks the silence.

Anna Rapp, a high-school junior completing a semester-long internship, enters the morgue. She fishes through the cabinet for a surgical gown, then ducks into the evidence room to obtain booties to cover her shoes. She braces herself by placing her palm on a table in the corner of the room—this evidence table against the wall contains the possessions that entered the hospital with Aaron. Three Beenie Babies—a turtle, a puppy, and a duck—along with a foam NASCAR sit on top of a baby blue blanket covered with white and yellow stars and half moons. He loved Beenie Babies, he loved life . . .

"The terrible twos," I note to Tobin as I finish reading the report, may have precipitated the violence that led to Aaron's death; the father admits to spanking the child several times for misbehavior during the week. The report contains the testimony of the father, whose story of the event changed with each subsequent telling in each subsequent interview with law enforcement personnel—typical in child abuse cases.

"Terrible twos," Tobin repeats in a monotone voice.

"You won't think about that phrase the same way after this morning." Tobin slowly shakes his head.

The father's first version has Aaron playing on a piece of playground equipment and falling five to six feet and landing on his head. After the impact, he lost consciousness, his eyes rolled back, he turned blue, and he stopped breathing. The father attempted to resuscitate him.

In the second version of his story, the father admitted more responsibility. While dressing Aaron, the boy disobeyed, arching his back and throwing himself backward. The father stated that he slapped Aaron and shook him, although the extent of the father's treatment would remain buried in the tangle of half-truths motivated perhaps by a father fearful of prosecution or shocked by his culpability in the death of a two-year-old boy.

In a follow-up interview, the father stated that, under the pressure of the moment, he snapped, picked up Aaron by the armpits, and shook him as vigorously as possible for ten to fifteen seconds.

As I narrate this sad saga while reading the report, Tobin glances at the analog clock high on the wall behind, which provides some perspective. He watches its second hand move through its progression. Fifteen seconds is a miniscule amount of time unless one spends it in pain or torture. Fifteen seconds—look at your watch and gaze at the second hand as it makes its way through fifteen notches and imagine a father shaking his son. Perhaps for the first time, you might realize how long fifteen seconds can be. Did Aaron feel pain? Did he know what was happening to him? Was he afraid? Did he cry out for his mommy? The ten to fifteen seconds is the father's estimate, taken in an interview after the fact. Perhaps he shook his child for less time—perhaps more.

Yet, even fifteen seconds of fairly vigorous shaking could have killed Aaron Michael Edwards. According to the dad's statement, Aaron lost consciousness, after which the father doused his face with water from the shower and attempted to revive him with CPR. He then placed Aaron on the couch and ran for the phone, during which time Aaron fell from the couch, hitting his head on the floor.

In yet another interview, the father admitted to hitting Aaron in the back of the head several times over the course of the week; perhaps a blow to the head combined with ten to fifteen seconds of shaking killed his son. As I sift through the police report containing the brambles of subterfuge created by these conflicting statements, the evidence echoes the same two things mentioned earlier this morning: the terrible twos and the bottom line that he killed the boy.

"So we want to know what happened to the child after he sustained the injury and for how long he was conscious," I note to Tobin, who has begun to suit up for this morning's autopsy. To answer these questions, the autopsy of little Aaron Michael Edwards will commence.

The assistant prosecuting attorney, the deputy sheriff, and Paul Davison chat in the conference room as they sip their cups of coffee, their voices muffled by the distance.

As noted previously, most visitors to the morgue immediately spot the sign on the wall above the floor scale: "No eating or drinking in the morgue." The presence of the sign nearly always conjures a remark. Medical examiner personnel like Paul know not to bring coffee into the autopsy room; breaking this rule could result in a hefty fine from the Occupational Safety and Health Administration (OSHA). Perhaps the coffee is worth the fine this morning, but he also realizes that, with each sip, he could possibly ingest any number of fatal viruses (see "Risks," chapter 1), so the three chat and drink their coffee in the conference room before the autopsy begins, before their focus returns to the twenty-five-pound child lying on the autopsy table.

Aaron's body will bear witness against his father—a Greek tragedy applied to twenty-first-century America—and it will speak volumes. His body is a tapestry loaded with injuries that together chronicle his short, tortured existence.

The autopsy begins with a detailed description of each injury, past or present. "Faint, well-healed scar above the left eyebrow," I narrate into the recorder. I note another healed scar on the left side of Aaron's forehead accompanied by a contusion and a bright orange streak—an unusual abrasion—on his left cheek. This is possibly a burn that was healing. A one-inch round contusion on Aaron's left forearm and two red dots on his left clavicle—a possible bite mark—add to the boy's growing catalogue of injuries.

I tug Aaron's right wrist and without assistance and with little effort roll Aaron onto his stomach to examine his back. Two long slices run down the length on both sides of Aaron's back; another two-inch cut appears between his shoulder blades. Paul Davison made these cuts post-mortem to determine the extent of the bruises that dot Aaron's entire back like purple polka dots and to document the "true bruises." Hemorrhaging in "true bruises" runs into the fatty tissue under the skin, I explain to the assistant DA and the deputy as Anna and Tobin observe. With my thumb and index finger, I spread open one of the slices to reveal the thin layers of yellow-white fat just under the skin. Tiny crimson blooms appear in the fat layer, like strawberries on a cheesecake—hemorrhaging from bruises.

With the scalpel, I excise a few tissue samples from one of the "true bruises" and drop it into a pink cassette Anna is holding open. No amount of evidence here can be redundant—no one wants to lose this case: an impending murder charge against Aaron's father.

After the examination and narration of Aaron's external injuries, Paul begins the autopsy by removing the various hospital treatment parapher-nalia including the catheter. He then removes the black sutures left from the organ harvest, and makes the standard Y-incision. No need for rib cut-ters, he explains to the prosecuting attorney, who watches as he cuts through Aaron's ribs with his scalpel (by two years the cartilage con-necting the ribs to the sternum has not yet fully calcified). Behind the plastic shield of her facemask, the prosecuting attorney's eyes widen as Paul lifts and removes the breastplate to reveal the organs underneath. The intestines, almost translucent and bloated with gas, fill the entire lower half of Aaron's trunk.

Minutes later, Paul has removed all of Aaron's internal organs, which now sit in a silver bowl on the surface of the workstation. I remove Aaron's heart and lungs and place them on the dissecting table where they sit awaiting examination—together, they are the size of a softball. The remaining organs barely fill the bottom third of the bowl in which Paul has placed them.

As the heart and lungs are dissected, Paul begins work on Aaron's head, creating a modified incision that will allow them to examine the underside of his scalp for hemorrhages, the presence of which would indi-cate deep bruising—evidence of recent physical abuse.

A series of purple hemorrhages, each the size of the head of a pushpin, dot the underside of Aaron's scalp. Invisible under Aaron's reddish brown hair, from the inside they become visible, conspicuous. I examine the underside of the scalp and cut out a small slice, placing the slice into another pink cassette; later, technicians will stain this sample for iron. The presence of iron in the tissue would indicate that the bruise is at least four to five days old, since the iron in red blood cells breaks down over time.

After collecting tissue samples, I return to the workstation to finish examining Aaron's internal organs while Paul continues his work on Aaron's head.

"Did you know that superglue was designed by a funeral home director?" Paul asks Tobin as he squeezes some glue from a tube over the incision left by the scalpel when the tissue samples were taken. The incision went through the skin and would appear on Aaron's face as a red slice, but the superglue will patch the wound—a professional courtesy from the Kent County medical examiner team, which Paul jokingly calls "a one and a half man department" on mornings like these.

The young assistant prosecuting attorney observes as Paul cuts through Aaron's skull with the Stryker saw. In the reflection on the plastic shield of her mask, Aaron's head bobs as Paul works the saw through the skull, but behind the plastic, her eyes widen, the autopsy of Aaron Michael opening them to the ugly side of human society.

"Did you find anything out of the ordinary?" Tobin asks.

"Everything is normal," I declare upon completing the examination of Aaron's internal organs. "The problem will be in his head," I note as Tobin watches Paul open the skull.

Paul removes the calvarium—the top of Aaron's skull (also called the skull cap)—to reveal hemorrhaging over the surface of the brain (what doctors call a subdural hematoma). The underside of Aaron's skull is caked with thick, clotted blood that looks like the color and consistency of barbecue sauce.

The amount of blood over Aaron's brain indicates that the head trauma he suffered caused torn blood vessels that affected normal functioning. If the brain is the human body's "motherboard," severe head trauma may result in severed wiring and fractured capacitors; without intact wiring to connect the various components of the circuit board, the "motherboard" ceases to function as a coherent whole.

This victim has a very swollen brain. One of the theories of shaken baby syndrome, or SBS, consists of a sinister chain reaction similar to the effects of a traumatic head injury such as a blunt-force impact to the skull (see "Contrasts," chapter 2). Severe shaking causes damage to the brain stem, which subsequently ceases to function. Since the brain stem controls the heart and respiration, the heart and breathing stop; without the pump and bellows to provide oxygen to the brain, the brain dies—and as noted earlier, "the brain stem is boss."

After snapping a few digital photographs with the morgue's camera, Paul removes Aaron's brain. He places the brain in a bowl and puts the bowl on the workstation for weighing and examination.

While the brain is weighed and the weight noted on the white board, Paul prepares to collect more evidence of what caused Aaron's untimely demise. . . . He will find the evidence he seeks in the boy's eyes. Using surgical clamps, he pries open the lids of Aaron's right eye, and with a pair of scissors he frees the eye by severing the connective tissue around the eye and the muscles that hold it in the eye socket. Cases of shaken baby syndrome, he explains, produce tiny pinpoint-like hemorrhages on the eyeball. These petechial hemorrhages represent evidence, so he will remove and process the eyes as forensic evidence.

The eye is very tough, Paul explains to Tobin, who watches intently as he continues the time-consuming process of severing the muscles. Just yesterday, they conducted the autopsy of a woman who committed suicide by shooting herself in the head with a shotgun. The force of the blast destroyed her head, leaving nothing intact above her mouth and throwing her eyes from their sockets. The eyeballs, though, remained unscathed— undamaged by the blast.

After a few more cuts, Paul removes the eyeball and holds it in the palm of his hand while Tobin studies it. About the size of a large, white marble, the pupil is on one side and on the opposite side is a red dot. In the center of the red dot, a small cord—the optic nerve—now severed, protrudes. The optic nerve is the wire that connects the eyeball to the brain.

Paul directs Tobin to find two plastic jars on the workstation next to the one on which I am examining cross sections of Aaron's brain. Each jar, about the size of a coffee mug, is filled with formaldehyde and contains a label on which Paul asks Tobin to write the medical codes for "right" and "left." He scrawls the numbers on the labels, unscrews the top of the jar that will contain Aaron's right eyeball, and holds it up in front of Paul, who slides the needle of a syringe into the right eye and draws back the plunger, removing the fluid—vitreous humor—inside the eyeball. As the syringe drains the vitreous humor, the eyeball deflates and flattens. Paul pushes the plunger and the vitreous humor in the syringe spills onto the autopsy table. He dips the needle into the jar, fills the syringe with formaldehyde, and then inserts the needle into the deflated eyeball, filling it with formaldehyde and restoring the circular shape of the eyeball, which now is translucent rather than white. The infusion of formaldehyde will "fix" or preserve the eye and the evidence it contains. He drops the eye into the jar.

Tobin fastens the lid and holds up the jar; inside the blue pupil floats in the column of fluid, dangling, bobbing in the formaldehyde. In life, Aaron may have wanted to close his eyes, to shield his consciousness from the pain of an existence with an abusive father; ironically, in death, these eyes that have witnessed so much pain, so much suffering, will testify against the perpetrator of that pain and suffering.

As Paul works to free Aaron's left eye from its socket, I prepare Aaron's brain for preservation. The unpreserved brain is soft and difficult to cut into slices; suspension in formaldehyde will solidify the brain, making easier the examination I will conduct in a few days. A white string that will be used to suspend the brain is laced beneath the artery on the brainstem (the basilar artery), and the brain is gently lowered into a plastic tub filled with formaldehyde. The lid of the tub is pressed closed and placed on the workstation.

A brief examination of the inside of Aaron's skull is conducted; no fractures appear in the skull, and the autopsy concludes with an official manner of death as "homicide"—a statement that in court could result in a sentence of thirty years to life in prison. Paul begins to reassemble the skull as the assistant prosecuting attorney and her police escort remove their masks and booties and throw them into the biohazard disposal bin, exchanging a curt dialogue about potential court dates.

All of a sudden, as if delivering a slap across the face by the ramifications of her statement, the assistant prosecuting attorney proclaims: "She has other children."

As they made their way toward the corridor leading to the exit, Paul looks up from his stitching, as he closes Aaron's scalp, and calls out to the assistant prosecuting attorney and her escort. "Get this bastard."

Davison couldn't have conjured a more perfect summary of the purpose of this morning's proceedings. The young assistant prosecuting attorney looked at Paul and nodded, then turned and disappeared into the corridor, off to fight for Aaron—and his siblings. She will leave the morgue this morning and return to charge the father with homicide.

Paul slides a compact disk into the stereo and the sound of Bruce Hornsby breaks the silence. Paul notes the unintended pun of the disk's title—*Halcyon Days*. "Halcyon" means "calm" or "peaceful." Halcion is an antidepressant drug, and the second victim on whom an autopsy will be conducted this morning died of a drug overdose. No fewer than two dozen brown plastic bottles of prescription medication accompanied her into the morgue. Among the barrage of medications on the evidence table in the corner of the room is a vial of Halcion. A physician prescribed Halcion to relieve stress so the victim could experience "halcyon," and perhaps dissatisfied, the victim turned to illicit narcotics in an attempt to achieve that "halcyon." Such coincidences make one disbelieve coincidences.

Behind the stereo, high on the wall of the autopsy room, the analog clock reads ten o'clock. The second hand begins its journey through another minute, ticking off the seconds. As you count to fifteen, imagine Aaron's final seconds of consciousness.

One . . .

Two . . .

Three . . .

Four . . .

Five . . .

Six . . .

Seven . . .

Eight . . .

Nine . . .
Ten . . .
Eleven . . .
Twelve . . .
Thirteen . . .
Fourteen . . .

Fifteen seconds—a lifetime. The time it took to count these seconds represents the duration Aaron's father shook him with all of his strength.

*****

Fate sometimes serves a dish of irony. In tonight's *Law & Order Special Victim's Unit* rerun titled "Shaken," investigators probe the case of a child who sustains a serious head injury as the result of a shaking. In the episode, which takes place in November (!), the medical examiner illustrates the damage done to a shaken child by placing a raw egg in a small glass jar. As the investigators watch in awe, and in horror, the fictional ME shakes the jar and the egg inside breaks, covering the glass with yellow yoke. Ultimately, the mother admits to shaking the child in a moment when the stress of life overwhelmed her. All of this sounds familiar, too familiar—like witnessing the confluence of fiction and reality.

BLUE HIGHWAY

Late Fall 2004
Spectrum Health, Blodgett Campus
East Grand Rapids, Michigan

It's Friday afternoon and the doors to the emergency room at St. Mary's—a small Catholic hospital situated in downtown Grand Rapids—give way to a gurney containing the body of a tall, thin black man. Friends found Marvell Green* forty-five minutes earlier lying flat on the floor of his residence. He was last seen alive at eight this morning, complaining of chest pains. Although his heart had stopped beating sometime in the interval, the emergency response medical technicians administered a cocktail of drugs—including atropine and epinephrine (adrenaline)—as they rushed Green to the nearest hospital, where medical personnel worked feverishly to revive his heartbeat and his life.

Within minutes of arriving and within forty-five minutes of when his friends discovered him unconscious, emergency medical personnel have in place the cardiac heart monitor. They place two large white pads, each the size of a large index card, on Green's torso—one on the left side of his rib cage and the other on his right side over his chest. Through these pads, they will administer an electric shock in an attempt to return his heart to its normal rhythm. About a dozen smaller, quarter-sized pads, each containing what looks like a snap, form rows across his chest. These nodes attach to a machine used to monitor the rhythm of his heart.

Unlike the handheld paddle version most often shown on television and in the movies, this type of electric shock via defibrillation cannot jumpstart a heart that has ceased to beat. This procedure can only correct an abnormal heart rhythm. For Marvell Green, whose heart stopped beating before he arrived at St. Mary's, the procedure represents a last-ditch attempt, a medical Hail Mary, to bring life back into his body. A vain attempt, though, as Green had left before he had arrived.

Two minutes elapse, but no response, no blood pressure, no pulse.

Two more minutes elapse, and the heart monitor pierces the silence with a high-pitched siren, as a flat, thin line runs across its surface.

The attending physician pronounces Marvell Green, fifty-six-years-old, dead. His pronouncement is just a formality, though; Green died before he left home, the victim of a heart attack.

Approximately fifteen minutes later, the attending physician makes his way to the waiting room, where Green's girlfriend anxiously awaits news of his condition.

The ECG (electrocardiograph) equipment will have a short rest. Emergency personnel will again call upon its magic, again in vain, in eight hours when John Michaels* arrives.

They may have casually bumped into each other at a local delicatessen down the road, or at the shopping mall; they may have even nodded in quiet deference as they passed by one another—two strangers acknowledging each other. Although they didn't know each other, Marvell Green and John Michaels had much in common, both in their lives and in their deaths. While one would harbor a forensic secret that will create a mystery for me this morning, fate would ultimately bend these two parallels lines, and they would converge in the unlikeliest of places: the morgue. Since both victims died without a witness, they will make one final stop before funeral directors work to make their exit from life's stage as graceful as possible; in the Kent County Morgue, by reading clues left in their bodies to piece together their final moments of life, I will work to untangle the physical knots left by two lives that ended prematurely.

The harsh wind howls outside the lobby of the Blodgett Campus hospital. Snow showers arrived early this year, leaving the ground a mottled fabric of white with patches of deep green grass and dark clusters of damp leaves. A thick blanket of clouds covers the sky; without the sun, the early morning takes on the darkness reminiscent of dusk.

Inside the autopsy room Tobin is chatting with Jason Chatman, the pathology assistant who will assist with this morning's autopsies. He has already changed into surgical scrubs and appears ready to begin the morning's investigation.

The two victims lie on the stainless-steel autopsy tables, one black, one white, but other than their superficial appearances, and the obvious age difference between them, they are mirror images. Both appear tranquil in death, their mouths hanging open, eyes closed, as if in a deep slumber. Green's hairline had receded to the middle of his head, and he wore the rest of his hair in braids fastened with colorful beads. Strands of steel-gray, which belie his age, had in his later years invaded his well-trimmed beard and the remainder of this hair. Michaels's hair has also receded, and a tuft of its hazel color is the last remnant of what was once his hairline. Both men are about the same height—six feet tall—with thin, but not emaciated, frames.

And both bear the marks of the desperate and futile attempts to restart their hearts: rectangle and square lines across Green's chest indicate where emergency personnel placed the heart monitor and ECG paraphernalia (Chatman removed the pads in preparation for the autopsy), and the pads still cover Michaels's chest.

First, I will probe the death of Marvell Green, whose case history contains a list of physical grievances he suffered before his fatal collapse last evening. In addition to hypertension, he suffered from diabetes. To police officers investigating Green's last hours, neighbors described him as a contentious man with many enemies; he would often come home, his fiancée explained to investigators, with black eyes and various contusions. Many enemies make many suspects, each with a motive should the autopsy provide evidence that the cause of death was homicide.

Jason pushes a button on the stereo, and a melodic tune from the Foo Fighters fills the room. He selects a scalpel, and with a smooth, rapid movement of his arm, a slice opens from Green's left shoulder to the center of his chest over the sternum, revealing a thin, dull yellow-white layer of fat the color of which presents a sharp contrast with the chocolate brown skin covering it. Another slice from over the left front deltoid to the same spot over the sternum forms the top portion of the "Y" incision; one final slice, from the point at which the two lines converge all the way down Green's stomach to a spot where the pubic hair begins, finishes the procedure.

Tobin watches, his arms folded across his chest, cradling a legal pad, as Jason pulls the flaps created by the Y-incision to the side, snaps through the ribs around the sternum with the "rib cutter," and removes the breastplate to reveal the inner mechanism of Marvell Green. In the background, the chorus to the soundtrack of today's proceedings seems to comment on what any outsider who visits this place must feel: "It's times like these you learn to live again. / It's times like these you learn to love again." While those who visit the morgue are inevitably exposed to death, its subsequent tragedy—a harsh reminder, like a slap across the face, of one's own mortality—the realization that life can be fleeting reminds them that life is not something to be squandered.

I place the handheld microphone on the desk and observe the organs within the body cavity in situ. Since Green probably died of a fatal cardiac arrhythmia, and his case history of hypertension would support this possibility, the heart will most likely provide the key clues to the ultimate cause of death in this case. A medical cliché best explains: "When you see hoof prints, look for horses, not zebras." In other words, the case history points to the likeliest cause of Green's death. Still, as past experience with zebras that came into the morgue with victims in previous cases indicates, sometimes a zebra is actually what made the hoof prints. They do, after all, have hooves.

They're just harder to catch.

"He abused alcohol," I note upon noticing the liver, which appears as a yellow mass in the upper-right portion of Green's torso cavity. Excessive intake of alcohol can cause "fatty change" in the liver; the fat accumulation within the cells damages them and changes the color of the liver from its normal dark brown to a golden yellow color (since fat has a yellowish hue). However, Green's diabetes (which also could have caused "fatty change") could have affected his liver in a similar way.

A few minutes later, the dissection of Green's internal organs begins in an attempt to find clues to his demise. The appearance of his lungs suggests that, in addition to frequent cocktails, the decedent also enjoyed his smokes. Small black dots tattoo the skin of his lungs and look like ink blots on a crimson-colored blanket.

The carbon or black patches on the lungs do not alone indicate that Green suffered from emphysema. Coal miners' lungs would blacken from inhalation of coal particles while in the mine, but they experienced no ill effects; their lungs would function as normal—unless they smoked. With a few deft snips with a pair of surgical scissors, Green's bronchi are open and offer more evidence of his physical woes: a ball of mucus appears.

"Strange to hear a forensic pathologist say 'yuck,'" Tobin remarks after hearing my reaction upon discovering the mucus in Green's lungs. The mucus represents evidence that Green suffered from bronchitis.

Smoking impedes the normal functioning of the lungs; it damages the bronchial glands that produce mucus. The mucus represents a manifestation of the bronchitis and often causes in longtime smokers, to the disgust of anyone in hearing range, a "wet cough."

The inside of Green's lungs show more damage done by years of habitual smoking. The interior of his lungs has a mottled appearance of alternating black and crimson blotches. To illustrate this damage to Tobin, with one hand I hold the cut surface of one of the lungs, the texture of which looks like the underside of a person's lip (although its color is a much deeper purple), and with the other I hold a small water hose. A gentle stream of water runs from the hose over the surface of the lung, exposing small, spongelike holes. Tobin can now report to his students that he has seen lungs affected by years of smoking.

The holes, bullae, result from damage to alveoli—the minute spaces in the lung where oxygen is absorbed into, and carbon dioxide excreted from, the blood. Inhalation of smoke, over a period of years, can destroy the blood vessel–containing alveolar walls, which line the air spaces (alveoli), impeding gas exchange and creating bullae from destruction of many alveolar walls. As a result, a person suffering from chronic emphysema may experience a shortness of breath even after a nonstrenuous task such as walking up a flight of steps.

Next begins the examination of Green's heart, which will most likely reveal evidence of the culprit that led to this victim's death. As we've learned, the heart is the pump that sends blood to the various areas of the body. Anything that impedes its function could prove fatal if the blood that courses through its arteries ceases to flow. Cholesterol can cause a buildup of plaque, which can curtail or block the flow of blood through the coronary arteries.

Arteries narrowed with plaque can also develop blood clots; the thickened lining of the artery can erode, forming the blood clots that may subsequently occlude (close up) the plaque-clogged artery. In such a scenario, the blood clot would impede or stop the flow of blood in the artery and could cause a fatal heart arrhythmia and often death. Coronary artery bypass surgery, during which doctors graft a segment of vein that "bypasses" the occluded section of the original artery, provides the most common solution for this problem. Nonsurgical treatments would include angioplasty (in which the blocked artery is reamed out) and stent placement (which involves the placement of a springlike coil into the narrowed artery; after placement, the spring is expanded, which results in the opening of the artery).

During the dissection of a heart, small incisions are made through each coronary artery to determine the degree of narrowing. An examination of Green's coronary arteries reveals that the most severe narrowing is about 20 percent. As a general rule, 75 percent of a coronary artery's lumen must be blocked in order to cause a fatal cardiac arrhythmia. Green died when his heart stopped, but *what* caused his heart to stop?

Let's explore the possibilities: he could have died from the effects of diabetes, so I will examine the fluid (vitreous humor) of his eyes—if Green died from the effects of diabetes, the eye fluid will contain the chemical proof. Then again, he could have overdosed on alcohol or drugs, which will appear on the toxicology screen.

Green's liver, which appears golden in color when it should appear dark brown, suggests that he may have imbibed much and often, although he did not have a clinical history of alcohol abuse. Sometimes we don't have a complete history. His liver seems to give away his secret. Next to the workstation, a glass cabinet contains bottles that accompanied victims to the morgue and looks like an out-of-place sideboard: a large bottle of Thunderbird, a pint of Canadian Mist, another pint of 5 O'Clock vodka. The bottles seem to provide a mute comment on the use and overuse of alcohol.

The diabetes from which Green suffered, though, blurs the picture of him as a heavy drinker or even an alcoholic, since the diabetes could also have caused the yellow discoloration. If caused by diabetes, though, damage to the kidneys would also occur, and a close examination of Green's kidneys has revealed no such damage.

In the background, Jason has begun the process of opening Green's skull. First, he slices through the scalp across the top of his head. He tugs the scalp and the top portion of Green's face forward to expose the top of the skull. A few minutes later, the grinding sound of the Stryker saw fills the autopsy room. Wisps of bone dust form small clouds in the air as Jason works the saw through Green's skull. He makes a pattern with a triangular notch on the top and a triangle on the bottom, so when he assembles the skull later and stitches closed the scalp, the skull will fit back together.

"Ah, Dr. Cohle." Jason has made a discovery. With a wedge of the skull removed, the top of Green's brain is visible. Instead of the usual off-white color, the entire left frontal portion of Green's brain appears as a thick, reddish brown mass that represents massive bleeding—a subdural hematoma. This discovery solves one mystery, but creates another. The bleeding indicates the dynamic that caused the victim's heart to stop, but raises the question as to what caused the head injury in the first place? If Green died of a head wound, what caused it? Did he suffer from a brain aneurysm, or a burst blood vessel in his brain? Did he fall over and strike his head? Or did someone strike him? Would this heart attack victim become a homicide victim?

Jason snaps a few photographs of this potential evidence of a homicide. If someone hit him in the head, most likely, but not always, some damage would appear on the outside of his head. Upon close examination of the scalp, though, I find no superficial damage. While a blow to the head with an object like a hammer would leave depressed fractures that radiate outward from a point, like a chip in a car windshield, a blow from a larger blunt object with a large surface area such as a board may leave the scalp and skull undamaged. In addition to dissecting the brain, therefore, I will study the inside of the skull for fractures that could determine what could have caused the bleeding.

"This case is not as it first appeared," Tobin remarks as I move over to the scale to weigh the brain before dissecting it. Perhaps he has just stepped into what will become a *Law & Order* or *CSI*-type investigation.

As an acoustic number from Dave Matthews Band hums in the background, I do not find a skull fracture, the absence of which does not preclude subdural hematoma, or a blow to the head. The victim has a thick skull, literally, so a blow with a blunt object could have caused the bleeding but not a skull fracture.

Regardless of what caused it, Green died from traumatic head injury.

The dynamics of Green's fatal head injury explain his last few hours. The hemorrhaging or bleeding causes pressure on the brain with resultant swelling. The brain stem, located at the base of the brain, passes through a hole in the bottom of the skull called the foramen magnum. When the brain swells, the brain stem becomes pinched into this narrow passageway, which causes it to stop functioning. As discussed in a previous chapter, when the brain stem stops functioning, the heart stops, and death results. From the initial blow, a clock begins ticking until the brain stem swells enough to shut down—a time that doctors refer to as "the golden hour." Had Green remained conscious after the head injury, and had he managed to reach a hospital, physicians would have worked frenetically to reduce the brain swelling by administering a series of drugs and drilling a hole in his skull to vacate the blood that would have accumulated. Generally, they must accomplish this task inside of "the golden hour." In Green's case, an estimated one to three hours could have elapsed from the onset of the head injury until death occurred.

I press the pedal labeled "Record," and narrate the specifics. "250 milliliters of subdural hemorrhage and subsequent compression . . . brain stem is herniated."

"You might find this interesting," I say to Tobin, who drifts closer to the workstation where I have removed the brain stem. I point to a little cordlike structure extending out from the brain—the "third cranial nerve." This nerve leads to the eyes and causes the pupils to expand (dilate) and contract. Brain swelling can cause pressure on this nerve, and it can cease functioning, which in the case of a traumatic head injury can fix the pupil in a dilated state. Fictional detectives and physicians sometimes refer to such fixed pupils as "eight balls" or blown pupils.

When checking patients with head injuries, physicians shine a bright light into the eye. Failure of the pupil to contract would indicate paralysis of the third cranial nerve (oculomotor nerve) from herniation of the brain. In this case, Green's left pupil would remain dilated, since the injury occurred on the left side and paralyzed the nerve.

The cause of death? He fell or was hit, which caused a traumatic head injury. Green could have lost consciousness or experienced a seizure brought on by his diabetic condition, or he could have passed out from excessive drinking, fallen, and struck his head on something like the edge of a chair or a coffee table. Or, a more ominous possibility looms: someone, with a score or vendetta to settle, struck him with the blunt edge of an object such as the flat side of a two-by-four. Although I found no evidence of foul play—no skull fractures, no bruising on the scalp, no evidence of bruising on the inside of the scalp—enough doubt exists to rule the cause of death as "undetermined." And then there's the tidbit about Green's belligerent and pugilistic tendencies. Now I will contact the police who will question Green's friends and relatives—although with little forensic evidence, they will be hard put to prove a homicide.

The toxicology report now represents a key piece of evidence; a high blood-alcohol level would indicate that Green could have drunk enough to pass out and hit his head, resulting in an accidental albeit tragic death. The final medical chapter of Marvell Green's life would come in the form of a toxicology report, as it did for another victim who lay on this very table almost five years earlier.

CYANOTIC

Their names are erotic, exotic, and enticing: blow job, buttery nipple, lemon drop, Jaeger Bomb (at the time of writing, a popular concoction consisting of a shot of Jagermeister dropped into a glass of Red Bull and generally gulped in one swig), oatmeal cookie—to name just a few of the infinite variety available to the thirsty customer.

And they feel so fine after a long day on the job. For many, they resurrect what should be resurrected and bury what should be buried; they make jokes sound funnier and bill collectors irrelevant; they bring out the humor in things and suppress the stress that often envelops adult life.

For some, they represent an antibiotic; for others, a painkiller; for still others, a drug, whose siren song proves irresistible. For millions of casual drinkers, they represent the lubrication that allows social gears to mesh. They are social KY Jelly.

Most casual drinkers know their limits because, at one time in their pasts, they went on a binge and traveled over the edge of their limits to spend a sleepless Friday night at the base of the porcelain god and a miserable Saturday huddled under the afghan on the couch, so sick that even slight movement hurts. Just one slip over Niagara Falls in a barrel and one learns how close all of us can come to the rapids without going over. It is a painful rite of passage that can prove dangerous—even deadly, as it did for Stephen Petz.

In order to belong, to become a brother, and to gain access to all of the perks the fraternity can provide, such as access to alcohol (particularly attractive for underage members whose "older brothers" will purchase liquor for them) and invitations to parties and other social events involving sorority sisters, a group of initiates assemble to play "The Wheel of Fortune."

Most of them are away from home for the first protracted period of time in their lives; some separated from their sweethearts who stayed home or attended other universities, but all of them are desperate to belong and for the comradeship that belonging promises.

The initiate spins the "Wheel of Fortune"—really a party roulette wheel modified for its new purpose—and watches intently as the ball lands in a slot marked with a four. One of the fraternity brothers lines up four shot glasses in front of the spinner, each filled to the rim with a potent mixture of vodka and lemon juice called a "lemon drop." Its lemonade taste belies its potency.

The first shot burns his throat, but they become progressively easier to swallow. After the fourth, he feels giddy and enjoys the warmth growing in his stomach, like a liquid version of sitting by the fire, as he watches each initiate take his turn. The basement is filled with "brothers" quaffing shots, mixed drinks, and plastic cups filled with beer.

Another turn arrives, and again he spins another four. Four more lemon drops follow, and he downs them in succession as the onlookers chant his name. One of the "brothers" chides him for slowing down, and without thinking about it, he turns his back to the "brother," unbuckles his belt, and moons him. The onlookers laugh. He feels like he belongs. He feels good. A "brother" tells a joke, and he can't stop laughing, as the other initiates continue to spin the "Wheel of Fortune."

Although he doesn't realize it, the last few shots have sent his blood-alcohol level over the legal limit to operate a car (0.08 in Michigan), although he may feel just slightly tipsy.

He stands up, adjusts his belt, and begins the trek across the smoke-filled room to the restroom, slightly dizzy. In the restroom, he finds one of his less fortunate peers huddled over the toilet, retching. The stench of bile fills the room.

When he returns, the "brothers" are singing an off-key rendition of "The Star Spangled Banner" that results in a guttural, inharmonious cacophony. He joins in the song until his turn arrives to spin the wheel again.

This time, he spins a six. Six more lemon drops. Two initiates disagree over something. One douses the other with his beer, and the other retaliates by throwing his, drenching those closest to the fray. The disagreement erupts into a shoving match until the two "brothers" are separated.

An hour has elapsed since the game began, and he has consumed fourteen shots. He feels seasick, and he squints in an attempt to read the scores scrolling across the bottom of the big-screen television in the corner. He reaches for the edge of the table to brace himself and knocks over a cup of beer, spilling its contents across the table. As the alcohol becomes absorbed into his body, he becomes more intoxicated and his physical coordination—his reaction time to stimuli, such as someone pulling out in front of him if he was driving a car—becomes severely inhibited.

Time seems to pass quickly as his turn arrives once again—a five this time. Five more lemon drops, bringing his total to nineteen shots, not including the beer in between. He feels very tired, and his speech is slurred. As hard as he tries, he cannot focus on the images on the big-screen television. He sees two of everything. He stumbles and begins to fall when a "brother" catches his arm. He loses consciousness; his revels have now ended. Two "brothers" carry him upstairs, place him on a bed, and scurry back downstairs; they don't want to miss the game.

The previous paragraphs detail what Stephen Petz may have experienced the night he died. On March 15, 2000, the nineteen-year-old Ferris State University student died of a lethal ethanol overdose, or alcohol poisoning; in other words, he drank himself to death.

On that fateful night, Petz participated in a hazing ritual involving a drinking game at an underground fraternity in Big Rapids—a small city located in mid-Michigan and home to Ferris State University. Following a tragic car-pedestrian incident following a party fourteen years earlier, the Tau Kappa Epsilon fraternity disbanded; its remaining elements evolved into the Knights of College Leadership, also known as Knights of College Lore—a fraternity not recognized by Ferris State University. Participants of the game called "Wheel of Torture" spun a roulette-type wheel to determine how many shots they had to consume.[1]

Petz vomited while playing the game, and fraternity members carried him upstairs to a bedroom, where they found him the next morning, unconscious and with a cyanotic (blue) complexion.

An autopsy was conducted on Petz, who died without witness, to determine what killed the healthy nineteen-year-old college undergraduate. In such an autopsy, we will see very heavy and congested lungs. The lungs become congested with blood, and furthermore, because of the cessation of breathing, there is an abundance of fluid that accumulates within the air spaces of the lungs. This is called pulmonary edema. The brain will swell. The determining factor in such a case is the toxicology report.

Eyewitnesses at the preliminary hearing to determine if charges should be brought against the hosts of the party estimated that the participants had consumed approximately ten shots of alcohol, although the toxicology report told a different story. As a point of reference, the legal blood level of alcohol for driving is less than 80 milligrams per deciliter (0.08%). In an average 70 kg (approximately 154 lbs.) person, about 5–6 drinks would bring a person to 80 mg/dl. On admission to the hospital, Petz's blood alcohol level was 372 mg/dl (0.372%). In an average person of 154 lbs. (and Petz was 150 lbs.), an average beer or mixed drink raises the blood alcohol level 15 milligrams per deciliter. Therefore, the math indicates that Petz had consumed twenty-five to as many as twenty-seven shots, as an estimate, in a two-hour period, and was at that time almost four times over the legal limit for driving a car—enough to kill Petz, although 400 mg/dl is the "rule of thumb" for lethal ethanol overdose (about 27 shots for a 150 lb. male). Whether the drinker is a 235-pound linebacker or a 98-pound gymnast, when the blood alcohol reaches 400 ml/dl, acute alcohol poisoning and death will likely follow. Because of a much lower body weight, the 98-pound gymnast would consume fewer beverages before reaching the "deadline" than the 235-pound linebacker.

Petz may have even consumed more than the twenty-five-to-twenty-seven-shot estimate since the body continues to absorb and process alcohol until the time of death, *if* he consumed some alcohol before the "Wheel of Torture" drinking game.

Sometime during the night, Petz progressed to the fourth stage, in which binge drinking becomes fatal. During the first stage (5–6 drinks), he is less inhibited; he may sing or tell jokes that he wouldn't otherwise tell while sober; he may hit on women, such as his buddy's girlfriend. In some individuals, intoxication may manifest as a tendency to fight. As he becomes more intoxicated (12–14 one-shot drinks), his physical coordination—his reaction time to stimuli, such as a driver pulling out in front of him—would be inhibited. The third stage (15–20) progresses into a decreased level of consciousness, decreased coordination. Speech and vision impaired, the drinker now has a risk of falling. Ability to steer a car is greatly decreased. The fourth stage, or the last stage, is unconscious-ness, progressing to death. The portion of the brain stem that controls breathing is depressed by the alcohol, causing a cessation of spontaneous breathing.

Petz's case is a tragedy but not an uncommon one. Ferris State University had experienced such tragedies before—and recently. In the two years before Petz's death, two fatalities rocked the campus; after a night of drinking, a twenty-year-old student fell from an apartment window, and a twenty-four-year-old former student died of alcohol poisoning after attending a party at a sorority house on campus.[2] While these incidents occurred in Big Rapids, with a slight alteration in details, they could have occurred on any college campus in America. At Michigan State University in East Lansing, for instance, a student died after drinking twenty-four shots.

Three members of the underground fraternity pled guilty to supplying alcohol to a minor, causing death, in the "dram shop" case, named after an old-fashioned term—dram—for volume. If a person dies from an ethanol overdose after buying drinks at a bar, the person supervising the bar can be charged. Among other evidence, prosecutors produced a photograph of two men pouring alcohol into Petz's mouth.[3]

*****

Her names range from cute to ominous and are as varied as the characters drawn to her charm: China Cat, Good and Plenty, Golden Girl, Galloping Horse, (Aunt or Witch) Hazel, Joy Flakes, Mexican Horse, Mortal Combat, Nice and Easy, Red Eagle, Reindeer Dust, Spider Blue, Sweet Jesus, Tootsie Roll, White Nurse. It can be taken in a variety of ways, including the Sandwich and the Speedball. Her allure is so strong that once a man meets her, he cannot resist her. He must come back to her. He will never stray too far from her and will always return.

Of course, some just call her Shit, perhaps the most appropriate name of all. Shit—aka Heroin, aka Witch Hazel. And John Michaels* knew her, and knew her well. Last night, paramedics rushed the twenty-two-year-old Michaels, found unconscious at his home, to St. Mary's Mercy Medical Center, where, at 11 PM, he was pronounced dead, possibly the result of his relationship with heroin. Michaels, an on-again, off-again student at one of the area's universities, lived what some might consider a bohemian lifestyle from his downtown apartment. His friends subsequently admitted that he had been using heroin.

Like Marvell Green nearly eight hours earlier, Michaels received emergency treatment in a last-ditch attempt to save his life. The ECG pads and silver heart monitor snaps still run across his chest, and his cargo shorts, leather sandals, and pager are neatly tucked into a plastic bag on the evidence table in the corner of the autopsy room.

The autopsy proceedings begin with a superficial examination of the body. First the case history is recorded, followed by a search for the needle or "track" marks that would appear on a frequent heroin user. The search of Michaels's arms results in nothing suspicious; no superficial evidence exists of needle punctures anywhere on Michaels's arms. Michaels's fingers make a cracking sound as they are pulled apart one by one. No needle marks between the fingers. No needle marks between the toes. No outward evidence of needle use anywhere on the man's body.

Although the circular marks on Michaels's chest indicate the hospital performed an ECG, this is surprising since his heart had ceased beating long before he arrived at the hospital. The purple, bruised appearance of his back caused by lividity suggests that Michaels died on his back at home.

To probe the veins for evidence of hemorrhage from previous injections, I make a deep incision in Michaels's left arm. If at one time Michaels used intravenous drugs, the veins in his arms might contain red or yellow staining from degenerating red blood cells caused by previous injections.

"Argh," I exclaim as a line of blood jumps out of the incision. "Guess we found a vein." The blood runs down Michaels's arm and forms a small pool on the stainless-steel autopsy table. The effort paid off; I found slight traces of past bleeding that I am able to confirm later using a microscope.

Although this examination resulted in only slight evidence of previous drug use, like Marvell Green's case, the toxicology screen will provide the key piece of evidence, unless Michaels's body harbors some ominous secret as Green's did. And so the internal autopsy begins.

While every indication suggests that he casually if not habitually used heroin, and possibly died from an overdose, Michaels's lungs do not support this possibility. Some narcotics, like heroin—which, according to Michaels's friends, was his drug of choice—impede the body's ability to breathe, and subsequently cause the lungs to fill with edema fluid. The lungs, therefore, become "heavy." In this case, the lungs are normal— light. If he died of a heroin overdose, he died rapidly, before he could develop pulmonary edema. I poke my index finger into the bright-pink lung (which presents quite a contrast to the outward appearance of Green's lungs) and the nipple-shaped depression disappears as fast as it appeared, the surface of the lung springing back into shape—like poking a finger into a Nerf football.

A drug like cocaine, on the other hand, which can kill very fast, would leave the lungs pink and aerated, as in this case. Perhaps Michaels experimented with other "ladies," and one of them killed him. Perhaps he died of a cocaine overdose. Of course, the absence of "heavy lungs" does not preclude the possibility of a heroin overdose, but it does argue against such a conclusion.

The remainder of the autopsy reveals no hidden surprises, no sign of foul play, no natural cause for Michaels's heart to malfunction. So I will wait for the toxicology report in the hope that it contains the answer to the puzzling question as to what stopped John Michaels's heart.

Both victims died last night. Both were pronounced dead after receiving ECGs in the same hospital on the same day. Both used substances that may have contributed to their deaths. And both paid the ultimate price for their choices; Marvell Green downed one drink too many, and John Michaels's affair with the White Witch turned deadly—she (the heroin) killed him.

At this point in the autopsy, the lower jaw of the plaster cast skeleton falls off and strikes the floor. Infer from this what you will . . . truth is stranger than fiction. Or perhaps this is an omen.

A few days later, the toxicology screen confirms that Marvell Green consumed enough alcohol that he could have passed out and struck his head, sustaining a fatal head injury. And detectives found nothing to suggest he died as the result of foul play. Officers interviewed friends, family, and acquaintances, and they found motives aplenty, but nothing else.

The toxicology screen for John Michaels confirmed the presence of heroin at a lethal level in his system when he died. Michaels sped down the blue highway—and crashed.

In mathematics, parallel lines never meet, but in human society, they do. While they did not live parallel lives, Marvell Green and John Michaels died parallel deaths.

BROKEN HEARTS

Early Winter 2004
Spectrum Health, Blodgett Campus
East Grand Rapids, Michigan

Emergency medical technicians respond to a 911 call and arrive at a large house on the near west side of Grand Rapids. The house, a large turn-of-the-century abode that, like its residents, has seen its better days—its roof shingles chafed, disintegrated with age, and edged with a deep emerald green moss patina; the paint on its once white, wooden siding yellowed and chipped with age.

Inside, they would find a shocking sight. The house interior appears as neglected as its exterior. Dishes fill the sink, the white ceramic stained with blood-red streaks of rust; and the smell, a mixture of mildew and something else, a sweet, pungent odor, increases as they approach the first-floor bedroom. It is a distinctive odor, one they have encountered on other occasions. As they open the door, the stench intensifies. One of the technicians buries his nose in his sleeve.

Next to bed, in a Lazy Boy easy chair, sits the source of the smell. A grotesque shape inhabits the chair—midsection bloated and appearing nine months pregnant, his arms, still resting on the arms of the chair. Jim

Benson* sat down in this chair—from the light spots on the arms of the chocolate colored upholstery, a favorite chair. Perhaps he felt dizzy or light-headed or exhausted, and sat down to catch his breath. He would never get up.

Mr. Benson died in this chair days earlier, even though his wife, bound to a wheelchair, had not left the residence.

But how did this happn?

*****

It is still dark outside at eight in the morning, a still, quiet morning with little movement in the hospital lobby. Outside a few flakes of snow dance on the wind. Beyond the perimeter of the hospital campus—along Plymouth and beyond—green, red, and white bulbs line pine trees and house gutters. A garnish of evergreen wreaths and boughs of mistletoe endow the lobby with a festive atmosphere, but without people, the lobby, decked out for the holidays, is reminiscent of an airport in the middle of the night: escalators and people-movers running, but without people to transport.

I arrive at eight thirty—on time this morning—because both Paul Davison and I have other plans for this afternoon. Outside, a light snow shower has replaced the dancing snowflakes and, after only a few minutes, has covered everything with a bright white sheet that this afternoon will become a blanket. Tobin appears in the corridor leading to the morgue wearing his black jeans and a blue gingham, long-sleeved shirt.

This morning, two autopsies, two investigations, will be conducted. One, an "advanced decomp"—forensic lingo for a body that, without refrigeration, has severely decomposed—will lend a nasty odor to this morning's business and will present a challenge to the morgue's visitors, especially Tobin. The presence of the "advanced decomp" will lead to the pervasive smell of wintergreen in the morgue once again (see "Red Sky in the Morning," chapter 4)—a smell that to Tobin has come to represent something disgusting. He told me that certain smells trigger the memory of that morning in the morgue when he first confronted an advanced decomp; he used to love to eat wintergreen mints, but now the mere scent of wintergreen makes him nauseous.

Tobin is certainly not alone in his aversion to the smell of human decomposition; it is one of the worst scents imaginable. The US military's nonlethal weapons division once invented the ultimate stink bomb that could be used to clear people, such as protestors or rioters, from an area. Scientists working on the "malodorant" experimented with the scents of, among other things, vomit, "US Government Standard Bathroom Malodor," and human decomposition.[1]

Last night, police arrived at the Benson residence in response to a 911 call, and upon entering the house they found Julia Benson* in the living room suffering from severe dehydration. In an adjacent bedroom, they found her husband, Jim, slumped in a brown recliner; the sixty-eight-year-old had died an estimated four to five *days* earlier. Not hours, but *days*.

Mrs. Benson, wheelchair bound and suffering from advanced Alzheimer's disease, depended on Mr. Benson for everything. When he didn't appear, she found him in the chair in their bedroom, sleeping, she thought. Hours turned into days, but Julia Benson lost track of time. Each time she returned to check on him, she assumed he was asleep. A neighbor noticed the smell and called the police.

While Mr. Benson rests in the morgue, somewhere in the hospital above, Mrs. Benson is receiving treatment for dehydration.

Benson died without a witness, so an autopsy must be conducted to determine the cause and manner of death. Although I suspect Benson may have suffered a fatal cardiac arrhythmia (massive heart attack), one aspect of Benson's case history casts a shadow over this supposition: a few years ago, Benson attempted suicide via an overdose of a prescription narcotic. A toxicology screen will determine if Benson took an overdose, but until the results become available, I will conduct an "autopsy of exclusion"—a search for any anatomical evidence of a history of heart disease and anything else that suggests a different fate.

I punch in the key code and open the door to the morgue suite. Once inside the corridor leading to the morgue, the pungent, bittersweet odor of human decomposition becomes pervasive—an invisible hand reaching out and grabbing the lapel of anyone about to enter—but less severe than that of our previous drowning victim (see "Red Sky in the Morning," chapter 4). Tobin grimaces as the smell envelops him.

Benson is lying on the table closest to the corridor, his legs jack-knifed, as if in a sitting position; dark red blood, the color of red velvet, has saturated the backside of his khaki slacks and plain white T-shirt. As every visitor to the morgue learns, the location of the "lividity" (pooling of blood in the body cavities) depends on the body's position and on gravity. In the decomposition process, blisters develop and the skin often ruptures, allowing blood-tinged fluid to escape, which accounts for Benson's soaked clothes.

A head full of loose curls, mostly white, interrupted by a few errant strands of auburn, creates a wild, unkempt look. A few tangles dangle over his forehead, nearly reaching his eyes, which are swollen nearly shut. Benson looks like a boxer after the twelfth round; swelling, another effect of advanced decomposition, has partially obscured his still-open but lifeless eyes. His jaw hangs open as though he died after one last gasp of breath. Streaks of dried blood run from the corners of his mouth down both cheeks.

I hand Tobin a pair of booties that he slips over his tennis shoes, and he shimmies into a pair of baby blue surgical pants and a surgical gown. Medical examiners and pathology personnel will often cover themselves with several layers; they, to use Paul Davison's advice, "double-up" when around "stinkers" because the stench of death tends to stick to clothes.

"Good morning, Paul," Tobin greets Davison.

"Is it?" He brushes past and disappears down the corridor and into his office, reappearing a few seconds later. Paul has a scheduled choir practice early this afternoon, one he may now miss because this morning the police are on the scene investigating another death. If the body arrives at the hospital before noon, he and I will conduct the autopsy.

A few minutes later Paul returns to the autopsy room, his demeanor changed from irritated to relaxed; perhaps he's resigned to the fact that it may be a long Saturday morning. He knows the nature of the second death, and perhaps he doesn't like the second of the Grim Reaper's double feature. Paul inserts a CD into the stereo, and to the faint rhythm of Los Lonely Boys' "Heaven," he removes Benson's clothes, cutting through them with a pair of scissors. The smell intensifies.

"Remember," Davison reminds Tobin, "breathe through your mouth.

Not your nose." The brown bottle of wintergreen Lorann oil sits on the table near the stereo—the only medicine available to treat the stench.

Now that Paul has removed Benson's clothes, the full ravages of decomposition on the human body become clear. His belly protrudes with an abnormal curve, giving him a pregnant appearance, caused by the buildup of methane gas in his abdominal cavity. The body looks much larger than the six feet two, 210-pound figure noted on his autopsy record. His torso has a marbled appearance of red, white, and blue hues, with large blotches of green, the color of aquarium algae, covering the front and sides of his stomach.

"Advanced decomposition," "foul odor," "massive discoloration of torso"—I have begun to record the condition of Benson's body as I notice Tobin hovering around the brown bottle of wintergreen oil, like a bee hovering over a flower.

The skin is "slipping" off Benson's arms—a key indicator in determining time of death; the condition of Benson's body suggests that four to five days have elapsed from the time Benson died until the discovery of his body. The skin on his arms and his torso is flaked, peeling, and long, thin, fingerlike blisters, filled with gas, run down the sides of his torso; the decomposition has caused the skin to acquire the overall appearance of a thin layer of cellophane, bubbled, torn, and flaking.

"What causes the emerald green color?" Tobin asks.

"Clostridium, a bacterium that lives in the intestines; upon death, it utilizes the body tissues as a growth medium," I explain.

"This will help with the smell." Paul inserts the twelve-gauge veterinary needle, which looks like the type of needle one might use to inflate a basketball only with a flared end, into Benson's scrotum (which we resorted to after the abdominal cavity failed to yield sufficient gas to burn). Gases have swelled the dark purple scrotum to the size of a softball. He lights a disposable lighter and holds the flame over the flared end of the needle, which results in a faint hissing sound—the methane gas escapes Benson's body through the needle and is incinerated in the flame. This escaping gas creates a blue flare that looks like the flame of a blowtorch. Paul tried the same strategy in an earlier case (see "Red Sky in the Morning," chapter 4), but there was insufficient gas left in the body.

"Do you see it?" I ask Tobin. "You have to get close."

Tobin hesitates for a second, and leans closer.

A slight hissing emanates from Benson's scrotum; the hissing sound represents the escape of the methane gas through the veterinary needle. Benson's scrotum noticeably shrinks, like a deflating balloon. The blue flame caused by the incineration of the gas, though, remains invisible under the morgue's fluorescent lights.

"Here." I turn off the lights in the morgue, and a brilliant, blue flame appears about a quarter of an inch long, emanating from the flared end of the veterinary needle.

I flip the switch and the fluorescent lights flicker and again bathe the morgue with their cold, white light.

"You may want to move to the other side of the room," Paul suggests as he carves a line down Benson's torso. He explains that the room's circulation pulls the air toward the corner, and when he makes the Y-incision, the gases will spill out of Benson's body into the corner, and out of the room—and around anyone standing between them.

As his scalpel pierces the cavity beneath, a burst of air escapes with the sound of a basketball punctured with a knife. The pregnant, bloated appearance disappears, as Benson's torso, like his scrotum a few minutes earlier, deflates.

The stench intensifies . . . and intensifies. It becomes palpable; the smell thickens the air in the room, and one can taste its bitter flavor.

Tobin darts out of the room, down the corridor, into Davison's office, where he pulls two pieces of tissue from a box on the desk, and then back to the morgue and to the bottle of Lorann oil. The latex gloves make the task of opening the bottle difficult; he struggles to open it, all the time reminding himself to "Breathe through your mouth. Breathe through your mouth." He crushes the two pieces of tissue in his hand, holds the wad over the mouth of the bottle, tips it, and then holds the wintergreen-scented oil over his mask.

By the time Tobin finishes with the wintergreen oil, I have begun examining and dissecting the throat structures, which had no evidence of strangulation-associated injury.

"That's his Adam's apple," I explain to Tobin, who has positioned himself behind me. Tapping the flat end of the knife against a hard bulb in the throat structure makes a hard, hollow sound like a knuckle rapping against a wooden table.

If Benson died as a result of a fatal cardiac arrhythmia, his heart would most likely contain evidence of heart disease. A series of transverse cuts along the coronary arteries in Benson's heart will determine the extent of blockage, which if severe would indicate that heart disease ended Benson's life. In cross section, the arteries look like tiny, pale white tubes; they appear like the cross section of tiny, uncooked macaroni noodles.

Among Benson's coronary arteries is a severely narrowed artery, an estimated 98 percent narrowed; this finding is an insurance policy. The more narrowed the artery, the more compelling the evidence becomes, and at 98 percent, the artery is virtually blocked or occluded. One blocked artery alone could lead to death. Should I find nothing else in the remainder of the autopsy, should the toxicology screen reveal nothing out of the ordinary, the "severely narrowed" artery would provide sufficient "anatomical evidence" for a determination that Benson *did* die as a consequence of a fatal cardiac arrhythmia.

In the background, the sound of holiday tunes a la Trans-Siberian Orchestra has replaced Los Lonely Boys; "Jingle Bells" in the morgue, which to Tobin must seem like an odd juxtaposition.

"He does have hypertension," I explain to Tobin as I place Benson's kidneys on the scale. The surface of Benson's kidneys exhibits a granular, dull appearance instead of the usual smooth exterior: the effects of hypertension. Hypertension causes narrowing of the small arteries in the kidneys, leading to decreased blood flow, which results in a gradual loss in kidney tissue. Numerous small scars replace the lost kidney tissue and impart a granular appearance to the surface. For the medical examiner, the granularity is as telling a sign as the scarlet "A" on Hester Prynne's clothing; the evidence of heart disease has begun to mount.

I call out the weight of each kidney, and Tobin jots down the number on the white board next to the workstation. Careful to avoid any potential exposure to blood-borne pathogens like hepatitis B (see "Risks," chapter 1), he has wrapped the blue marker—its barrel streaked with dried blood—inside a paper towel.

The refrigerator door opens, and a late middle-aged man in street clothes, Conveyance Specialist (body transporter) Dick Washburn, enters cradling in his arms something bundled in a white bedsheet—an infant; Washburn and two Kent County sheriff's deputies have just returned from a scene the presence of which has soured Paul Davison's morning and his planned choir practice. Washburn gently sets down the bundle on the second autopsy table opposite Benson, whose body has become a cavernous, empty shell.

"Looks like he died of a heart attack?" Tobin asks, although he appears distracted by the bundle now lying nearby.

"Heart attack is a generic term." I explain that "heart attack" represents one of two specific conditions: myocardial infarct—or a dead heart muscle—and arrhythmia—or an irregular heartbeat—both of which can prove fatal. An arrhythmia, unlike an infarct, leaves no physical evidence to tell the forensic pathologist that it occurred.

Tobin should know this; he has observed the autopsies of several victims who died from various heart problems, but something else is on his mind. Several times as I explained the medical conditions that define the generic term "heart attack," he glanced over his shoulder to the bundle on the table. He hasn't seen its contents, but he knows what lies inside. He has not yet observed the autopsy of an infant—a sight that even hardened law enforcement officers avoid if possible.

The autopsy of Jim Benson continues with an examination of his skull and brain. The discovery of a skull fracture and/or subdural hematoma would present a nasty surprise and negate the possibility that Benson died of a fatal cardiac arrhythmia. The presence of such a fracture would suggest that someone struck him with an object like a bottle, inflicting a traumatic, fatal head injury.

The decomposition has also affected Benson's brain, and I must assist Paul in removing it from Benson's now-open skull. The insidious forces of decomposition have caused the brain to soften; the brown-sugar-colored mass slides through the wedge-shaped gap Paul cut with the Stryker saw and into a bowl I hold behind Benson's neck.

"Here's what most students' brains look like," I chide Tobin, a high school teacher during the week, morgue volunteer on weekends.

"I didn't think most of them had brains," Tobin retorts with a smile that quickly disappears. He glances at the bundle; his smile is merely a front, a façade and a hollow attempt to hide the tears that have begun to well in the corner of his soul. When an outsider first enters the morgue, he may marvel at the comics taped to the glass windows, finding their presence hard to understand; but humor in the morgue serves a purpose, which perhaps Tobin can understand because now he is leaning on it like a crutch.

I examine the contents of the bowl containing Benson's brain—a flattened mass filling the bottom of the bowl. Tumors tend to better survive the ravages of time and decomposition, so they could be easily found if present. No tumors here, though. And no skull fractures, either.

Tobin moves toward the bottle of wintergreen Lorann oil, swipes a tissue over its mouth, and dabs the oil on his facemask. Even if a person dislikes the sweet scent of wintergreen, it's a much-preferred alternative to the stench of rotting, fetid flesh. This "decomp," though, does not smell as bad as the other "stinker" ("Red Sky in the Morning," chapter 4); much of the stench escaped the corpse, and the morgue, via the veterinary needle, a lighter, and the Y-incision. With the earlier drowning victim, the methane had leaked from the tissue, and no tricks would relieve the morgue of the smell.

The examination of Benson's internal organs provides more evidence of a lifestyle that may have ended his bid for longevity. Charcoal-black blotches cover his lungs, and the discoloration and the damage to the alveoli inside his lungs—evidence of emphysema—indicate that in life Benson enjoyed cigarettes.

Meanwhile, Paul Davison unwraps the body of the infant cocooned in the bedsheet. The baby is clad in blue pajamas over a white onesie; baby blue socks match the pajamas, and another pair of socks, white socks, cover his hands. Davison gently rests the boy on the table; wisps of jet black hair contrast with the dull shine of the stainless steel under the morgue's fluorescent lights. His eyes are closed; a circular EKG pad on his upper left thigh appears huge, oversized on the child who is shorter than the length of my arms.

As I pierce Benson's stomach with a scalpel, a thick, yellow-brown porridge spills from the incision, oozing into the stainless-steel tureen sometimes referred to as a "gut bucket" used for collecting stomach or "gastric" contents. A glance at the gastric contents reveals what Benson ate before he died; the semiprocessed meal looks like chicken soup, with discernible slivers of bright orange—fragments of carrot. Benson's last meal consisted of carrots, celery, and chicken.

With the collection of the gastric contents, Benson's autopsy comes to a conclusion.

"Cause of death?" Paul asks, information needed for the official report.

Pending the results of the toxicology screen, which I expect will be negative (and which ultimately did prove negative), ASCVD.

"ASCVD?" Tobin asks; he doesn't know the acronym.

"Arteriosclerotic cardiovascular disease." It is a common cause of death, but one that causes the heart to stop beating.

BROKEN HEARTS

In mid-April 2005, a Federal Express package arrives at Spectrum's Blodgett Campus. The return address label suggests that it came from Dr. Thogmartin—a Florida medical examiner. Using a pocketknife attached to my keychain, I slice through the packing tape and remove the contents: a large, leak-proof plastic tub, about the size of a popcorn bucket, the type forensic pathologists typically use to fix and suspend brains in formalde-hyde (to harden soft, decomposing brains for ease in later examination). Inside the bucket, wrapped in formalin-soaked rags, awaits a heart. Dr. Thogmartin, of district six in Florida (Pinellas and Pasco counties), hopes that another pathologist conducting a second examination of the heart will find evidence to answer a question that has transfixed the nation for the past few weeks. Media coverage flooded the public with the debate about Terri Schiavo's fate, but this morning I will examine her heart to discover what caused her condition.

Unlike a cardiovascular surgeon, I don't fix broken hearts; I examine broken hearts to determine what caused them to break. I'm one of several forensic pathologists (along with Mike Bell, Mike Graham, Sam Gulino, and others) who are known for their expertise in cardiovascular pathology and sudden cardiac death. When a particular case has stumped a medical examiner—in other words, when the standard gross and microscopic autopsy, drug screen, and the history and scene investigation fail to disclose a cause of death (a "negative autopsy")—some of my forensic pathologist colleagues may ask me to examine the heart, or they will consult me when they want an unbiased expert opinion in high-exposure cases in which a heart-related concern exists.

What types of cases stump medical examiners with regard to the human heart? Some subtle diseases and conditions of the heart exist that upon further investigation may become apparent, but recognition often requires the examiner to have a special interest and expertise in these subtle diseases and conditions.

A brief tour of the heart mechanism will help to explain the problems that can lead to a broken heart.

The heart functions as the body's pump, sending blood to various parts of the body, including the body's computer, or brain. A relatively small organ (the average heart is about the size of a large apple, or 310 grams), the heart is an incredibly strong muscle, which contracts as many as eighty times per minute. The heart contains four chambers, two atria and two ventricles, that like reservoirs fill with blood; each time the heart muscle contracts, they contract. From the ventricles, the blood flows into the arteries carrying it to the various parts of the body. The atria sit on top of the ventricles and connect to them by valves (mitral valve for the left atrium and ventricle and tricuspid for the right). Nerves and specialized heart cells (the conduction system) function like an electric battery powering this extraordinary pump; they cause the heart to beat regularly, rhythmically, and speed up during times of physical activity and slow down during periods of physical inactivity.

Large conduits—the veins and arteries—bring blood to and from the heart; the superior and inferior vena cavas bring blood into the heart, while the largest conduit of all, the aorta, carries blood from the heart. The pulmonary artery is the conduit that connects the heart with the lungs; through it, blood travels to the lungs, picks up oxygen, and reenters the heart to be transported via the aorta to various parts of the body.

This description of the heart is, of course, a generalized depiction of a very complex machine; when any one of the machine's parts malfunctions, the consequences for the human body can be severe. Therefore, when I examine a heart, I must examine all the parts of this complex mechanism to determine which one broke. Typically, I begin on the outside and work in. First, I will study the outer surface of the heart, then the arteries for narrowing (which most often occurs when plaque builds up and narrows the lumen of the artery). Next comes the heart muscle, the valves, the lining of the heart, the openings of the coronary arteries (called ostia), and the portion of the aorta that accompanies the heart—the same procedure I follow in all autopsies.

As stated above, because of its extreme complexity, the heart may fail when any one of its parts malfunctions. Narrowing of a coronary artery, for example, can result in insufficient delivery of blood to the heart muscle, causing injury that in turn can be the site of a lethal heart rhythm. An insufficient supply of blood to the brain can lead to irreversible brain damage and death.

Other diseases can lead to broken hearts as well. For example, diseases of the specialized heart tissue that initiates electrical impulses causing the heart muscle cells to beat synchronously (cardiac conducting tissue) can cause sudden death. In particular, the two areas of the conducting tissue that initiate electrical impulses that control the heart rate are known as the sinoatrial (SA) node and the atrioventricular node (AV). The AV node itself may be obliterated by a tumor (known as an AV node tumor or a mesothelioma of the AV node), or the artery supplying the AV node may become severely narrowed. Either of these may lead to a sudden cardiac death.

In addition, other more subtle problems may be missed upon first examination; a careful examination by a cardiovascular pathologist of a previously dissected heart may yield findings that would explain the patient's death. Examples of this include a very localized area of severe narrowing of a coronary artery that may have been missed by the original pathologist during a routine autopsy, or a localized area of coronary occlusion by a disease known as coronary artery dissection, characterized by a bleeding into the wall of the coronary artery with compression of the artery opening (the lumen).

The reason I was consulted about Terri Schiavo's heart was because in 1990 Schiavo had "a major event," presumably a cardiac arrhythmia, that resulted in anoxic encephalopathy, or severe brain damage from lack of oxygen. The heart as the body's pump sends blood to the brain, but when the heart malfunctions (arrhythmia, for example), and the body's pump ceases to function, the brain, without the oxygen it needs to survive, begins to die. The longer the brain starves without oxygen, the more damage it sustains. The technical name for this starving is anoxic encephalopathy.

When Terri Schiavo died in 2005, one of the issues to be addressed by her autopsy was the cause of the cardiac arrhythmia that led to the anoxic encephalopathy—what caused the pump to stop? Since the heart examination by the Florida forensic pathologist, Dr. Thogmartin, showed no heart disease and thus no cause for her presumed arrhythmia, he consulted an outside opinion. Perhaps the cardiovascular pathology specialist could find a cause for Schiavo's heart event that he could not. Dr. Thogmartin wanted to make certain that there was no subtle cardiac disease, particularly in the conducting tissue (the specialized cells that can initiate electrical impulses that spread synchronously through the rest of the heart muscle to cause the heart to beat regularly). He sent the heart to me for a general examination, particularly of the conducting tissue. The intense public scrutiny of the Schiavo case in part led Dr. Thogmartin to send the heart to a distant expert to obtain an opinion unbiased by Florida politics.

Did Schiavo's heart contain evidence that could shed light on the event that she experienced in 1990, the one that created the irreversible brain damage?

What did my examination uncover? Nothing. The heart had no abnormalities. No structural abnormality in the heart led to the disastrous episode that placed her in a vegetative state. Whatever caused Terri Schiavo's brain to be deprived of oxygen, it was not a structural heart abnormality. Her physical problems came from another source, such as a drug or chemical not detected in a test done (if any) after her 1990 collapse.

With this examination completed, I carefully packaged Schiavo's heart in formalin-soaked rags, placed it in the plastic tub, and addressed the package to Dr. Thogmartin in Florida.

Other hearts await examination. Recently, I acted as a consultant to the pathologist investigating the death of Thomas Herrion, an NFL football player who collapsed after an exhibition game in Denver in late August 2005 and died that evening, an hour after the game ended. At the time of this writing, in the morgue's evidence room sits a Styrofoam package. The package contains formalin-soaked rags that envelop like a blanket portions of another athlete's heart, this time the heart of a high school swimmer who collapsed after a practice and, like Herrion, died shortly thereafter.

When a person thinks of heart disease, the television screen in his mind conjures up images of an elderly gentleman with a walking cane, whose pacemaker and time on earth expire. Heart disease is, after all, a disease of the elderly. The powerful heart muscle does not malfunction after just twenty or thirty years of work.

Yet this image does not capture the entire story.

Just recently we had a case of a twenty-something who died of coronary atherosclerosis.

Such deaths horrify, terrify, and mystify. Such young people should not die of a "broken" heart. Yet hearts do "break," and physicians do what they can to repair them. When surgeons cannot repair the heart, pathologists do what they can to explain what went wrong. And when they cannot, they call me.

But I don't always answer the question of what went wrong when I examine a heart from a negative autopsy. Families are incredulous—obviously, something went wrong. Their loved one is dead. Sometimes, though, even with a meticulous gross and microscopic exam and a negative toxicology screen, I can find no explanation for the death.

There are a number of possibilities: biochemical abnormalities, termed channelopathies, are characterized by abnormal proteins lining the channels through which sodium and potassium ions pass into and out of the heart muscle cells during the electrical process that causes the cells to contract and pump blood. Abnormal flow of these ions can cause the heart to fibrillate, resulting in sudden death. The best known of these disorders is long QT syndrome, (LQTS). Because genetic mutations cause the abnormal proteins, many cases of LQTS are inherited, so it is vital for surviving family members of LQTS victims to be screened for the abnormality by their physicians.

Other subtle causes of cardiac death include Wolff-Parkinson-White syndrome, which can lead to lethal arrhythmia, and less common channelopathies such as Brugada syndrome. If the victim was exposed to a substance not identified on the drug screen, such as would occur from huffing typewriter correction fluid, the autopsy would reveal no cause of death. "Huffing" is the act of pouring or spraying a volatile substance (typewriter correction fluid or Freon) into a bag and inhaling the vapors from the bag.

*****

A beep sounds and Paul Davison opens the morgue's refrigerator door. A radiology technician wheels into the morgue a portable x-ray machine that looks like a photocopier with a large arm that she positions over the infant. X-rays are standard protocol for the autopsy of a child; they reveal if the infant sustained any fractures. After a few x-rays, the technician wheels the machine back into the hospital through the double-wide refrigerator doors.

The infant appears peacefully asleep on the autopsy table. As any parent can attest, peace personified is a child asleep, and in this child's face, it becomes too easy to see one's own child . . . but this child will never awaken. I can see the tragic scenario that led to his death: the baby wakes in the middle of the night, completely reliant on his caretaker, who, desperate for a few more minutes of sleep, takes him back to bed, and in the midst of a deep sleep, rolls over.

The technician reenters the morgue through a different door, removes the x-ray sheets from an oversized manila folder, and places them onto a viewbox. An image appears: the image of the tiny skeleton inside the body lying on the table behind.

"A radiologist examined the x-rays and found no fractures," the technician explains to Tobin, who stands, mute, staring at her, mouth agape, speechless, unsure of what to say or how to respond. The technician has mistaken him for a pathologist!

The technician shrugs. "Maybe you see something different."

Paul, having observed the short exchange, smiles. "You're talking to the wrong person," he explains. The technician smirks and leaves. Paul laughs. "You should have told her that you noticed something on the x-rays."

By the desk, the two deputies provide a briefing on the circumstances of Cedric Wright's* death. Last night, his father brought his two-month-old child to bed with him; in the morning, he awoke to find his son face-down, his face buried in the bed's soft bedding. The day before, his grieving mother explained, Cedric received immunization shots. Did he die of a reaction?

Not likely, I explain to the deputies. Fatal reactions to immunization shots are very, very rare. More likely suffocation—the nightmare of any parent. A body of evidence suggests that suffocation results when an infant rolls into something, such as a crib bumper, that impedes the airflow. The infant doesn't suffocate from a lack of oxygen but rather breathes in its own exhaled carbon dioxide, paralyzing the breathing center of the brainstem. In this case, Cedric rolled onto his stomach, and unable to roll onto his back and lacking the strength to keep his neck elevated for a prolonged period of time, he died of asphyxia.

Perhaps the father, a big man, rolled onto the child and suffocated him—one of the deputies raises the specter of an accidental death. Or did something more insidious occur? Yet the father seemed very shaken, his grief genuine, the other deputy notes.

I study Cedric's body, which Paul has stripped and placed on the floor scale on top of a blue blanket, and note no outward signs of abuse; I begin dictating notes as the autopsy of little Cedric Wright begins.

After his external examination, Paul turns Cedric onto his stomach and with a scalpel makes two long slices running the length of his torso—test cuts to determine the presence of bruising that could have resulted from abuse (just as he did in the case of the two-year-old boy in the earlier chapter). The slices allow for a cross-sectional view of the layers on Cedric's back; just under the tooth-white sliver of fat, the dark red color of muscle appears, but no bruising. There is no bruising, no evidence of abuse.

After collecting fluid samples from Cedric's eyeballs (vitreous humor) and spine (spinal fluid), Paul makes the Y-incision, peels back the flaps of skin created by the incision, and slices through Cedric's ribs. No need for rib cutters; at two months of age, the rib cartilage is soft and uncalcified. Under the ribs, the organ that runs the human machine appears in miniature with the addition of the thymus—a gland just under the upper chest.

"See these petechial hemorrhages?" Paul asks Tobin, pointing to the pinpoint-sized red spots that dot the thymus and lungs like blood spatter. "Typical of SIDS cases."

To determine if a bacterial infection may have caused Cedric's death, a lung culture must be taken, and today Tobin will cross over the invisible line between observer and practitioner. He will take the culture. First comes the creation of a sterile area. I turn the knob on the small, green tank, like a miniature scuba tank, that contains a supply of propane. A faint, almost inaudible hiss results as the gas begins to flow from the copper hose, under the nozzle of which I hold the yellow disposable lighter Paul used to clear the methane from Benson's body forty-five minutes earlier. Once lit, a bright blue jet flickers from the nozzle. I hold the flat end of what looks like a stainless-steel spatula under the flame to heat it, then press the blade against the purple pleura (covering) of each lung; the resultant seared, rectangular patch on each lung represents a sterile area.

Next, I tear open a foil pack that looks like a condom wrapper and hold the wrapper in front of Tobin. The foil pack contains a long, thin blade that comes to a point at one end, like a penknife blade. "Take the blade," I instruct, as he plucks the blade from the package, being careful not to handle the end.

As instructed, Tobin jabs the blade into the sterilized patch on one of Cedric's lungs and twists to create a small, gaping hole. Penetrating the lung feels like stabbing a ballpoint pen into a slice of gellatin; once it punctures the pleura, the blade slides into the lung tissue.

Next, I hand him a sealed plastic tube that contains a long, sterilized cotton-tipped swab. He twists off the top of the tube and removes the swab. As directed, he inserts the tip of the swab into the wound he just created with the blade, twists once, and removes the swab. Tobin slides the now pink-tipped swab back into its tube. He repeats the process for the other lung. The two plastic tubes containing these lung cultures will leave the morgue in a large Baggie assigned to Cedric Wright's case, along with our samples of his bodily fluids. The samples will travel to various laboratories in the hospital where a litany of tests will determine if Cedric suffered from a potentially fatal bacterial infection.

With his organs removed, the empty shell of Cedric's body lies on the table—an image that would thaw the coldest of hearts.

"You'll have to add the thymus." I point at the white board where, in dry-erase blue marker, Tobin scribbles numbers as I place each organ on the scale and read out the number of grams each weighs: heart, liver, rt. lung, lt. lung, rt. kidney, lt. kidney . . . and now thymus gland.

This reddish yellow gland, which looks like two triangles that join in the center like a clamshell, produces white blood cells called lymphocytes that stave off infection. As the child ages, the thymus atrophies or shrinks; by adulthood, the thymus has virtually disappeared.

While I dissect the internal organs, Paul makes an incision across Cedric's scalp. Under the scalp, the large, radial hole appears in the skull—the "soft spot." Paul doesn't need the Stryker saw to access Cedric's brain; he cuts through the skull with a pair of scissors, which results in a cracking sound (imagine cutting through a thick sheet of plastic with a scissors). Davison places the brain in a bowl as Tobin and I watch.

"Ladies and gentlemen," I announce in a mock officious tone that silences the room (oh, shit, the detectives are thinking), "here we have [a pause to raise the dramatic tension] a completely normal brain." A collective sigh of relief follows.

No one wants to see this case become anything other than a tragic SIDS death, and no evidence was found to contradict this supposition. Still, to verify the validity of the father's account, I will request that the detectives re-create the scene using a "surrogate baby"—either a doll or a teddy bear—with which detectives can determine the likelihood of suffocation or asphyxia death in soft bedding.

While I dissect Cedric's brain, Paul peels the dura from the underside of Cedric's skull with a forceps. Removing the protective membrane makes easier the discovery of any linear skull fractures the child could have sustained from a fall. Under the brain the skull contains an assortment of ridges, in the middle of which lies the pituitary gland that produces and regulates the body's hormones.

"Hold out your hand," Paul asks Tobin.

Tobin places his hand in front of Paul, palm up, and Paul drops into it the tiny, bean-colored pituitary gland, about the size of half a peanut. Without moving his hand, like a dancer on a floor of eggs, Tobin moves across the morgue toward the workstation where I am dissecting Cedric's brain. He takes the pituitary and places it on the workstation shelf next to the stock jar containing various samples of Cedric Wright. Evidence. Just in case.

With the morning's autopsies concluded, one by one, the detectives leave the morgue, off to the Wright household to conduct the re-creation. Tobin waits in Paul's office in the morgue suite, while I change in the restroom. On the floor sit two bottles of liquor—Christmas gifts from various funeral directors around the Grand Rapids metropolitan area who frequently work with the Kent County medical examiner's team.

Paul and I appear in the doorway a few minutes later.

"Odd gifts for the medical examiner?" Tobin remarks about the small pile of boxes on the floor. Perhaps he is thinking about the glass cabinet of liquor bottles, each of which came in with an unfortunate victim most of whom died in one way or another as the result of the bottle he or she carried.

"Any Bailey's?" I ask as he plucks a box containing a bottle of Irish crème liqueur from the pile.

"You like Bailey's?" Tobin asks.

"Steve likes a chardonnay, too," Paul chides.

The gifts from the funeral directors serve as reminders that somewhere above this underworld, songs create the festive atmosphere that most associate with the holidays. Christmas is just a few days away, but under one evergreen tree sit presents intended for a child who will never open them. For many, the song "White Christmas" encapsulates their holiday experience, but for one couple, a poem written by an Englishman named Robert Herrick in the seventeenth century offers a more fitting narrative of the short life and death of Cedric Wright:

Upon a Child. An Epitaph
—Robert Herrick
BUT born, and like a short delight,
I glided by my parents' sight.
That done, the harded fates denied
My longer stay, and so I died.
If, pitying my sad parents' tears,
You'll spill a tear or two with theirs,
And with some flowers my grave bestrew,
Love and they'll thank you for't. Adieu[2]

OF ZEBRAS AND HORSES

Early Winter 2004
Spectrum Health, Blodgett Campus
East Grand Rapids, Michigan

W hen it comes to diagnosis, doctors use a medical proverb: when you see hoofprints, look for horses, not zebras. In other words, look for the most probable conclusion, not the most unlikely one. Arthur Conan Doyle's Sherlock Holmes says it another way: when one eliminates all other conclusions, what is left, however unlikely, must be the solution. In *Sign of the Four*, Holmes explains to Watson: "How often have I said to you that when you have eliminated the impossible, whatever remains, *however improbable*, must be the truth?"[1]

When we arrived at the Kent County Morgue this morning, we found hoofprints running across the white tile floor. While one expects to find a horse at the other end of the hoofprints, years of looking for horses and occasionally finding zebras keeps the pathologist from making assumptions about cause of death. Many zebras have passed through the Kent County Morgue in the past: the victim of a house fire who upon examination had bullets embedded in his back and a "suicide victim" who somehow managed to shoot herself in the head twice (see "The Hand of God," chapter 11).

Zebras could have found their way into the morgue with Elliot Mayfair* in a number of ways. Friday night, Mayfair settled onto the living-room couch with his daughter Crystal* to watch one of her favorite movies: *The Wizard of Oz*. It was his weekend with his daughter, who must have seemed an elixir from a hectic week of work as a retail manager. Mayfair left for the kitchen and never returned. When the Wicked Witch of the West appeared a few minutes after her father left, the frightened four-year-old went to the kitchen to retrieve her father. She found him lying on his back, spread-eagle, on the kitchen floor. She called her mother, who called 911, and when the emergency response technicians arrived a few minutes later, they found Mayfair with a slight pulse. An hour later, despite attempts to resuscitate him, Mayfair was pronounced dead at 9:00 PM.

Since he died a death without witness, his last surgery will consist of an autopsy this morning, because the forty-one-year-old could have met his end in any number of ways. His ex-wife could have decided to poison his favorite snack—cheesecake—in which case the toxicology screen will show a fatal level of cyanide or arsenic. If the former, when Paul Davison opens his body this morning, the faint smell of bitter almonds (which could still prove virulent if too much is inhaled) would waft from the body. Even the surgical masks with plastic face shields would not protect their wearers from this danger.

Or she could have hired a professional hit man to eliminate the pain that her ex had become. The hit man could have sneaked into the apartment through the partially open sliding door leading to a second-floor balcony and strangled Mayfair with a towel, which would have left little or no physical evidence. More than likely, though, Crystal would have heard a struggle.

Or a disgruntled employee (or customer, take your pick) could have followed Mayfair home from work and clubbed him in the head, causing a skull fracture, bleeding, and the initiation of his "golden hour."

Or the hoofprints belong to a horse; Elliot Mayfair may have died from a fatal cardiac arrhythmia—the most common lethal complication of a heart attack. All of the circumstantial evidence surrounding Elliot Mayfair suggests this tragic end to his life's story.

The labels on the dozen orange bottles sitting in a circle on one of the stainless-steel tables tell the story of Mayfair's health, and it's a sad tale of a short life filled with physical hardship. Among many others, Elliot Mayfair took Norvase, Atenolil (for high blood pressure), Lipitor (for high cholesterol), and Metformin (for diabetes). The medical detective can sift through these plastic vials and deduce that Mayfair suffered from heart trouble. Do the bottles represent harbingers of his ultimate fate? The autopsy will soon answer this question.

And Mayfair appears fit to play the role of heart attack victim. At five feet seven and 330 pounds, he looks like he ate himself into an early grave. In medical terms, his height and weight place him at the top of the obesity pyramid as "morbidly obese"—the category name says it all. A side mystery here, one that will remain unsolved forever: When he left his daughter Crystal for the kitchen last night, what did he want? Was this the last trip of thousands to the refrigerator for a beer, to the freezer for ice cream?

Mayfair is lying naked on the autopsy table nearest the corridor leading into the morgue. His midsection, covered with dark wisps of hair, protrudes six inches above his head and looks like a sanitary landfill, and one wonders if this simile extends beyond mere superficial appearance. Did he frequent the buffet restaurant in the shopping mall in which he managed a retail store? Did the managers of the buffet want to close the doors when they saw him coming?

I examine Mayfair and note various details into my recording device. Dark tangles of loose curls cover his head, which appears too small for his body. His eyes are closed, and the corners of his closed mouth are slightly upturned, like he smiled one last time before he died, giving him the appearance of dying a not-too-painful death. If he did suffer a massive and sudden fatal cardiac arrhythmia, he likely felt little pain. He may have felt dizzy and simply collapsed into unconsciousness on the kitchen floor.

Paul and Tobin struggle to roll Mayfair onto his side to examine his back, but they manage. Mayfair's entire back appears "bruised"; the reddish purple appearance, as we know, is caused by lividity (the settling of the blood without blood pressure) and indicates he lay faceup for several hours after death. No cuts, perforations, gouges, or holes; whatever happened to Mayfair, it didn't result from being stabbed or shot in the back.

The superficial examination reveals nothing unexpected, so the autopsy will move into its second phase—the internal examination—during which we hope to determine the nature of the hoofprints running across the morgue floor.

While the circumstantial evidence seems to make this an "open and shut case," the medical examiner knows better than to leap to a hasty conclusion. Sometimes, as past cases illustrate, a zebra comes through the morgue. One did in August 2000, when the autopsy was performed on Richard Dunn.

DAVID VERSUS GOLIATH

As the saying goes, you can't fight city hall. Just ask Barbara Dunn; in the fall of 2000, she found herself up against formidable opponents: the United States Department of Defense and BioPort. Richard Dunn's untimely death would evolve into a classic David versus Goliath story, with Barbara Dunn and I jointly playing the role of David (my middle name, by the way).

The story has all of the ingredients of a thriller: two dissidents—a forensic pathologist and an aggrieved widow—pitted against a pharmaceutical giant allied with the monolithic US Department of Defense.

But it all starts with an envelope. An ordinary 5-by-8½-inch envelope arrives addressed to you in blue ink. There's no return address.

You open the envelope to find a sheet of paper. You remove and unfold the sheet, which is blank, and notice at the bottom of the envelope what looks like some brown dust. You hold up the envelope and sniff, but the dust has no odor. You shrug and throw the envelope into the trash, forgetting about it.

The next day, you discover that you have a cold. Your nose is running and you're tired, fatigued.

You wake up the next morning and pull yourself out of bed. Despite nearly ten hours of sleep, you still feel exhausted. Nonetheless, you must go to work. At work, you begin to cough. It's a slight cough at first but then it turns into a more severe hack by the afternoon. By the end of your shift, you experience pressure on your chest that feels like an invisible hand pushing against you.

And then, you begin to feel better; you have entered into the eye-of-the-hurricane period in which the symptoms lessen.

You don't know it yet, but *Bacillus anthracis*, a spore-forming bacterium more commonly called anthrax, has waged war against your body. You inhaled the spores—a weaponized form of anthrax, the Vollum strain discovered in England before World War II—bringing them into your lungs, where they sit on the wet surface and begin growing. Once growth begins, the pathogens spread from the lungs into the bloodstream.

Since you inhaled the spores in the mysterious envelope, your immune system, like a battalion of soldiers, has battled the invading bacteria. This war they will ultimately lose; by the end of the week, your symptoms will return and become progressively more severe until you succumb to a fatal case of pneumonia, but not before you vomit frothy, bright-red clots of blood—hemorrhage from your devastated lungs. While two FDA-approved antibiotics exist—Cipro and doxycycline—that can fight anthrax after an exposure, they cannot help you since you have contracted the most deadly form and don't realize it until it is too late.

This drama nearly became reality in the months after terrorists leveled the twin towers of the World Trade Center on September 11, 2001—a date that changed many things in America, including the government's attitude toward anthrax immunizations. After terrorists mailed anthrax spores in envelopes to several government officials, the threat posed by weaponized anthrax became a harsh reality.

Bacillus anthracis occurs naturally in certain animals, such as cattle, sheep, goats, and camels, but can also infect humans exposed to infected animals or their hides—in England, the disease became known as woolsorter's disease. The most common form of infection occurs when the bacterium enters a cut or abrasion on a worker's hands. The infection at first looks like an insect sting: a raised bump that within two days becomes an ulcer with a black center that represents necrotic or dying tissue. With the proper treatment, most would survive a cutaneous (skin) infection of anthrax.

A person can contract intestinal anthrax by consuming the meat of an infected animal. The bacteria inflames the intestinal tract, leading to stomachaches, fever, vomiting, and severe diarrhea. The intestinal form of anthrax will kill approximately 25 to 60 percent of its victims.

When the spores are inhaled, though, *Bacillus anthracis* makes the perfect weapon. Its spores kill quickly, approximately 99 percent of its victims die, and its effects at first appear like an innocent cold. By the time the symptoms progress to more serious manifestations, nothing can help the victim. The disease is not contagious, so the damage of anthrax as a weapon is limited to the area in which it is disbursed. And a little goes a long way. As the British discovered in 1942, a pound of anthrax spores can destroy thousands and render an area uninhabitable for decades.

During World War II, the British, fearing that the Germans might attack with biological weapons, began to experiment with anthrax. Their research culminated in a 1942 test that would prove the potential damage of anthrax as a weapon. On the 520-acre Gruinard Island, in the middle of Gruinard Bay, Scotland, British scientists infected a group of sheep with anthrax by exposing them to a bomb that when detonated scattered the anthrax spores. Three days later, the sheep began to die. Yet the scattered spores kept Gruinard dangerous, and the infected island would remain quarantined for forty-eight years. A massive attempt to disinfect Gruinard took place in 1986. Topsoil around the bomb site was stripped and removed in sealed containers, and 280 tons of formaldehyde, diluted by 2,000 tons of seawater, was used to soak the soil. In 1992, the British government proclaimed Gruinard safe after carefully observing no ill effects in a flock of sheep allowed to graze on the island after the decontamination effort. As of this writing, none of the sheep have become infected with anthrax. The Gruinard experiment proved the viability and tremendous damage anthrax could cause if used as a weapon.

A vaccine for anthrax, which does not contain any live or dead anthrax bacteria, does exist; it consists of three shots two weeks apart, followed by a series of three shots given six, twelve, and eighteen months after the initial three. Annual booster shots follow this sequence.

Only one company in the United States, BioPort Corporation, possesses a license to manufacture anthrax vaccine; it enjoys a very lucrative monopoly. In 2004, the parent company that owns BioPort, Emergent BioSolutions, began construction on a plant to produce vaccine in Frederick, Maryland.[2] Emergent BioSolutions has become a giant, but like all giants, it began as a fledgling child. With infusions of capital from the US government via several anthrax vaccine deals, it grew, and grew, and grew.

In 1998, the state of Michigan owned the Lansing plant—up to that time the only plant in the United States licensed to produce the anthrax vaccine—and despite the fact that the Pentagon gave the state of Michigan $20 million for equipment upgrades and repair and over the previous years $100 million in contracts, Michigan decided that it would sell the company since it failed to produce a profit.[3] A team of investors led by a German businessman named Fuad el-Hibri—and backed in large part by his father, a Lebanese businessman—purchased the plant and named the company BioPort. Although el-Hibri was considered friendly to the United States, foreign investors now controlled the only licensed source of anthrax vaccine in America (since the purchase, though, Fuad el-Hibri has become a US citizen).

BioPort purchased a problem, because the Lansing plant had failed to pass Food and Drug Administration (FDA) muster. But it did control the only plant licensed to produce anthrax vaccine, and as a condition of the purchase from Michigan, BioPort became the owner of $7.9 million in vaccines that the plant had produced for the US government. Shortly after the sale, BioPort brokered a new deal in which the Pentagon agreed to purchase $45.1 million in vaccines and provide $16 million to renovate the Lansing plant.[4] And, most important of all, BioPort enjoyed a monopoly as the *only* US company licensed to produce the vaccine.

By June 1999, BioPort had not yet obtained FDA approval for the Lansing plant, and once again, the Pentagon bailed the company out with a $24.1 million infusion in the form of a new contract. This new contract, in addition to paying the company's debts, also agreed to an increase in the per vaccine price from $4.36 to $10.64.[5] National security demanded that the Pentagon have access to anthrax vaccine—a favorite among terrorists who would develop and use biological weapons.

For the next three years, BioPort produced anthrax vaccine even though it had not yet secured the blessing of the FDA. And the Pentagon paid for this vaccine.

When Richard Dunn died on July 7, 2000, the United States government had its attention focused on Iraq and the fear that Saddam Hussein had amassed an arsenal of "weapons of mass destruction" that might have included weaponized anthrax. The military was concerned about bioterrorism and germ warfare, and anthrax is endemic in the Middle East. The Department of Defense had just begun a program requiring all military personnel to receive anthrax inoculations. Thousands of troops received anthrax immunizations from BioPort, and the complaints of illness arising from the vaccine began.

Richard Dunn, sixty-one years old, worked at BioPort laboratory. According to Barbara Dunn, "Dick" worked with guinea pigs that BioPort used to test the anthrax vaccine. Although he worked mostly with guinea pigs, she does remember on one occasion when her husband came home with a scratch from a monkey.[6] Since Dunn worked with laboratory animals infected with anthrax, he received anthrax vaccinations.

In the eight years that Dunn worked at BioPort, he received eleven doses of vaccine. After many of his vaccinations, though, he experienced discomfort consisting of swelling and pain at the vaccination site. He also experienced arthritis and tenderness following the vaccinations; these adverse reactions caused him to miss work for three months. He began to suspect that something in the vaccine was causing his discomfort. According to Barbara Dunn, he didn't want to take the last vaccination before he died, but he was told if he didn't, he would lose his job.[7]

"To this day, I say, he knew he was going to die," she explains. "He would say, 'If I take another shot, I know I'm going to die.' He was well-read, very knowledgeable about anthrax."[8] Dunn, a hunter and skier, loved to read. He would read three to four newspapers a day; he would go to bed at seven in the evening and read to late at night, often books about the Civil War.

Though not one to complain, during Desert Storm, he had quite a fit when the news media reported the location of BioPort. He feared a terrorist attack on the only plant licensed to produce the vaccine, which appeared could play a vital role if the United States became engaged with an enemy that deployed viruses as biosoldiers.[9]

Still, the pain didn't go away. He was exhausted. He would stop on the way home from work to take a nap. Something was wrong. Eventually, on May 13, he consulted a doctor because of his discomfort. BioPort referred Dunn to Sparrow Occupational Health, where Dunn was treated for an allergic reaction to the vaccine.

On the morning of Friday, July 7, 2000, Richard Dunn went into the bathroom of his home to shave. He may have felt dizzy and decided to sit on the toilet seat to steady himself. Seconds later, he collapsed. Barbara found him unresponsive on the floor of their bathroom, the razor still in his hand. He was pronounced dead at home.

At the funeral home, Barbara Dunn approached her husband to give him one last kiss on the forehead, one last kiss good-bye, when she noticed something odd in the coffin: a bottle of Bud Light, a pack of cigarettes, and a Dave Brubeck LP. Her two children placed these items in their father's coffin "for his trip home."[10]

But what caused Richard Dunn's death?

"The man had never been to a doctor," Barbara Dunn explains. "Never been sick other than the flu."[11]

Dr. Joyce, the Ionia County medical examiner, ordered an autopsy. So Richard Dunn arrived at the Kent County Morgue housed in Spectrum Health's Blodgett campus.

At first, Dunn appeared as one of millions who eventually succumb to a fatal heart arrhythmia, or a heart attack. Upon examination of Dunn's heart, however, I found evidence that more than the usual type of heart disease caused his death.

Dunn's coronary arteries—those arteries that supply blood to the heart—had vasculitis. Vasculitis is inflammation of a blood vessel, usually caused by an autoimmune disease, or one in which the body makes antibodies to its own tissues; the body's defense system—the antibodies—in essence, turns on the body it is assigned to protect. This vasculitis involved arteries in the prostate gland, the testicles, and the small intestine as well.

In medical terminology, just what caused Dunn's heart to stop? I believe that the vaccine that he received caused his immune system to react in such as way that (1) the antigen-antibody complexes deposited in the arteries and the subsequent reaction of the body's immune system caused damage which resulted in narrowing of the arteries on the heart's surface (coronary arteries), or (2) the antibodies produced to fight the anthrax vaccine cross-reacted to the tissue in the blood vessels, causing damage and injury and subsequent narrowing of the blood vessels.

Your body's immune system, in other words, represents an army, poised to attack anything it considers "foreign" or adverse to your system. The antibodies can fend off an assault by an influenza virus, for instance. Sometimes, though, they can confuse the body's own tissue with foreign tissue, attacking it, which often leads to a friendly fire casualty. This same reaction can occur with organ transplant recipients. A recipient of a kidney transplant must take medicine that prevents the soldiers (the antibodies of the patient's immune system) from attacking the foreign invader—in this case the new kidney.

Like the good little soldiers they are, Dunn's antibodies detected the presence of the vaccine, and they attacked. As a result, Dunn sustained damage to his coronary arteries, which subsequently became narrowed. When they narrowed to the point that an insufficient amount of blood flowed through them, portions of the heart died from insufficient blood supply. The resultant scar tissue, or myocardial infarcts, led to a fatal heart arrhythmia. The most common cause of a myocardial infarct is the narrowing or occlusion of a coronary artery, often caused by atherosclerosis, which results from too many cheeseburgers and chili cheese fries (the cholesterol in them creates plaque that clogs the arteries; think of the PVC pipe below your kitchen sink after years of service), but in Dunn's case, the inflammation created by the vaccine caused his coronary arteries to narrow. Richard Dunn died of friendly fire from his own body's army.

Yet this diagnosis posed a challenge. Dunn died of an abnormal heartbeat—a ventricular arrhythmia—caused by the narrowing of his coronary arteries, but what caused the narrowing in the first place? How could it be determined that the vaccine caused the narrowing rather than another factor, such as the decedent's diet?

I formed the opinion that the vaccination led to the arteritis based upon his complaints of swelling and tenderness at the vaccination sites. This indicated a very strong immune reaction to the vaccine. Dunn also had some serum tests when seen in the hospital a few weeks before his death that suggested he suffered from an immune disease. The other factor I considered in forming the opinion that the anthrax vaccinations played a role in his arteritis was the review of the medical literature which linked some other kinds of vaccinations, such as influenza and hepatitis B, to arteritis. Arteritis has never been reported as a complication for anthrax vaccination, making Dunn's case very rare indeed.

This theory created a fight in which I would play David to the Goliath of the United States military and the BioPort Company. Goliath consisted of some very powerful opponents who came armed with teams of scientists and pathologists who posited that the vaccine did not cause any fatal damage to Dunn's heart. Instead, they offered another theory: they proposed that the cause of Dunn's coronary artery narrowing was an unusual but recognized disease called polyarteritis nodosa—a natural disease that occurs independent of the vaccine. The Department of Defense had just begun a program requiring soldiers to receive anthrax immunization shots, and the Pentagon considered suspending the immunization program.

The military's suspension of its anthrax immunization program may have crippled the BioPort Company, given the fact that prior to Dunn's death it had experienced financially troubled waters, even though the Department of Defense had floated BioPort with a multimillion-dollar raft through several revamped contracts; but the raft soon after began to sink.

Then came the disastrous events of September 11, which underlined the threat of terrorism to America. This was followed by several suspicious envelopes mailed to members of Congress. The envelopes contained anthrax spores, and fear of biological terrorism reached a fever pitch. In one respect the terrorists succeeded: they terrified the public.

In January 2002, BioPort regained its license to produce the anthrax vaccine.

In the last few years, a number of deals have turned the once-fledgling company into a giant, a veritable Goliath. Two years after 9/11, the price of the vaccine had doubled; the Pentagon paid $22 a dose.[12] In 2003, the Pentagon entered into yet another new contract with BioPort. And the

Department of Health and Human Services signed a contract with Bio-Port for five million doses of anthrax vaccine at a cost of $122.7 million.

Somewhere in the middle of this fracas, Mrs. Dunn fought her own battle: she sought worker's compensation benefits on behalf of her husband, but she was denied these benefits based on insufficient evidence to prove the link between the vaccination and arteritis.

In one of the many depositions given during this case, I explained that the conclusion reached—that the anthrax immunizations caused the vasculitis in Richard Dunn's heart, which ultimately killed him—was based on a theory. With the data that existed during Dunn's autopsy, it was a reasonable conclusion.

In other words, my opinion was, well, just an opinion, a hypothesis, but one that was reasonable. The odds of an extremely rare disease, polyarteritis nodosa, occurring in one of the relatively few people receiving anthrax vaccinations, are very long. The facts that his symptoms began only after the onset of his vaccinations and that other vaccines have caused arteritis added weight to this opinion. One infectious disease expert opined that Richard Dunn died of the affects of rheumatic fever, and according to Barbara Dunn, this belief prevailed.

After Richard Dunn's death, numerous complaints, leveled against Bioport and the Department of Defense by military personnel who took the vaccine, began to emerge—a macabre satire of a military parade. In one instance that occurred in 2000—the same year in which Richard Dunn died—a navy captain developed symptoms of amyotrophic lateral sclerosis (ALS), often known as Lou Gehrig's disease, within a week of taking the anthrax immunization. He died just before turning forty-five—ALS seldom kills younger victims.[13]

After receiving his second anthrax immunization, another navy man became physically ill and fell into a state of severe depression from which he would never emerge. After spilling gasoline on his pants, apparently confused, he accidentally ignited himself by lighting a cigarette, sustaining burns over 80 percent of his body. A year later, he died from the burns.[14] Whether the fact that these deaths followed anthrax immunizations is circumstantial, or whether a causal link binds the anthrax immunization to the maladies such as ALS and mental illness remains speculation.

Barbara Dunn received no settlement from BioPort, and she also received no worker's compensation. She lives in Ionia, Michigan, where she works as an emergency room technician and struggles to pay for the bills that accumulated in her fight to secure compensation for Richard's death.

Emergent continues to grow. In January 2005, it inked a deal with the British government to produce tetanus, toxoid, and botulism vaccines, and purchased another company that produces various vaccines, including an anthrax vaccine.

On her late husband's birthday, Barbara Dunn travels to the cemetery to visit his grave, always bearing the same gift. She pours a bottle of beer over his grave—Bud Light, his brand—her way of saying "this Bud's for you."[15]

The Pentagon never suspended its anthrax immunization program.

Mrs. Dunn and I could not fell Goliath.

Goliath won.

Or did he?

Now the vaccine carries a warning label suggesting that arteritis is a possible complication of the vaccine.

*****

Paul opens Mayfair's chest with the ubiquitous Y-incision. Obese patients complicate autopsies. Fat tends to invade body organs, making the pathologist's job much more complicated. A huge, two-inch layer of yellow fat appears like a warm blanket on top of the red muscle underneath.

"This guy was a walking time bomb," Paul notes as he works through Mayfair's ribs with the rib cutter.

Paul exposes the heart and points out a stent, which one can feel by pressing the outside of the heart. Mayfair's history of heart trouble extended to one or more surgeries in which a cardiologist implanted stents used to force open a partially blocked artery. If the bottles of medication and Mayfair's obesity represent circumstantial evidence that a heart attack killed him, the stents represent witnesses to the crime; in the heart perhaps lies the smoking gun: severely blocked or occluded arteries. The stents feel slightly rough to the touch, like touching a wire mesh fence.

Mayfair's heart appears yellow in color, discolored by fat. Tobin places the heart on the scale and jots its weight, 750 grams, in blue pen on the white board by the workstation. The weight of the heart provides more circumstantial evidence that Mayfair's end came because of some catastrophic cardiovascular event. A quick glance at a photocopied sheet of paper taped to the wall—"Normal Heart Weight"—and a quick calculation indicates that Mayfair's heart is enlarged.

Normal Heart Weight	
2 x body weight in grams	
Males	0.45–0.5% of body weight
Females	0.40–0.45% of body weight
1SD =	28 g for women
1SD =	35 g for men
2 SD are physiologic	

NOTE: SD = standard deviation

Although Mayfair weighed 330 pounds, an ideal body weight for him would be 220 pounds (100 kiligrams). Therefore, his maximum ideal heart weight would be up to 500 grams, two-thirds of his actual body weight. Mayfair's heart, at 750 grams, is markedly enlarged.

During the examination of Mayfair's heart, I find no fewer than seven stents placed during two different episodes to keep open partially blocked or occluded coronary arteries. The stents appear as silver-colored wire mesh embedded in the tan coronary arteries.

I have never seen a partially occluded stent. In other words, the tiny devices almost always do their intended jobs. Implanting a stent offers the patient one option for keeping a coronary artery open. A bypass surgery, during which a surgeon uses a segment of a leg vein to bypass the blocked section of a coronary artery, offers another option. The seven stents indicates Mayfair's extensive history of heart trouble.

Next, an examination of the coronary arteries follows, which I study by incising them, periodically pausing, placing the scalpel on the white cutting board, and dictating my findings into a microphone that hangs over the station like a silver vine. He should have had a heart transplant. As expected, the murder weapon, the smoking gun, that killed Elliot Mayfair was inside his heart: enough blockage in the coronary arteries to warrant a finding that Mayfair died from a lethal cardiac arrhythmia. Unless we uncover evidence of a more compelling cause of death, such as massive subdural bleeding or a skull fracture, the certificate of death will read that Mayfair died from arteriosclerotic cardiovascular disease (ASCVD).

But no such surprise would appear.

No subdural hematoma, no brain aneurism.

No knife wound in his back.

A few days later, the toxicology report reveals no alcohol or drugs in his body and no poison either.

In short, the hoofprints on the morgue floor this morning came from a horse, not a zebra.

ENDINGS

Early Winter 2005
Spectrum Health, Blodgett Campus
East Grand Rapids, Michigan

E ndings. Every book has one. They're hard to write, hard to imagine. Everyone wonders how the last page of their life's book will read, but some, dying of the suspense perhaps, or just tired of waiting, choose to end their stories prematurely, by authoring the last page . . . with a suicide. The final pages of tormented lives ended by suicides could make an interesting tome.

In 1962 the actress Clara Blandick, who portrayed Auntie Em in *The Wizard of Oz*, took an overdose of sleeping pills and fastened a plastic bag over her head; she suffered from severe arthritis.

A poet named Harte Crane said his farewell and leaped over the side of a steamship in 1932. Another poet, Vachel Lindsay, downed a bottle of lye in 1931. Thirty-one years later, Sylvia Plath, poet and author of *The Bell Jar*, committed suicide by asphyxiating herself in an oven. She swallowed a bottle of sleeping pills and gassed herself in her kitchen, but only after sealing the kitchen and opening windows of her flat to protect her children.

Lillian Millicent Entwistle, a silent film star, jumped off of the "H" in the HOLLYWOOD sign (HOLLYWOODLAND in 1932, when Mrs. Entwistle scripted her last page of life).

The writer Eugene Izzi hanged himself out of an eleventh-floor window in a downtown Chicago skyscraper. He may not have intended to die, though; some believe he was conducting research on a scene for an upcoming book.

Dr. Horace Wells, a famed nineteenth-century dentist and a pioneer in the use of general anesthesia (nitrous oxide) in dentistry, became a user of chloroform; under its influence on his thirty-third birthday, he threw acid on two prostitutes. While in jail for the assault, Wells held a rag soaked in chloroform over his mouth and cut open his thigh with a razor. He bled to death. Ironically, a pioneer in anesthesia anesthetized himself when he inked the final page in his vita.

The curious reader can find many such macabre endings in *The Hollywood Book of Death: The Bizarre, Often Sordid, Passions of More Than 125 American Movie and TV Idols* by James Robert Parish. But one doesn't have to look to the stars for premature endings. They occur everyday, as people in mental or physical anguish, or a combination of the two, take pen in hand to write their final pages. Sometimes, they write bizarre endings by choosing an elaborate or creative method of suicide; sometimes, they choose old standbys. One common element ties together these pages, though: they are all tragedies.

*****

Grand Rapids this morning is colder than the proverbial witch's kiss (seventeen degrees Fahrenheit with a stiff wind). The two bodies in the morgue this morning belonged to tormented souls who, like those in the above anecdotes, chose to end their mental anguish by extinguishing their lives—each in a different way. To each his own, as they say.

Everything at the hospital seems asleep this morning, including the portable coffee stand, which is sleeping under a blue tarp. Tobin is sitting in the hospital waiting when I arrive (he describes waiting to enter the morgue as like sipping a cup of suspense, and today I let the bag steep for thirty minutes—a double shot of anticipation).

Detective Scott Johnson from the Walker Police Department meets us on the stairwell. A few days ago, a thunderstorm, rare for a January in Michigan, melted the snow cover and left Grand Rapids under the threat of flooding. Johnson, a tall, thirty-something with blond, cropped hair and round glasses, explains that Walker, a city on the western fringe of Kent County, experienced a flood of its own last night—a flood of suicides.

As we enter the morgue's conference room, Johnson provides a briefing on the particulars of each suicide and the relevant case histories. A few minutes later, Joel Talsma pokes his head into the conference room, his earring glistening under the fluorescent lighting, and listens to the case histories detailed by Detective Johnson. Deborah Weiler*, a fifty-three-year-old mother of two daughters, who had made several suicide attempts before, was found dangling from a tree in a wooded area; she hanged herself with her dog's leash. The dog, loyal to the end, sat under the tree until found by police hours later. John Carl May*, a forty-three-year-old bachelor, lived with his parents, who heard a gunshot shortly after May went upstairs to his room. He shot himself in the forehead with a .44-caliber Magnum revolver with an eight-inch barrel containing "varmint load" bullets.

Detective Johnson continues his briefing as Tobin and I make our way down the corridor and into the morgue. May lies on the table nearest the corridor, a neat, dime-sized hole in the center of his forehead. His short, wavy hair—once white, now a deep reddish purple—had become a mop for his blood. His eyes are open but have fallen back, pulled by gravity into their sockets.

John Connolly, a Colonel Sanders look-alike and a retired pathology assistant who still works as a medical examiner investigator, appears in the morgue and explains the details of Weiler's case history. Deborah Weiler, whose body lies on the far table, struggled with alcohol and drug abuse and was on the cusp of losing custody of her two children. She left two suicide notes, one addressed to her teenaged daughter that ends with the heart wrenching "I'll miss you. Love forever." She signed the note, "Mom XOXOXO."

Naked, she looks tall and thin; her jacket and clothes sit in a bag on the floor at the corner of the table. Under her locks of auburn hair, which obscure part of her forehead, her eyes are closed.

The three most common methods of committing suicide, I explain to Detective Johnson and Tobin, are shooting, hanging, and drugs. We have two of the three in the morgue today.

"Few females shoot themselves," Johnson adds. "They prefer pills."

Not Deborah Weiler, who entered the morgue with her dog's purple leash still around her neck.

The examination begins with my recorded description of Weiler's body. In the background, Joel snaps a series of photos that will provide a visual record of the damage John Carl May inflicted on himself with his .44 Magnum. Now that Joel has washed the dried blood from his head, May's reddish brown hair shines in the fluorescent light. Above his long, thin nose, centered in his forehead, is that dime-sized hole—the bullet entry wound. Lines of deep brown—almost black—blood drip down both cheeks, tiny streams of blood that drip off of his face, , creating two small, widening circles on the autopsy table.

Now that the description of Deborah Weiler's body is finished, Joel cuts away the dog leash wrapped around her neck—her makeshift noose. The pressure of the leash has left an inch-wide indentation, a groove really, pressed into her neck. Her eyes are closed, her lips open, her tongue clamped between clenched teeth. Weiler and John Carl May provide an in situ illustration of a statement made earlier, a statement that summarizes the causes that bring victims here, to the Kent County Morgue: where there's a will, there's a way.

As Joel prepares to begin Weiler's autopsy with the initial Y-incision, I dictate the description of May's body. I note the gunpowder residue around the bullet hole that suggests "loose contact" between the gun barrel and May's forehead; he held, but didn't tightly press, the barrel of the .44 to his forehead. In the narration, I refer to the varmint load bullet that tore through May's brain and ended his life; this description confuses Tobin, who has no idea what a varmint load cartridge is.

Detective Johnson explains that varmint load bullets, used to hunt small game, contain a plastic tip filled with tiny pellets, like the shot of a shotgun shell only smaller in diameter. John Connolly, who overheard the conversation, gestures to the conference room, where a glass case contains bullets of various types and calibers, including a varmint load cartridge.

Connolly—Joel Talsma's predecessor—was the senior pathology assistant in the autopsy room for thirty years. One can detect the Boston native's accent, and like most Bostonians, he feels passionately about the Red Sox and the Patriots. He moves through the corridor, with Tobin in tow, and into the conference room, where he stops in front of the glass case filled with bullets standing on end. He points to a bullet with a bright blue plastic cone on its tip. That, he says, pointing a long, bony finger at a bullet about three quarters of an inch long, is a varmint load bullet, only a much smaller caliber—a .22. The translucent blue cone contains dozens of tiny lead balls. Varmint load bullets work like shotgun shells; when the gun discharges, the cone ruptures and the shot spreads. The .44-caliber bullet that ended John Carl May's life would be much larger than this one—twice the size in fact—but would have also contained lead pellets inside the blue plastic tip.

In the autopsy room, Joel has wasted no time in beginning Weiler's autopsy; he has removed many of her internal organs for examination.

John Carl May's injuries, specifically the bullet wound, are described for the official record; the pellets entered his head as a group, en masse, and spread out once inside the brain. Two x-rays, lit up on the far wall behind Joel—who continues to excise Weiler's internal organs, placing them in large stainless-steel bowls he will use to convey them to the dissecting table—tell the story of the damage caused by the varmint load pellets as they tore through May's brain. The image on the x-rays, side and back views of the man's head, illustrate the damage May inflicted on himself last night; dozens of white dots—the shot from the varmint load bullet—litter the inside of May's skull like stars in the night sky. The image on the x-ray looks like a Lite Brite toy with its many white pegs inserted into a black grid.

It is a shocking image.

A diagram is needed to illustrate the gunshot wound on May's head, so I ask Tobin to select the proper diagram. He shuffles over to a set of shelves mounted on the wall that contain photocopies of anatomical drawings used to create sketches of various injuries for the autopsy record. After locating the proper diagram, titled "Head, surface and skeletal anatomy, anterior and posterior views," Tobin plucks the sheet of paper from the shelf.

"I need to sketch the bullet hole," I explain, placing the diagram on a clipboard.

Tobin leans closer, a few inches from the hole, while I sketch a few lines with a blue ballpoint pen. The hole made by the .44 Magnum is circular with a squared bottom—a thumb shape. The squared bottom suggests that the victim may have held the barrel to his forehead at a slight angle with the barrel just touching the skin, not pressed—the distance indicated by a rim of black soot. If the victim had fired the gun a few inches from the skin, a larger entrance wound with a scalloped, "cookie cutter" look would appear, resulting from the mass of pellets beginning to spread.

Yet oddly, the hole in the skin of May's forehead does not match the hole in his skull, Tobin notes. Skin is elastic, and the skin may slip, so the bullet wound often does not line up with the hole in the skull underneath it. To demonstrate, I pull down the skin to reveal a gaping black breach in May's skull where the varmint load pellets penetrated bone and began to spread; the hole in the skull is larger than the hole in the skin.

With May's external wounds described and catalogued, and with the internal organs of Weiler removed, the examination of Weiler's internal organs begins.

Still, no ME can rule out homicide without a thorough examination, and an examination of Deborah Weiler's organs would reveal some bizarre wounds.

"What did you find?" Tobin asks as he watches the dissection of Weiler's throat structures.

Hangings leave little physical damage, little forensic evidence, I explain. Sometimes, if something is wedged between the skin and the noose, like clothing or a towel, the medical examiner may find no external injuries, so once again context becomes everything. And of course, Weiler did come into the morgue wearing the dog leash—the purple leash now on the evidence table in the corner.

"So there might be nothing to find?" Tobin asks.

One never knows what one will find, though. "We had a case a few years ago," I note as I dissect Weiler's throat structures, "where a husband murdered his wife and then tried to cut out her tongue—a symbolic act."

Tobin chuckles.

As expected, no hemorrhaging (bleeding), which would appear in throat muscles if someone strangled Weiler.

Apart from evidence of a mild case of emphysema found in conjunction with the small black spots on the lining of her lungs that reveal the victim's history of smoking, I find nothing unexpected thus far. In the background, accompanied by songs from The Who's *Who's Next*, Joel has already opened May and removed his internal organs. He makes a few cuts on May's head and tugs his face forward; only with the skull exposed does the massive damage done by the .44-caliber varmint load bullet become evident. The discharging of the bullet forced gas into the skull; the subsequent pressure of the gas created the six-inch-long fissure running the entire length from the top front to the top back of May's skull.

On the opposite wall, the illuminated x-rays hang like a road map of the damage they will find inside May's head. The side view of May's skull provides a clear picture of the damage caused by the gas from the gunshot; the x-ray shows a gap behind the forehead—a black recess—where the force of the gunshot and the resultant gas forced the brain backward.

"What did you find?" Tobin asks, noticing me holding a tiny fragment of blue plastic on the tip of my gloved finger—a fragment from the plastic cone that held the shot of the varmint load bullet. On the inside of the scalp, around the skin by the bullet hole, I point to other tiny blue fragments of the shell tip adhering to the tissue. Again, Tobin leans forward for a closer look.

Under the skull, an even more graphic picture of the fatal wound materializes.

"This is interesting," I explain. The dura, the tough membrane attached to the underside of the skull, was blown clear from the skull and now appears as a thin, white membrane covering the brain. The placement of the dura underscores the sheer force of the gunshot. As with previous autopsies, pathology assistants peel the dura from the skull with a forceps, and they manage to remove it only with a good deal of effort.

Joel places May's brain in a bowl; Tobin joins him and the two peer into the bowl. The pellets from the varmint load bullet—the stars in the night sky of the x-ray—become visible under the fluorescent lighting of the autopsy room; the tiny metal fragments, embedded in the yellowish red mass, appear with a dull shine. Joel reaches into the bowl and removes a tiny clear plastic cap, like a small, thick contact lens. "That's part of it there." He has found the plastic tip of the bullet.

The examination of Deborah Weiler's internal organs continues, and the discovery of a troublesome anomaly results—forensic evidence that does not belong to a hanging suicide. Severe hemorrhaging has turned the tissues around her spleen into a deep purple almost black color.

"You have something to talk to the boyfriend about," I note to Detective Johnson, whose interest now appears piqued. The hemorrhaging, I explain, indicates that sometime in the hours before she died, Deborah Weiler sustained a blow to the abdomen, like someone punched her in the stomach. The hemorrhaging suggests that she received a severe blow, one that could have left her immobilized.

I can conceive a sinister scenario (I explain to Detective Johnson who listens intently) in which someone struck Weiler in the solar plexis, rendering her immobile, then strung her up to make it appear as though she hanged herself. Husbands have done stranger things to their wives, which reminds me of the anecdote of the husband who attempted to remove his wife's tongue after he murdered her—a horrific story that now seems like an eerie premonition.

THE HAND OF GOD

The voice that helped to convict a man of first-degree murder came from the victim herself. Sandra Anne Duyst spoke about her homicide from beyond the grave. "If anything has happened to me look first to David Duyst, Sr.," read a note written to her sister, written more than a year before her death. "He could be my killer. I would never commit suicide. He may have killed me."[1]

On March 29, 2000, Kent County sheriffs responded to a 911 call. David Duyst told investigators that he was asleep on a couch in a room adjacent to their bedroom when he was startled awake by the sound of a gunshot in an adjacent room. According to Duyst, inside the bedroom he found his wife, Sandra Duyst, lying on her left side atop blood-spattered sheets, a Smith & Wesson 9 mm pistol lying on the bed in front of her. He picked up the gun, returned it to the bed, and called 911.

David Duyst told investigators that his wife had been depressed since her accident a few years prior, on November 19, 1998. An equestrienne and horse trainer, she had been kicked in the head by one of the quarter horses she trained. David Duyst worked as an investment and insurance agent in downtown Grand Rapids, Michigan, with Sandra's father.

Sandra Duyst appeared to have a single entrance wound to the right temple between the eye and ear, but two apparent exit wounds were visible on the left side of her head—a scenario that, while rare, occurs sometimes with "jacketed bullets." Jacketed bullets consist of a lead core with an outer copper "jacket." When passing through the body, the core and jacket may separate, causing individual exit wounds.

The pattern of gunpowder residue around a bullet entrance hole can tell the forensic pathologist the distance from which the fatal bullet was fired:

Range	*Findings*
contact	bullet hole—often radial skin tears if over bone
fraction of an inch	burning around the wound margin
up to 6 inches	soot and powder stippling; the powder may lie loose on the skin or clothing or be driven into the skin (tattooing)
6 inches to 3 or 4 feet	powder stippling
more than 3 to 4 feet	bullet hole only, no soot or powder

These estimates, though, are approximate and will differ somewhat from weapon to weapon (e.g., those from a .22 pistol will differ from those of a .30'06 rifle). A shotgun fired at a person's face from a few inches away would destroy the victim's face, while a .22 pistol would leave a small, neat bullet hole. If a precise estimate of range of fire is needed, firearm examiners must test-fire the weapon with the same type of ammunition used in the shooting. A tight contact wound (one that results when the gun is pressed against the head) with a small caliber weapon (.22 or .25 caliber) may not cause splitting of the skin around the wound.

The pattern of gunshot residue around the wound can indicate the distance between the pistol muzzle and in this case the victim's head. If, for instance, the pistol is pressed against the skull, the gases that discharge with the bullet have nowhere to escape but between the scalp and the skull, bursting the skin and creating a star-shaped wound around the entrance hole. This type of wound only occurs when a gun barrel is pressed against skin that is stretched over bone, such as the skull and the sternum. Shots fired from less than an inch from the skull will leave a hole rimmed by residue including soot and partly burned flakes of gunpowder; a few inches more, up to six inches away, and the residue becomes like a soot peppered around the entrance wound that may or may not be "driven into the skin," called "tattooing" because the myriad of tiny black dots cannot be removed—the blast tattoos them onto the victim's scalp. Suicide victims, though, typically press the pistol tightly against the head or just a slight distance from the head; therefore, the bullet wounds are characterized by singed, burned skin.

The entrance wound in Sandra Duyst's head was a tight contact wound, indicating that she pressed the gun against her head, which is consistent with suicide victims even though firearm suicides are less common among women than are suicides by other methods.

Oddly, upon examination of Sandra Duyst's body, I did not find any blood on her hands or arm, even though the gun had blood on it—quite strange for a victim who shot herself in the head.

While incising Sandra Duyst's scalp in preparation for removing her brain, the pathology assistant, Paul Davison, found a second entrance wound in the right temple above her ear and behind the hairline (the hair obscured this second entrance wound). Sandra had been shot not once, but two times in her right temple. Two autopsies were conducted simultaneously on this date, so the relatively confined morgue was filled with medical and law enforcement personnel. Everyone in the room fell silent at Paul's discovery. The second entrance wound literally silenced the room.

Why? Because Sandra Duyst could not have shot herself in the head twice. The first wound would have left her comatose. A second shot? Impossible.

Impossible. An impossible suicide. In other words, a homicide made to appear as if it were a suicide. The routine autopsy had turned up a concealed homicide. One of the detectives assigned to the case, present at this autopsy, told me that he never before heard a doctor use the word "impossible," as I did at that moment. The first shot would have left Sandra Duyst incapacitated instantaneously. Given the placement of the first shot, she could not have shot herself a second time. The existence of the second entrance proved that someone else must have pulled the trigger.

Nonetheless, the Kent County prosecutor, Greg Boer, solicited the opinion of an expert on gunshot wounds to the head, who confirmed this analysis—Sandra Duyst could not have shot herself in the head a second time given the placement of the first wound.

With the cause of death listed as a homicide and supported by other independent experts, the Kent County sheriff's department launched a thorough investigation. Suspicion fell onto David Duyst, Sandra's estranged husband, who discovered the body. However, many in the community could not (and to this day still do not) believe that this active church-going man would be capable of murdering his wife. Investigators found tiny spots of blood on the shirt David wore that night, and DNA testing confirmed the blood to be Sandra's.

The Kent County prosecutor then sent detectives to Portland, Oregon, to work with Rod Englert, one of the nation's leading blood-spatter experts (a forensic scientist who specializes in the patterns created by blood in various circumstances). Englert was not new to high-profile cases or Michigan law enforcement. He testified in the O. J. Simpson trial and again at the trial of Detroit police officer Walter Budzyn, convicted of second-degree murder for his role in the death of Malice Green. Englert's analysis of blood on the victim's windshield indicated that Green had been beaten by two different people.

Englert examined the shirt Sandra Duyst wore and the bedsheets on which she was lying when she received her fatal wounds. The blood spatter that misted the bedsheets exhibited a telltale pattern with a blank spot or shadow created by an obstruction, such as someone's outstretched arm, which a re-creation of the event confirmed. In a motel room, Englert and investigators re-created the murder scene and determined that the blood-spatter patterns, on the bed sheets and on David Duyst's shirt, were consistent with someone standing over Sandra and firing two shots into her head from a distance of a few inches.

Englert found spots of blood on the shirt David Duyst wore when his wife allegedly committed suicide; the tiny spots of blood, found only after thirty minutes of inspection under powerful lights with a magnifying glass, were caused by the mist of blood that, like a cloud, hovers around a victim immediately after the high-velocity impact of a bullet. These spots would appear on the shirt only if the man wearing it stood within four feet of Sandra when the trigger was pulled. This discovery placed Duyst *inside* the bedroom when the fatal shots occurred, not in an adjacent room as he initially told detectives.

In the cinematic version of the Agatha Christie masterpiece *Death on the Nile*, Peter Ustinov's Hercule Poirot explains to Simon Doyle, the murderer, that firing a gun deposits minute amounts of burned powder on the hand firing the weapon, and a paraffin test, which he calls a moulage test, can indicate if a person has fired a gun. But could such a test prove if Sandra Duyst fired a weapon? Or if David Duyst did? No. Such tests are not reliable; not even the FBI uses them anymore.

Despite a growing mound of evidence pointing to him, David Duyst steadfastly denied his guilt, and the investigation continued.

And then in April came a telephone call and a revelation.

Sandra Duyst must have suspected her husband, because she took out an insurance policy of her own; she wrote a note and placed it in a china cabinet—the kind of note that can sway a jury. She needed a beneficiary, someone who would know about the note buried in the china cabinet, someone like her sister Mary Ellen Spring.

Around Easter 1999, Sandra called Ms. Spring to tell her of the note's existence, but at that time she did not reveal its explosive contents. Almost a year later, Sandra's sister contacted detectives and told them about the note, presumably still tucked in the china cabinet where Sandra Duyst deposited it.

One of the detectives working the case found himself in Jackson, interviewing the sister, who told him, ominously, that Sandra Duyst told her if anything happened to her, she would leave a note to her sister in the china cabinet.

A long drive and a search warrant later, the detective executed a search of Sandra Duyst's china cabinet that had become a repository of "stuff" over the years. After an exhaustive search, the detective found Sandra Duyst's note to her sister.

In the note, Sandra Duyst indicted her killer. "On November 19th, my accident was no accident," the note read. "David beat me with a hammer/ax. He came from behind while I was in Dexter's stall. He hit me repeatedly. Only when I told him I would sell my horse and support him in leaving the partnership he had formed with my dad would he let me go."[2]

Sandra Duyst reported the incident in the stable as an accident at the time, despite the fact that the wounds on her head were inconsistent with the blunt-force trauma that would have resulted from a horse kick. The "accident," the note alleged, was in fact a homicide attempt masked as an accident, and her husband had forced her to report it as an accident.

The note also pointed at David should Sandra Duyst become the victim of a strange accident or "suicide" and therefore provided the last major link in a chain of evidence against David Duyst, which included ample evidence of his motives. Detectives uncovered an affair between Duyst and a coworker, Linda Ryan, that began in July 1998—a few months before the November incident in the horse stable. They also uncovered evidence of David Duyst's financial difficulties, which, coupled with the $579,000 in life insurance on his wife, payable even in the event of suicide, offered a powerful motive.[3]

Although the note did not provide hard evidence for investigators, it did provide valuable background on the relationship between David and Sandra Duyst, *if* the note could be authenticated. An investigation confirmed the handwriting belonged to Sandra Duyst, and a DNA analysis on the saliva that sealed the envelope proved it to be hers.

A body, a motive, opportunity, evidence—all of which led to a murder trial.

I testified about the forensic evidence at the subsequent trial. When the prosecutor asked me about the manner of death, I looked steadfastly at the jury and responded "homicide."

Throughout the five-week-long trial, David Duyst professed his innocence and insisted that his wife committed suicide. Duyst testified that he found his wife on the bed with her finger still inside the pistol's trigger guard.

Furthermore, Sandra Duyst had attempted suicide on previous occasions, he told the jury, and she had refused to seek psychiatric help. Since her accident in the horse stable, Sandra Duyst had taken Paxil and Prozac—antidepressant drugs. These two drugs have reputed adverse side effects, and during the trial the defense claimed that 10 percent of all patients who take these drugs exhibit suicidal tendencies.

Throughout the investigation, though, detectives questioned friends, family, and acquaintances of the victim, and no one—not one of the more than one hundred interviewed—knew of any previous suicide attempts, as Duyst alleged in his testimony. The only one who claimed that Sandra Duyst attempted suicide was her husband.

The defense staged a re-creation of its own: David Duyst's version of events in which he runs into the bedroom and discovers Sandra after she fired his 9 mm above her right ear. Whereas Englert used a mannequin in his reenactment, the defense used live models to make its case. In the videotaped reenactment played for the jury, a model representing Sandra is lying on a bed; a model David Duyst enters the room, takes the gun from her hand and removes the clip, and then places both back on the bed. He leaves and returns a few seconds later, leaning over her body to determine if she is breathing. The video reenactment, though, almost mocked the re-creation done by Englert in Portland, Oregon, because Englert's re-creation and analysis of the blood patterns proved a different version of the events that occurred on March 29, 2000.

David Duyst just couldn't shed the blood on this shirt, which spoke in a stentorian voice, and the jury couldn't help but hear it. Whoever wore the shirt must have been within four feet of Sandra when the shots were fired, Rod Englert told the jurors.[4] The spots of blood on the shirt proved it.

Furthermore, Englert testified, the absence of blood on the victim's hands and arms indicated that she didn't fire the gun.[5] If she pointed the gun at her head and pulled the trigger, blood would have sprayed her hands and arms as it did the bedsheets. If someone shot her while she was asleep, with her hands and arms at her side, no blood *would* appear on those parts of her body.

And Duyst and his defense could not dodge a bullet: the second bullet. As I testified, the first bullet would have incapacitated Sandra Duyst, and its location precluded the possibility that her hand fired the second bullet. A firearms expert testified that the 9 mm semiautomatic pistol did not misfire. The expert also testified that the firing mechanism inside the Smith & Wesson 9 mm weapon made a misfire impossible. Not unlikely, but *impossible*. Someone had to fire that second bullet.

The defense called an expert who countered with another theory that suggested Sandra Duyst could have shot herself in the head a second time. Reflex action caused her to fire the second bullet, the expert argued.

The jury didn't buy the explanation, and in late March 2001, just about a year after Sandra Duyst's death, the members convicted David Duyst of first-degree murder. He is now serving a life sentence, and all appeals brought on his behalf have failed.

Still, David Duyst maintains his innocence and has accumulated evidence that he believes warrants a new trial. During the investigation that led to his conviction, he submitted to three polygraph tests, two of which he passed (the other was inconclusive) as telling the truth when asked if he killed his wife. These tests, though, were not presented to the jury because polygraph evidence is not admissible in court.

The blood on David Duyst's shirt, according to a blood-spatter expert his current attorney consulted, could have occurred from Sandra Duyst choking on the blood in her throat and coughing. And they claim the bedsheets have no evidentiary value either, because they were originally discarded when authorities believed Sandra Duyst committed suicide.[6]

As for the second bullet, one firearms expert consulted by Duyst's defense claims that the Smith & Wesson pistol could malfunction and discharge twice. Thus, according to this expert, one pull of the trigger could account for the two bullet entrance wounds.

The two tight-contact entrance wounds, though, seem to argue with this conclusion. The wounds suggest that whoever shot her pressed the barrel of the gun in front of her right ear and fired, then pressed the gun against her head an inch and a half above and fired a second shot. If the gun accidentally discharged a second time, the second shot could not have been a tight-contact wound.

David Duyst's claim of innocence raises some interesting possibilities, however. Duyst's defense has posited one scenario in which a vengeful Sandra Duyst used suicide as a vehicle for framing her husband.[7] In this scenario, the china cabinet note placed David Duyst inside of a macabre frame. Another possibility: someone else murdered her.

Of course, one burning question remains, despite the guilt or innocence of David Duyst: If Sandra Duyst didn't commit suicide, *why* did the perpetrator fire a second shot? Since the murder investigation began in the Kent County Morgue with the discovery of the second entry wound, if the perpetrator hadn't fired a second bullet, one of the detectives involved with the investigation surmised, Sandra Duyst's killer would have literally gotten away with murder.

"I believe it was the hand of God," someone involved with the case later suggested.

Another, more scientific explanation exists. Victims of gunshot wounds to the head often do not die immediately. They sometimes have seizures and may take terminal breaths; such activity may lead the assailant to believe that the victim may survive. I believe this victim didn't die right away, so the killer shot her a second time to ensure her death, even though the first wound was in fact fatal. In this case, a homicide masked as a suicide, the autopsy uncovered a crime; this case unfolded from the inside out, but the autopsy cannot answer the lingering question: Why the second shot?

*****

Until more evidence arises in the case of Deborah Weiler, I am ruling her death a suicide.

As Detective Johnson listens about a potential homicide, Joel lays a towel over a faux wood cafeteria tray. He places the spleen and stomach—the organs that contained the hemorrhaging—on the tray and takes it to "BA57: Photography" adjacent to the autopsy room. In the closet-sized room, its appearance made smaller by the black cinder-block walls, Joel removes the organs from the tray and places them onto a large blue plastic square below a digital imaging system.

With the examination of Weiler's internal organs complete, I ask Tobin to gather the pieces of dissected organs from the corner of the workstation and gently place them into one of the large bowls. Handling the organ sections, which is like trying to handle live fish while wearing latex gloves, is tricky, but after a few minutes, he manages to place the remaining pieces into the bowl. The once baby blue cuffs of his surgical scrubs are now rimmed with crimson stains, and the once beige latex gloves are covered with bright red streaks.

Next, as directed, Tobin carries the bowl to the body; Joel watches as he tilts the bowl and its contents pour into the plastic bag lining Weiler's torso cavity. With the investigation over, the organs go back inside her body; at the funeral home, embalmers will discard them.

Within thirty minutes, the examination of May's internal organs is complete; except for a head shattered by the varmint load bullet, May receives a clean bill of health—no unexpected injuries, no fatal disease the discovery of which would have provided some explanation for his suicide. Nothing, except for the hideous damage he inflicted on himself, the ultimate self-hatred.

Detective Johnson says good-bye as he peels the foot protectors from his shoes. He's off to question Weiler's boyfriend, although ultimately he will find no evidence of foul play. Behind him, two figures lie on the autopsy tables, two whose lives ended prematurely. *What people do to themselves.* A few minutes later, the living emerge from the morgue into an overcast, frigid late Saturday morning—another day in the books of their lives. The ends to their stories have yet to be written.

HORSEPLAY

Midwinter 2005
Spectrum Health, Blodgett Campus
East Grand Rapids, Michigan

A group of friends assemble at a party Thursday night to perhaps watch sports, play a few hands of Texas Hold'em, and drink. Large snowflakes dance in the wind of the night sky outside, as a light snow has begun its assault on northwestern Michigan. Temperatures outside fall below freezing when the sun sets, but inside the house the alcohol warms stomachs and spirits. Tonight, the friends will enjoy a large draught of life, and as tragedy strikes, they will quaff another large draught—of death. . . .

As the night progresses, their play degrades from discussion of sports and cards to "horsing around," as several of the revelers engage in impromptu wresting matches, oblivious to the obstacles the living room presents for physical activity.

One of the friends, twenty-six-year-old Jacob Dillon*, hits his head a few times on the edge of a coffee table, but after several cans of beer and a few shots of whiskey, he doesn't feel the pain; he continues to horse around with his friends, until he collapses and loses consciousness. Later, his friends would characterize his breathing at this point as like snoring. He is rushed to the local hospital, where Jacob Dillon is pronounced dead.

But how did he die? How, his shell-shocked friends wonder, did their party turn fatal?

This morning, an autopsy will occur to determine what force or forces took the life of a twenty-six-year-old with no known physical ailments. My forensic network covers much of Michigan's western lower peninsula—an area with a population of approximately two million. Many cases come as referrals from other counties. The hospital in which Dillon died does employ pathologists, but none with forensic experience. The medical examiner who examined Dillon does not have any forensic pathology training; so he will perform a toxicology test and a cursory external examination of victims of suspicious deaths. If these tests fail to yield a sufficient cause of death, he will refer the case for an autopsy. The tests on Dillon's blood revealed that he had consumed a substantial amount of alcohol the night he died; his blood told of consumption that led to a .24 percent blood-alcohol level, or three times the legal limit to operate a motor vehicle within the state of Michigan, although this amount would not have killed him. But it could explain why he may have fallen and struck his head. A preliminary exam, however, did not establish a cause of death.

So Jacob Dillon lies on the nearest table to the corridor leading into the autopsy room. Paul Davison has prepared the body for autopsy by undressing it; on a third stainless-steel table, kept in a corner of the room, lie the clothes Dillon wore the night he died. A single sheet of paper details the clothes and personal effects brought in with Dillon: a pair of work boots, a black T-shirt, a pair of blue jeans, and a large red plastic bag for the transportation of Dillon's clothes and personal effects either to his family or to a central evidence depot if the autopsy uncovers evidence of foul play in Dillon's death.

The key to Dillon's death is probably in his head. Possibly, Dillon hit his head harder than most of those at the party realized, and he sustained a fatal head injury. His "golden hour" came and went without a notice.

"Would that make his death a homicide?" Tobin asks.

"Possibly. I'll bet he has some nervous friends awaiting the results of this autopsy." If he died of a head injury, authorities would consider it an accident, albeit a tragic one. If he died of something else, such as asphyxia, charges of manslaughter could result. So, depending on just what type of "horseplay" occurred that night, one or more of Dillon's fellow partygoers could face a negligent homicide charge.

Dillon's autopsy begins, and the electric Christmas music of Trans-Siberian Orchestra provides a faint soundtrack to this morning's work. I circle Dillon's body, holding a red ballpoint pen and clipboard containing a page with an outline of a human body with front, or "anterior," and back, or "posterior," views. Dillon had auburn hair, and the tide of time had pulled his hairline back to form a sort of widow's peak in the center of his head; his well-groomed mustache and goatee are redder than his hair, almost orange.

A small detail about Dillon provides an interesting side note about the subjectivity of eyewitness statements. Eyewitness testimony can prove as reliable as the weather in Michigan. After days or even months pass, an eyewitness to a homicide may "see" something different than he or she did as the event witnessed actually occurred. Paul Davison, early in the examination, described Dillon's hair color as "brown," but in fact his hair is red. The beard and goatee provide the deciding factor. Had he committed an armed robbery, one eyewitness may describe him as a brunette and another as a red head.

Dillon's eyes, lifeless, seem to stare up at the fluorescent lights from behind partially closed eyelids—not like he is squinting in bright sunlight, but with heavy eyelids, like he has just pulled an all-nighter. Having been found facedown, the lividity has stained his head and face a deep purple that looks like ice cold personified.

An examination of Dillon's mouth results in a surprise. I pry it open and find not teeth, but nubs—the decayed remains of once healthy teeth. For the forensic pathologist, these rotten teeth represent evidence of a possible drug habit; crystal methamphetamine users and abusers, for example, notoriously exhibit signs of poor hygiene, such as rotten teeth— a condition sometimes called "meth mouth." This autopsy will include a toxicology screen. The presence of "meth" (methamphetamine) in Dillon's blood could explain what occurred a few nights ago. Use of the drug can lead to a stroke or cause the heart to beat erratically, which can lead to a fatal cardiac arrhythmia. Users of methamphetamine, though, will often have scabs or sores on their bodies, because the drug produces the feeling of bugs, "crank bugs," crawling on the skin. From the appearance of his nude body, Jacob Dillon did not feel invisible bugs crawling on his arms and legs.

But the toxicology screen, done on blood taken from Dillon postmortem, will reveal what drugs he may have ingested the night he died. With a vial of your blood, a doctor can read your health like a book.

And blood does not lie—or does it?

Experts would ponder this question in the case of *The People v. Ernest Stiller*

BAD MEDICINE

At a few minutes after six on the evening of February 4, 1997, Michael Cluster, a Three Oaks police officer, entered Loretta Sloan's apartment in response to a 911 call made by a neighbor, Rebecca Peterson. He found Sloan, unconscious, lying on a foam mattress, with Dr. Earnest Stiller, wet with perspiration, performing CPR on her. A catheter in her chest led to an IV bag—an important detail that Officer Cluster recounted later in court.[1]

The scene must have come as a surprise: Dr. Stiller was performing a type of CPR that takes two people, and CPR protocol calls for a hard surface under the victim, whereas Loretta Sloan lay on the soft surface of a foam mattress. The presence of syringes, vials, and no fewer than seventeen prescription drugs must have made the apartment appear like a makeshift ER.

A few minutes earlier, despite the presence of a telephone in Sloan's apartment, at approximately six, Dr. Stiller knocked on Peterson's door and requested she call 911 for help (Dr. Stiller would later explain that he didn't want to place the call for fear that it would interrupt the CPR).[2] The 911 operator requested more information, so Peterson peeked into her neighbor's apartment. Sloan's skin appeared gray. Dr. Stiller asked her if she knew CPR, and Peterson later recounted that Dr. Stiller was attempting to resuscitate the comatose Loretta Sloan.[3] An emergency technician arrived a few minutes later, and a paramedic joined the effort to revive Sloan at 6:18, but with no success.

Loretta Sloan died shortly after, raising the inevitable question: What killed the 35-year-old licensed nurse? According to Dr. Stiller, a longtime friend and physician to Loretta Sloan, he had treated Sloan in her apartment that afternoon for "flu symptoms.[4] She complained of chest pains and passed out. She had a pulse of 200 beats per minute that Dr. Stiller knew to be a heart malfunction called an atrial flutter. Ultimately, she died from respiratory failure, but what caused her heart to speed up to the point of failure? Did Sloan die of influenza: a rare occurrence for a thirty-five-year-old? Or did heart disease claim her life? The numerous medicine bottles present in her apartment suggested that Sloan suffered a serious malady. The labels on the seventeen bottles, all dating from within the month prior to her death, appeared to indicate the recent onset of disease, but in fact the decedent's medical problems began years earlier, and so did her association with Dr. Stiller.

Loretta Sloan suffered from a recurrent leg infection that resulted from an injury she suffered in 1987, which brought her in contact with Dr. Ernest Stiller, at that time an Indiana physician. He treated Sloan for an infection, and although a close friend later testified that Sloan appeared not to be in any pain at the time, Dr. Stiller prescribed the painkiller Lortab—a combination of Tylenol and the narcotic hydrocodone.

She suffered from a more serious problem in September 1994, however, when a rapid heartbeat led Dr. Stiller to recommend that she go to the hospital. At the hospital, it was discovered that she had experienced a life-threatening condition: an irregular heartbeat called supraventricular tachycardia.

Perhaps this part of Sloan's case history would provide the clue to what killed her just over three years later. An autopsy would likely reveal the identity of Sloan's killer, be it heart disease, influenza, or some other possibility. Nineteen hours after she died, on February 5, an autopsy was conducted in the Kent County Morgue to determine what disease or injury led to her death.

A thorough examination of Sloan's internal organs revealed no evidence of injury, and no heart disease, or any other cause of death. Her blood, taken as part of the autopsy procedure, told a different story, however. The toxicology screen revealed that Sloan's blood contained a cocktail of prescription medicine in alarming amounts: the painkiller hydrocodone (most know this drug by its brand name, Vicodin), in a concentration of 146 nanograms per milliliter; the antidepressant Prozac, in a concentration of 930 nanograms per milliliter; and the antihistamine Benadryl (a decongestant taken by allergy sufferers), in a concentration of 3,000 nanograms per milliliter. Although at trial an expert testified that he knew of one published case where 130 nanograms per milliliter of hydrocodone proved fatal, in most cases, the concentration of each individual drug in Sloan's blood would not lead to an overdose; together, though, this drug cocktail could kill her. Since Sloan's body provided no evidence for any other cause of death, I concluded that Sloan died from this potent mixture of medicines—a mixed-drug intoxication.

Excessive amounts of hydrocodone can slow the functions of the brain stem, the part of the nervous system that controls respiration and heartbeat. Benadryl can have a similar effect. The effect of the two drugs combined can be additive; in other words, taking the two drugs in combination is like taking one of the drugs at a higher level. In fact, too much Benadryl can lead to a cardiac arrhythmia, which is also a side effect of Prozac—a drug also found in Sloan's apartment. If this drug "cocktail" affected Sloan's breathing, carbon dioxide would have accumulated in her bloodstream and, in tandem with an arrhythmia, led to Sloan's death. Toxicologist Bernie Eisenga confirmed these findings.

Sloan had access to more than enough medicines to lead to this potent drug cocktail. Remember those seventeen plastic medicine bottles found in Loretta Sloan's apartment the night she died? The list, entered into evidence at the subsequent trial, reads like a medical alphabet soup.

One (1) plastic pill bottle of Zofran 8 mg tablets. Nine (9) tablets left of 40, prescribed by Dr. Stiller, 01/05/97
One (1) plastic pill bottle of Phentermine 37.5 mg tablets. Twenty-nine (29) tablets left of 30, prescribed by Dr. Stiller, 01/08/97

One (1) plastic pill bottle of Eldepryl 5 mg capsules. Seventy (70) capsules left of 120, prescribed by Dr. Stiller, 01/14/97

One (1) plastic pill bottle of Procardia XL 60 mg tablets. Forty-eight (48) tablets left of 60, prescribed by Dr. Stiller, 01/14/97

One (1) plastic pill bottle of Thioridazine 50 mg tablets. Ninety-two (92) tablets left of 120, prescribed by Dr. Stiller, 01/14/97

One (1) plastic pill bottle of Prozac 20 mg Pulvule. Four (4) capsules left of 120, prescribed by Dr. Stiller, 01/14/97

One (1) plastic pill bottle of Propranolor 120 mg capsules. Ninety-one (91) capsules left of 120, prescribed by Dr. Stiller, 01/14/97

One (1) plastic pill bottle of Levoxyl .3 mg tablets. Fourteen (14) tablets left of 30, prescribed by Dr. Stiller, 01/14/97

One (1) plastic pill bottle of Diphenhydramine 50 mg capsules. Fifty-three (53) capsules left of 100, prescribed by Dr. Stiller, 12/02/96

One (1) plastic pill bottle of Mevacor 40 mg tablets. Forty-three (43) tablets left of 60, prescribed by Dr. Stiller, 1/14/97

One (1) plastic pill bottle of Trazodone 50 mg tablets. Seventy-three (73) tablets left of 100, prescribed by Dr. Stiller, 1/14/97

One (1) plastic pill bottle of Dilantin 100 mg Kapseal. Seventy-five (75) capsules left of 90, prescribed by Dr. Stiller, 01/14/97

One (1) plastic pill bottle of Hydrocodone—APAP 7.5/500 tablets. Twelve (12) tablets left of 65, prescribed by Dr. Stiller, 02/01/97

One (1) plastic pill bottle of Alprazolan 2 mg tablets. One and one half (1½) tablets left of 65, prescribed by Dr. Stiller, 01/11/97

One (1) plastic pill bottle of Thioridazine 50 mg tablets. Thirty (30) tablets left of 100, prescribed by Dr. Stiller, 01/11/97

One (1) plastic pill bottle of Compazine 10 mg tablets. Sixty-nine (69) tablets left of 100, prescribed by Dr. Stiller, 01/11/97

One (1) plastic pill bottle of Phentermine 37.5 mg tablets. No tablets left of 60, prescribed by Dr. Stiller, 01/11/97[5]

One common thread weaves these drugs into a deadly web—Dr. Ernest Stiller, licensed to practice medicine only in Indiana, prescribed all of them—and Michigan resident Loretta Sloan, for whom Dr. Stiller wrote these prescriptions, would fall into this web, never to emerge. The labels on the medications indicate that area pharmacies filled over half of the seventeen—nine prescriptions—in one day alone, January 14, 1997!

The dangerous web created by these seventeen bottles and the fact that a physician unlicensed in Michigan prescribed them, other suspicious circumstances that occurred in the early evening hours of February 4, and the results of the toxicology test placed Dr. Ernest Stiller in front of a jury on charges of second-degree murder and the unauthorized practice of medicine.

For a jury to find a defendant guilty of second-degree murder in Michigan, evidence must exist that the person acted with "malice," defined in this context by applicable case law as "a defendant's wanton and willful disregard of the likelihood that the natural tendency of his behavior is to cause death or great bodily harm."[6] In other words, for the jury to find Stiller guilty of second-degree murder, evidence must exist that he recognized or should have recognized that his actions could lead to his patient's injury or death ("the likelihood of . . . ") and "threw caution to the wind." In contrast, a reckless act, such as a practical joke turned deadly, would qualify as manslaughter and carry a shorter prison sentence.

Because the law entitled Dr. Stiller to prescribe medicines in Michigan only if he practiced medicine in Indiana, for the prosecution to find Stiller guilty of the unauthorized practice of medicine, investigators needed to delve into the defendant's life in La Porte, Indiana. Investigators discovered that Dr. Stiller did not practice medicine in Indiana; he only served as an expert witness in worker's compensation cases. In Michigan, though, he dished out medical advice and prescriptions to anyone, it seemed, who inquired.

During the trial, the prosecution offered as evidence a calendar of prescriptions Dr. Stiller wrote for Loretta Sloan; the calendar offers a startling chronicle of Sloan's treatment that would provide the jury with more than enough evidence of "malice" in Stiller's actions. The portrait that emerged from a parade of witnesses depicted a reckless doctor with a restless pen for writing prescriptions. The seventeen bottles present in Loretta Sloan's apartment represent only the last page in this chronicle of questionable and dangerous medical advice that began years earlier, and like seventeen witnesses for the prosecution, they would help to seal his fate.

In November 1996, at Dr. Stiller's request, an expert in infectious disease, Dr. Mark Harrison, examined the infection that had continued to vex Loretta Sloan. He proscribed Vancomycin—an intravenous antibiotic—and because Sloan experienced difficulty with IVs, implanted a catheter under her collarbone. He also suggested that Sloan not take Gentamicin or any related drugs, because these drugs would not help her bone infection and they could cause kidney damage. Later, Dr. Harrison would discover that Sloan had been taking not only Gentamicin but also a related drug called Tobramycin. Another fact bothered Dr. Harrison: at the time, Sloan lived in the same residence with Dr. Stiller, her physician—an obvious breach of medical ethics.

After a disagreement over Sloan's treatment, Dr. Harrison terminated his treatment of Sloan; Dr. Stiller, however, did not, and the prescriptions he wrote for his patient reached a fever pitch by January 1997.

In the four months before Sloan died, Stiller prescribed for her massive quantities of hydrocodone—a painkiller dangerous if taken over a long duration—despite having no medical reason for doing so. In a three-day span in January, area pharmacies filled prescriptions for Sloan that Stiller wrote or called in that amounted to three hundred 7.5 milligram tablets of the narcotic. In one month's duration (from January 2 through February 1), Stiller's prescriptions for the narcotic amounted to 750 tablets, an average of approximately twenty-five tablets a day.[7] This is a staggering amount that would leave anyone who took this quantity staggering, literally.

One pharmacist noticed this excessive amount, and during Stiller's trial, she testified that on one occasion she warned Stiller about the large amounts of hydrocodone and even gave him some medical literature about the drug, but he did not heed her warning and continued to prescribe the narcotic, and other drugs.

A professor of internal medicine, Dr. Jeffrey Stross, examined the calendar of Dr. Stiller's prescriptions and concluded that if Sloan took the medicines as prescribed, she would run the risk of tremendous harm.[8] And some of the medications made no medical sense whatever. One of the medicines during the prescription frenzy of January 14, 1997—Levoxyl—is used to treat thyroid problems, but Sloan's history indicated no such trouble. A prescription for Eldepryl, a medicine used to treat Parkinson's and Alzheimer's, was filled on the same day, but Sloan suffered from neither malady.

In addition, Dr. Stiller had prescribed a diet pill called phentermine. Levoxyl, Eldepryl, and phentermine could cause the heart to beat faster—a dangerous possibility given Sloan's history of arrhythmia. Two other medicines prescribed for Sloan, Procardia and Inderal, could lower the blood pressure, and Sloan had experienced problems with low blood pressure in the past.

Between October 1, 1996, and February 4, 1997, Stiller wrote Sloan two prescriptions for Benadryl, and in one day alone, January 14, 1997, Stiller wrote ten prescriptions for Sloan that included the drugs Eldepryl and Prozac: two drugs that when taken together can be harmful, as Stiller admitted in court. Sloan's blood, the report produced by the Blodgett toxicology department revealed, contained no trace of Eldepryl, although investigators discovered that thirty of the Eldepryl tablets were missing. While the combination of these two drugs did not cause Sloan's death, the simultaneous prescriptions illustrate Stiller's lack of medical sense that created a risk for Sloan.

At Stiller's trial, another expert witness testified that some of the medications he prescribed would place Sloan at a greater risk because she had a history of cardiac arrhythmia. Another expert witness stated that the drugs and the amounts Stiller prescribed created not just the possibility of great harm to Sloan, but a probability, and a likelihood, if she consumed the drugs he prescribed. Dr. Stiller countered; Loretta Sloan was a licensed nurse who acted responsibly when it came to taking her medications.[9]

The excessive prescriptions alone did not place Dr. Stiller on the hot seat in court; his actions on the day Loretta died raised a few eyebrows among the prosecution. On that day, the apartment manager, Melody Cummins, during her lunch hour, visited Sloan to inquire about a bad check. Dr. Stiller answered the door, standing in the doorway so as to block Ms. Cummins's view into the apartment; during testimony, Cummins described him as agitated and covered with sweat.[10] Dr. Stiller told Cummins that Sloan was very sick. Thirty minutes later, at 1:30 PM, Cummins observed him leaving Sloan's apartment and returning half an hour later with an IV (intravenous) bag. At the trial, though, Stiller contended that he left and returned at 2:30 PM and did not bring with him an IV bag.

And the appearance of Sloan, as described by Officer Cluster and Rebecca Peterson, with an ashen gray skin tone, suggested that she had slipped into a coma far earlier than Dr. Stiller suggested, raising an interesting series of questions: Did some time elapse between the time Loretta Sloan slipped into a comatose state and the time Dr. Stiller knocked on Rebecca Peterson's door? If so, how much time? And *why* would he wait?

Furthermore, during the investigation and subsequent trial, Dr. Stiller claimed that he was treating Sloan for osteomyelitis, an infection of bone, and for this reason he had inserted a permanent intravenous catheter (in her subclavian vein); the autopsy, though, showed no osteomyelitis. The presence of the shunt suggested that he fed her drugs through the IV, which would make an overdose a greater possibility since the drugs enter the bloodstream directly. According to Dr. Stiller, the osteomyelitis left Sloan in tremendous pain, hence the prescriptions for hydrocodone.[11]

Why the tremendous amounts of painkillers he prescribed at various times? At the trial, Dr. Stiller offered an explanation: he believed that Sloan had been giving them to Carol Smythe, who at the time of Sloan's death was Dr. Stiller's fiancée.[12] And Dr. Stiller had also written prescriptions for the drug for Smythe.

Despite the quantities of drugs he prescribed for Sloan, Dr. Stiller maintained that Sloan did not die of a mixed-drug intoxication; she did not consume enough in his estimation even though the drug levels in her blood indicated otherwise.

To prove this claim, Dr. Stiller used himself as a guinea pig for an impromptu experiment. Over a two-week period, he consumed ten Prozac a day; in one day alone, he took ten hydrocodone tablets. A blood test revealed a concentration of 155 nanograms per milliliter of Hydrocodone and a 1,579 nanograms per milliliter concentration of Prozac.[13] He videotaped himself to prove his lucidity by performing tasks one would expect a police officer to require of a suspected drunk driver, such as reciting the alphabet and walking in a straight line. The amounts he took hadn't killed him; therefore, similar amounts could not have proved lethal to Loretta Sloan.

During the experiment, though, Stiller did not consume any Benadryl—the third drug in Sloan's system when she died. Since he had written prescriptions for all three drugs during the period just before Sloan died, the mixture of the three may have created the lethal "drug intoxication." His decision not to take Benadryl in his experiment is a curious omission that he explained in court: he had nothing to do with the Benadryl Sloan apparently took before she died.[14]

Furthermore, as Stiller's defense argued during the trial, he did not hold down Sloan and force her to take the medications. The defense invoked case law, specifically *People v. Kevorkian*. Jack Kevorkian, also known as "Dr. Death," faced criminal charges after assisting a patient with committing suicide; the Supreme Court found that a person is not guilty of murder if he or she provides the vehicle a person uses to commit suicide. Simply because Stiller prescribed the medications does not mean he forced his patient to take them. Unlike Kevorkian, though, Stiller was not helping Sloan to commit suicide.

In fact, by his own admission during testimony, out of a concern for her well-being, he monitored Sloan during the day she died.[15] Therefore, she most likely did not overdose by accident or as a means of committing suicide, but the evidence suggests she believed the medications would make her better. Most patients assume that their doctors have their best interests in mind, that doctors would not prescribe medicine in combinations and quantities that could result in a fatal overdose. Perhaps Sloan should have questioned her doctor, should have researched the drugs he prescribed, but her faith in his expertise, however blind it may have been, does not eliminate the fact that his prescriptions, even if out of ignorance or absentmindedness, led to an overdose, and as a result, her death. In short, malice.

But the blood doesn't lie . . . does it?

The defense attacked the forensic evidence. The theory that Sloan died of a "mixed-drug intoxication" depended on the results of a toxicology report based on blood drawn from the right subclavian vein six or seven inches from the heart. The concentrations found in the blood sample placed the hydrocodone and Benadryl in dangerous concentrations, but not the Prozac. Stiller's defense argued that a condition known as postmortem redistribution skews the drug levels in a victim's system after death, making them more elevated after death than before death. Because this phenomenon, recognized in the medical community, elevated the concentrations of drugs in Sloan's system, no forensic evidence proved that she died of a drug overdose, the defense argued.

During life, many drugs accumulate in the heart muscle. After death those drugs are often released into the heart blood. In other words, upon death, the heart muscle releases the drugs into the heart blood. Therefore, a sample of blood taken from the heart itself may contain a level of drug up to two to three times the actual level of the drug in the blood at the time of death. Because of this effect, the optimal site for acquiring postmortem blood samples for toxicology is from a "peripheral" site such as the femoral vein or a subclavian vein. The accepted location to obtain blood for a blood screen is (1) femoral, or (2) subclavian (which is second best). Did postmortem redistribution skew the forensic evidence? This became a central question in the case.

A battle of experts followed.

I testified that I knew of one article which indicated that levels of some drugs may be higher in the subclavian vein compared with veins farther from the heart. However, I still believed that this combination of drugs, especially in the absence of other causes of death, led to her demise. In the absence of evidence supporting any other cause of death, I stood by my opinion that she died of a drug overdose from the combination of the three drugs: hydrocodone, Prozac, and Benadryl.

Several toxicologists testified, which amounted to a battle of theories about postmortem redistribution. One testified that the three drugs found in Sloan's system could appear elevated in a postmortem sample. Benadryl, for example, could be as much as twenty-one times more concentrated in a sample taken after a victim's death than before. Prozac could also be more elevated.[16]

Another toxicologist testified that he knew of one case in which the level of hydrocodone found in Sloan's system led to a fatal overdose. He also testified that he knew of a case where a blood sample taken from the femoral artery in the leg revealed a higher level of Benadryl than did a sample taken from the subclavian vein.[17] This testimony corroborated the belief that the blood sample I took accurately reflected the amount of drugs Sloan ingested on the day she died.

All three drugs can appear elevated in samples taken after death, argued yet another toxicologist, who testified that, in his opinion, the drug levels found in Sloan's body after her death did not accurately reflect what was in her system when she died. As a result, he contended, the finding that the mixture of the three drugs led to her death was inaccurate.[18]

Two more experts called by the defense, a toxicologist and a Missouri forensic pathologist and medical examiner, Dr. Miles Jones, agreed that the toxicology screen was most likely distorted. Dr. Jones argued that the questionable results should result in a cause of death listed as "undetermined."[19] A conduction system study of the heart, he opined, may have revealed the true cause of why Sloan's heart malfunctioned, but in cross-examination he admitted that he could not dismiss the possibility of a mixed-drug intoxication.[20]

Yet none of the experts could say without question what effect redistribution had, if any, on the drug levels found in Sloan's system after death. Without another cause of death, though, the diagnosis of mixed-drug intoxication became a diagnosis of exclusion. It was the only proposed cause of death that made sense given the evidence available.

In the end of this cacophony of expert medical opinions, the jury heard the voices of the medical experts consulted by the prosecution. The expert testimony, coupled with the overwhelming evidence that Dr. Stiller prescribed massive amounts of drugs in combinations that could lead to a fatal overdose, led the jury to find Dr. Stiller guilty on both counts— second-degree murder and the unauthorized practice of medicine. The case progressed to Michigan's Court of Appeals, which supported the lower court's ruling. Dr. Stiller is currently serving concurrent terms of two to four years for unauthorized practice of medicine and eight to twenty years for second-degree murder. While eligible for parole since 2004, at the time of writing, Dr. Stiller still resides in a Michigan correctional institution. His maximum discharge date is 2014.

Yet one question remains: Why? What motivated Dr. Stiller to prescribe such excessive and dangerous amounts of drugs? Is this a case of "bad medicine," in which Dr. Stiller did not realize or acknowledge the danger in his actions? Or did some other, more insidious motive lie under the mountain of prescriptions given to Loretta Sloan? It was speculated that Dr. Stiller had some motive for killing Sloan, but no evidence existed to support such a claim.

According to Berrien County prosecutor and chief trial attorney Mike Sepic, Dr. Stiller's rather enormous ego accounts for the plethora of prescriptions he doled out to Sloan—and who knows what medications he prescribed to other patients. He felt as though he could treat what ailed Sloan, and he felt as if he could do no wrong.[21]

Ernest Stiller liked to help people, according to the prosecutor. Sepic characterized Dr. Stiller as a highly charismatic individual who possessed a "very gregarious personality."[22] He once practiced medicine in Indiana, but for the few years prior to his arrest, he worked as an expert witness in worker's compensation cases in La Porte, Indiana, commuting from his residence just across the border in Three Oaks, Michigan.

In fact, Dr. Stiller acted like a medical philanthropist—the medical world's version of Albert Schweitzer. Although he no longer practiced medicine, Stiller liked to help people and often provided medical advice for free to casual acquaintances who sought it, often at a Three Oaks restaurant/bar; when he deemed it appropriate and necessary, he wrote prescriptions for these casual acquaintances.

Loretta Sloan didn't meet Stiller in a Michigan tavern, though; she sought Dr. Stiller's help when he did practice medicine from an office in Indiana. She was and remained his patient, despite the fact that he no longer worked in the Indiana practice and Sloan lived in Michigan, a state in which Dr. Stiller did not possess a license to practice medicine. According to applicable law, Dr. Stiller could legally write prescriptions in Michigan, though, if he were licensed in Indiana and practiced there. However, since he did not practice medicine in Indiana, he could not legally write prescriptions in Michigan.

Ernest Stiller may have been trying to help his patient, Loretta Sloan, in accordance with the Hippocratic Oath, but this help proved fatal. Ultimately, his fate in court would balance on an argument of forensic experts regarding blood, and if it can in fact lie.

In the late nineteenth century, before the birth of modern medicine, salesmen sold patent medicines. These medicines—with colorful names such as Ayers Cathartic Pills, Drake's Plantation Bitters, Merchant's Gargling Oil, Ring's Vegetable Ambrosia, and Wright's Indian Vegetable Pills—supposedly cured any ailment in existence. Ayers Pills, for example, provided "an unfailing remedy for constipation, indigestion, dyspepsia, biliousness, heartburn, loss of appetite, foul stomach and breath, nausea, flatulency, dizziness, headache, numbness, loss of memory, jaundice, diarrhea, dysentery, and disorders of the liver." And people, ignorant of the contents in the bottles, purchased them with the hope that the medicines would cure whatever ailed them.

Unknown to many who relied on them, these panaceas often contained harmful substances. When divers salvaged a few crates of intact bottles of Drake's Plantation Bitters from a Civil War–era shipwreck half buried in a river bottom, chemical analysis revealed that Drakes contained, among other substances, the poison strychnine.

We've come a long way . . . or have we?

*****

Will Jacob Dillon's blood provide the answer to what caused his death, or will the autopsy reveal another cause of death? The physical examination of Jacob Dillon continues. . . .

A small hole, the circumference of a ballpoint pen, sits on the left side of Dillon's chest. It's nothing sinister like a bullet entrance wound where a .32 slug tore through his heart: the hole represents a test done postmortem during the initial examination at the hospital that admitted him.

"What are you doing?" Tobin asks as he watches me stretch Dillon's left arm to the side, where the arm remains fixed, frozen in space and time.

"I always look on the forearms and wrists for evidence of intravenous drug use or previous suicide attempts." No such evidence exists, though, but I do find an abrasion on the underside of Dillon's arm that I sketch onto the clipboard.

I also note a scrape on Dillon's left shoulder and sketch it on the diagram. Thousands of pale red dots—broken blood vessels, or petechiae—cover his back. Unlike in "The Rough Sex Case" (see chapter 4), though, these broken blood vessels (called Tardieu spots) likely did not occur as a result of a crushing force applied to his torso—the pattern does not fit. In this case, the broken blood vessels resulted from the lividity, or the settling of the blood after death.

Apart from the scrape under Dillon's left arm, which could have resulted from the impromptu wrestling at Thursday's party, nothing suspicious is found; the autopsy now moves to the internal examination.

Paul Davison slices through Dillon's chest, creating the Y-incision. He cuts through the ribs around Dillon's sternum and pulls off the breastplate to reveal the organs under the protective rib cage. "We follow the same procedure for every autopsy," Davison explains to the high school intern who watches in awe as he lifts the purple lungs out of he cavity. "We check for fluid in and around the lungs."

Paul collects various fluids with a needle the size and appearance of which would make anyone flinch (the syringe's barrel or tube is nearly the size of a half dollar in circumference): urine from the bladder and femoral-vein blood for toxicology testing; bile from the gall bladder to confirm, if necessary, blood levels of a drug; and fluid from the eye (vitreous humor), which is used to test for alcohol and other conditions such as diabetes and is aspirated through a smaller bore needle. Kent County tests each victim for the presence of HIV. Paul holds up a card, like a square index card separated into four quadrants, with four quarter-sized blots of blood—one in each quadrant. The Kent County pathology team, as a routine procedure, always takes DNA samples of each victim for later reference. The most common use for such cards is to confirm identity; DNA testing could also be performed to confirm paternity.

Next, Davison reaches under the top flap of the Y-incision and inserts his right hand into Dillon's throat from the inside of the body cavity to remove the upper part of the airway (larynx or voice box) and the first part of the esophagus (the pharynx) to check for patency (openness) and disease. "I have to be careful to not cut the carotid arteries," he explains. "The funeral home will need them for embalming."

Paul works quickly; in fifteen minutes, he has removed most of the internal organs and placed them in large, round stainless-steel bowls.

While Paul, using a pair of scissors, opens Dillon's intestines in the washbasin at one end of the autopsy table on which the deceased rests, I begin the examination of Dillon's heart. After the lengthy examination, during which I made a series of cuts along the coronary arteries to determine the presence of narrowed arteries, no evidence of heart disease is found, and thus, there is no reason to believe that Dillon could have died of a heart attack.

Heart disease in a twenty-six-year-old would be a rare, but not impossible discovery. We autopsied a twenty-six-year-old a few weeks ago who had severe coronary arteriosclerosis, but this was an inherited condition. In other words, you would not want to be related to that young man.

As I progress through my examination of each organ, Davison prepares Dillon's head for removal of the brain for dissection and examination. Paul slices through Dillon's scalp. He grips the front flap with both hands and tugs it down and forward to expose the off-white cranium. Inside Dillon's cranium could lie the culprit (such as a subdural hematoma) that led to his untimely demise.

The Stryker saw grinds as Davison works its circular blade back and forth through Dillon's skull. After completing the incision, he inserts a small wedge into the crack to pry open the calvarium, or skullcap. With a little effort, the calvarium comes off with a sucking sound. Under the protective dura membrane that lines the underside of the skull he can find no evidence of hemorrhage. Although Dillon's brain is swollen, he did not suffer from a traumatic head injury or brain aneurism that could have led to his death. So what killed him?

The absence of subdural hematoma, or bleeding under the dura that would indicate he sustained a potentially lethal blow to the head, is disappointing, and disturbing, because the internal examination revealed no other possible cause of death. An old medical proverb states, "When you hear the sound of hooves, look for horses, not zebras." In reference to forensic pathology, a zebra represents an unusual cause of death. Forensic pathologists don't like to find zebras in their morgues, because corralling them can prove very difficult.

Continuing the internal examination of Dillon's organs, the spleen is bread-loafed (cut into cross sections) on the cutting board with a large knife. I lay out a slice of liver to conduct the "finger test," which pathologists will conduct to determine if years of heavy alcohol consumption have caused severe scarring (cirrhosis).

"Poke your finger into the liver," I tell Tobin, whose furled brow indicates his confusion about my request. He gently pokes his finger into the liver, which creates a shallow indentation that disappears as quickly as it appeared.

"Like this."

A firm jab with my index finger into the liver punches a button-sized hole through the slice. The liver of a person with alcoholic cirrhosis becomes very tough; one cannot perforate it with a finger jab. Cirrhosis also occurs as a terminal complication of hepatitis. The "finger test" indicates that this victim suffered from neither alcoholic nor hepatitis-induced cirrhosis.

Next comes the examination of Dillon's stomach contents, which are emptied into a large, plastic beaker. A thick, pink-beige mixture fills the tube—the victim's last meal, digested. The stomach contents can provide a rough guide to the time of death. Generally, it takes about two hours for a meal to pass from the stomach to the small intestine, but pathologists must be careful not to draw conclusions based on this general principle. Certain circumstances can impede digestion. For instance, stress, such as that experienced by the victim of an abduction, may cause the last meal to remain in the stomach. I would not want to send someone to prison estimating the time of death on the stomach contents alone. I use stomach contents to date time of death as a ballpark figure only. I cut open the stomach and spread its thin surface across the cutting board. The inside of it—a pink-brown color—looks like the inside of an old PVC pipe used as a sink drain.

Pathologists sometimes do err by drawing conclusions based solely on stomach contents, a situation that occurred just recently when a forensic pathologist on a nonfiction television show drew an erroneous conclusion of time of death based on stomach contents.

Next, I section Dillon's brain into slices, each about half an inch thick. Nothing in the brain—no "ruptured berries," no hemorrhages—indicates that Dillon hit his head hard enough to cause a lethal injury.

Would the hippocampi provide some answers about Dillon's

untimely death? The seahorse-shaped hippocampus (named after the Greek word for seahorse) is tiny and can fit inside the palm (the human brain contains two hippocampi). The hippocampus contains the recent memory systems of the human computer, and is a primary area destroyed by Alzheimer's disease. Anoxia, or the lack of oxygen to the brain, also causes damage to the hippocampus, so this portion of the brain offers vital information to the forensic pathologist. With a suffocation or some other cause of death that deprives the brain of oxygen, the cells of the hippocampus will show damage if the patient survives for about twelve hours or longer.

Throughout this autopsy, the same nagging question keeps arising like an echo off the morgue walls: What killed Jacob Dillon?

Perhaps a drug overdose. We know he had a high blood-alcohol level, which, when mixed with a drug such as Oxycontin, could kill him. Everyone else involved in this case realizes that homicides complicate matters; they lead to charges, court dates, and appearances to testify. The discovery of evidence leading to a cause of death as an accidental drug overdose would provide the easiest solution for the medical and legal professionals involved. But the most convenient answer does not always fit the circumstances or the forensic evidence.

Another possibility: when horsing around, if two or three men pounced on him and compressed his chest, he could have suffocated. I will contact the authorities and urge them to conduct a thorough interview of witnesses about exactly what occurred that night, because context may help explain what force took Dillon's life.

The report that Dillon's breathing sounded like snoring—snoring respirations—is consistent with an anoxic brain injury, or one in which some force, such as a drug overdose, results in a decreased flow of oxygen to the brain.

Perhaps his blood will answer the question. And so all involved in this case will await the results of the toxicology screen before I can rule on the cause of death. Dillon's blood should answer the question, because blood does not lie.

A few days later, the results of the toxicology report prove, like an exclamation mark at the end of a sentence, that Jacob Dillon's tragic and untimely demise came as a result of a mixed-drug intoxication; the com-bination of Oxycontin and alcohol overwhelmed him. Like Loretta Sloan, the mixture and quantity of drugs in his body proved too much. The proof? An examination of his blood.

And blood does not lie.

THE LAST CHAPTER: LIFE

Midwinter 2005
Spectrum Health, Blodgett Campus
East Grand Rapids, Michigan

Note to the reader: this chapter concludes the case of Richard Sullivan,
which began in chapter 4, "Red Sky in the Morning."

Almost five months to the day after the body of Richard Sullivan arrived at the Kent County Morgue, Ottawa County prosecutor Ron Frantz would do his best to bring justice to the bereaved relatives and to the slain; the final chapter of Sullivan's tragedy would be written in the next few days, with the murder trial commencing at one o'clock this afternoon. The trial represents a final chapter in a different context as well; Tobin will be watching as I offer expert testimony, this being the medical examiner's final responsibility in a process that begins with the discovery of the victim's body. My testimony will also mark the conclusion of a case Tobin followed from its very beginning, and it will also mark the final chapter of this narrative.

Approximately five months earlier, in August, Richard Sullivan was found dead in his home, his hands bound behind his back with a lace from his running shoes. Police tracked a suspect through stolen credit cards and Sullivan's missing Pontiac Aztec to the Chicago area, where they arrested Michael Brancaccio. Brancaccio made a partial confession when he claimed that Sullivan lured him to his home on the pretext of a job opportunity and then made a homosexual pass, after which Brancaccio, in a rage, strangled Sullivan. Prosecutors, though, believe that Brancaccio killed Sullivan during an alleged robbery of the victim's house, fueled by his drug habit. The forensic evidence collected during the autopsy detailed in chapter 4, "Red Sky in the Morning," will play a vital role when later this afternoon prosecutors reconstruct what they believe occurred in Sullivan's house.

This first day of the trial, the Kent County medical examiner team's workday began at eight at the morgue. By ten thirty, when Tobin arrives, this morning's cases have not yet been finished. Inside the autopsy room, both autopsy tables are occupied—their tenants laid open by Y-incisions. I am at the workstation flanked by two fourth-year medical students—Jill Jennings and Vincko Zlomislic—watching over my shoulder as I delve into the mysteries posed by the deceased. Paul Davison and Joel Talsma are present, as well—a lot of bodies for the relatively small room. The pale blue color of hospital garb moves about the room, giving the room the feeling of incessant motion. A buzz is in the air—literally—as a high-pitched noise indicates that Paul, wielding the Stryker saw, has begun to open one of the victim's skulls. All occupants are in appropriate attire (masks, gloves, booties) since the room is considered a biosafety hazard zone during autopsies. Tobin remains in the conference room. From the conference room at the opposite end of the corridor leading to the autopsy room, the buzz becomes audible.

The conference room table contains the mundane tools of the medical examiner's daily grind, although anyone who has shadowed the world of a medical examiner, as Tobin has during the past eight months, would question the accuracy of the word "mundane" (nothing in this underworld seems mundane). A pile of papers includes a document titled "Burial-Transit Permit" and four different death certificates—one-page documents that carry the heading "Certificate of Death" above the state of Michigan logo of a shield flanked on one side by an elk and on the other by a moose. The shield contains the scene of a hunter holding a rifle and standing next to a lake, under the word *Tuebor*—Latin for "I will defend."

From the number of death certificates on the table, Tobin can deduce that the Grim Reaper worked overtime yesterday. Although confidential, the papers lure him like sirens—forbidden fruit for the curious. Paging through the death certificates, though, is like eavesdropping on an intensely personal conversation.

In the background, faint sounds emanating from the autopsy room provide a narration to the proceedings. The rustling of a plastic bag—the entrail bag—suggests that the autopsies have neared conclusion since Davison has begun to prepare the bodies for transport to the funeral homes. A cacophony of voices—casual conversation among coworkers broken by the occasional laugh—punctuates the end of the autopsy procedure like the period at the end of this sentence. With the autopsies concluded, I will soon move to the afternoon's work: testifying in court about the Richard Sullivan homicide.

A rubber stamp, used to place a facsimile signature on official documents, lies next to a stack of CD-R disks labeled with the names of victims and associated law enforcement agencies. The name on the top disk—"Deb Weiler"—is familiar because this was the suicide victim with the anomalous hemorrhaging in her midsection that led to speculation about her boyfriend's potential role in her death. Next to the disks, almost as if it were another "tool" of the medical examiner, sits a beige, checkered shirt and matching tie—my attire for this afternoon's trial. Jackets and a large blue backpack—personal effects of the medical students in the other room—cover the other end of the table.

Paul Davison shuffles past and enters his office—a room adjacent to the conference room. He recently returned from a ski trip to Colorado, and he is taking a short break before they begin the autopsy of a third victim—they've had a busy day.

With the third autopsy complete, the medical examiner personnel and the fourth-year medical students trade their scrubs for their day's attire (for me, a suit) and head for the hospital cafeteria. After a brief lunch, the two medical students, Tobin, and I will make the forty-minute drive to Grand Haven and the Ottawa County Courthouse, about a half an hour late.

"I have a radar detector in my car," Jill offers as we pull out of the hospital parking structure.

"I have a subpoena, which is just as good," I respond.

Tobin laughs.

The actors who play medical examiners on television often appear in short snippets wielding knives and explaining the cause of death to the detectives, but they spend little "screen time" in court. At the Ottawa County Courthouse, I will perform a vital function: testifying about the death of Richard Sullivan. Like a detective, a medical examiner collects evidence from the body of the victim and, based on that evidence, formulates a theory that re-creates the final moments of the victim's life. Detectives often rely on eyewitnesses to tell the story of a suspicious death. Petechial hemorrhages, skull fractures, and other physiological evidence provide the eyewitnesses on which I rely.

Trial by jury, though, involves a panel of twelve unbiased people—but people nonetheless, whose passions and preconceived notions during a trial sometimes create a vortex that swallows fact, fiction, and occasionally innocent victims.

Unless they have toured the world of the medical examiner, as Tobin has, their preconceived notions of forensic science come primarily from well-scripted television dramas. The proliferation of crime shows, manifest in the wildly popular *CSI* and its spin-offs, offers to the thirsty audience real stories and real portraits, but veiled by a medium that requires a solution be found within an hour. Actors play roles; fact becomes buffered in TV land by the need to entice audiences with twisted plots, compelling characters, and satisfying conclusions (conclusions sometimes fail to satisfy, indeed, quite the opposite may be intended, but have you seen a television show that lacks closure?).

Most who watch crime dramas will admit to a certain morbid fascination with forensic science, particularly true-crime junkies. And they have many fictional and nonfictional shows from which to choose: *Law & Order, American Justice, City Confidential, Cold Case Files*—they queue like police officers in a true-crime parade across the television set. Viewers have been to many fictional morgues but not real ones. While good fiction suspends disbelief, it remains fiction. The audience can always pad a morose conclusion with the terse truth that what they have watched unfold was just a TV show.

For a shot of stronger stuff, viewers may turn to a reality-type show like *Dr. G Medical Examiner*, but here again one finds a reality tempered by the limits of the television medium. And as authentic an experience as the producers attempt, television delivers an experience in two sensory dimensions only; the viewer still can't feel, smell, or taste the business of forensic pathology—unless Smell-o-rama makes a dramatic and unexpected comeback, television cannot express the smell of a "decomp" or a "stinker."

And sometimes these telepathologists make mistakes that go uncorrected, and the television audience cannot ask questions. Indeed, viewers without experience in forensic science, which would include the vast majority, wouldn't know what questions to ask in the first place; they eagerly swallow and digest like junk food this "junk science," as some have come to call it, and like junk food, it is not good for one's health—especially if you are a prosecutor.

Juries, after digesting "junk science," can enter a courtroom with a warped sense of forensic science based on what they've observed on television. Many prosecutors worry that this effect, which some have dubbed the "*CSI* effect," has begun to affect the business of the courtroom, as juries demand that prosecutors produce evidence such as DNA comparison—even when it's not warranted.[1] Taken to the most dangerous degree, some prosecutors fear juries may vote to acquit based on a lack of what they consider necessary evidence to prove guilt—the "*CSI* effect." Without a DNA link between Marvin Gabrion and his alleged victim, Rachel Timmerman, such as a skin particle embedded underneath her fingernail, for example, today a jury might vote to acquit, despite other powerful evidence pointing to his guilt (see chapter 4, "The Oxford Lake Death Penalty Case").

The "*CSI* effect" has another potentially dangerous manifestation; juries may view anyone who dons pale blue surgical scrubs or white lab coats as an "expert," despite questionable credentials, dubious experience, or even a complete lack of suitable knowledge. Of course, this effect may have existed well before the proliferation of forensic-type television programs.

While this "*CSI* Effect" may or may not have played a role in the 1992 trial of Larry Souter (*Law & Order* first aired on NBC in 1990), the case of the "Message in a Bottle" presents an excellent example of when the presentation of forensic evidence can lead to tragic consequences. Sometimes the evidence appears to assume a personality all of its own.

MESSAGE IN A BOTTLE

At three o'clock on the morning of August 25, 1979, two truckers found a nineteen-year-old girl lying unconscious in the middle of the highway. Later that morning, Kristy Ringler died of severe head injuries. Dr. Steven C. Bauserman conducted an autopsy during which he found two large lacerations on her head: a five-inch wound on her forehead and another on the right side of her head. Ringler died when she sustained a fatal brain injury caused by blows from some sharp-edged object. Something or someone struck her with a sharp-edged object that cut her scalp but did not fracture her skull. Dr. Bauserman believed that either someone struck her with a sharp-edged object or a car hit her.[2]

At the scene, Deputy Sheriff John Sutton interviewed Larry Souter, the last person who saw Ringler alive at a party they attended down the road at the home of Anna Mae Carpenter. After the interview, Sutton drove Souter, who was drunk, to his friend's house.

The next morning, a police officer found an empty pint bottle of Canadian Club whiskey in a ditch by the house where the party had occurred the night before. Souter admitted to police that the bottle belonged to him, and he cooperated with the investigation by giving investigators the boots he wore the morning Ringler died; perhaps if he did kill Ringler and carried her body as the prosecution alleged, his boots might contain spots of her blood or strands of her hair (Souter's clothing contained no visible spots of blood). The bottle would play a key role in answering a question that would remain unresolved for twenty-five years: What happened to Kristy Ringler?

An analysis of the bottle turned up blood on the label, which cast suspicion over Souter, who steadfastly denied any part in Ringler's death and told investigators that he cut his finger on a door handle at the Carpenter home during the party. Since both he and Ringler shared the blood type found on the bottle label—type A—the presence of the blood proved nothing. Type A blood is very common and is shared by 43 percent of the American populace.[3]

Investigators also found glass on Ringler's jeans, but further analysis revealed that the glass did not fit the type used in car headlights, and it didn't come from the whiskey bottle either, because it was not brown in color. Perhaps the glass came from something like the side mirror on a vehicle.

The chief investigator, Detective Charles Foster, did not believe that a car hit Ringler.[4] Except for a small pool of blood under the victim's head, the small amount of blood at the scene and on her clothes suggested to him that she was killed elsewhere and then placed on the road. The police consulted a forensic pathologist, Dr. Laurence Simson, who disagreed with Foster and opined that Ringler's injuries did indeed suggest a car struck her.[5] The Newaygo County prosecutor decided not to pursue criminal charges against Larry Souter, and the question of how Kristy Ringler died remained unanswered. The case went cold.

Four years later, the bottle would reappear as Detective Foster presented his case to Dr. Ronald Graeser, the Newaygo County medical examiner. Dr. Graeser studied the autopsy photos by projecting them onto a wall; he concurred with Dr. Bauserman's conclusion that Ringler was struck with a sharp-edged object, but in matching the bottle with the wounds, Dr. Graeser claimed that the whiskey bottle could have caused her fatal head injuries. After reviewing the slides (but not the bottle), I concurred that, if the bottle in fact had a sharp edge, it could have caused the injuries to Ringer's head. Still, no charges against Souter followed. The case went cold again.

Then in 1991 a newly elected sheriff vowed to bring justice to the county's unsolved homicides. The death of Kristy Ringler was reopened and original witnesses were interviewed again, but no new evidence surfaced. Dr. Graeser reviewed the forensic evidence and wrote a report in which he opined that the whiskey bottle caused Ringler's injuries and stated that the idea Ringler was struck by the side mirror of a car was "virtually impossible."[6] Despite the lack of any new evidence to support such a claim, and after nearly thirteen years had passed since the young woman's death, Larry Souter was arrested in November on second-degree murder charges. In the trial that followed, the jury would consider two vastly different scenarios of what occurred that night.

According to the prosecution at Larry Souter's 1992 trial for second-degree murder, a drama such as the following played itself out in the wee hours of August 25, 1979, with Souter cast as the jilted-turned-murderous paramour and Kristy Ringler as the girl whose birthday bash turned into a tragedy.

They meet at the Lamplight Inn, where she works, on a balmy evening in late August 1979. She is celebrating her nineteenth birthday, but after the Lamplight closes, they decide to continue the party at the home of a friend. After a few more drinks, they both have few worries and even fewer inhibitions; their party, which has now become intense and personal, moves to the yard, where they kiss. He hands her the brown glass bottle—a pint of Canadian Club Whiskey—and she wraps her lips around its mouth. The whiskey burns her lips, and her throat for a few seconds after she takes a drink, then a warmth appears like a bonfire in her stomach.

She hands the pint back to her paramour, who takes a sip from the bottle, then places his hand on the back of her neck and gently tugs her toward him. As they kiss, he caresses her back with his arm. He is still holding the whiskey bottle. After a few seconds, their passion carries them to the ground.

After a few minutes, she experiences a change of heart and pushes his chest, attempting to free herself from his grasp. She will go no farther down this road with him. Not tonight. Not without a clear mind.

He doesn't understand. Her entire body seemed to acquiesce to his advances. He pulls her toward him; she struggles, but the more she struggles, the tighter his grasp becomes. Their tryst has degenerated into an impromptu wrestling match.

He feels a surge of anger and remembers the bottle he holds in his hand. As if a reflex he cannot control, he raises the bottle and smashes it against her head. As she realizes what is happening, she gasps for breath, the raspy, muted sound inaudible over the sounds of the party in the background. The bottle strikes her skull with a hollow ring. Her body becomes limp, and she falls to the grass in a pile, blood from the five-inch wound on her forehead shining under the moonlight.

What happened? he wonders as he looks at her body on the ground beneath him. He can feel his heart beat against his rib cage as he ponders his options. He wants to call for help, but when he opens his mouth, no sound emerges. He looks around but sees no one.

Then his devious side takes control. No one in sight: no witnesses. A two-lane highway runs past the mobile home: the perfect alibi. He slides the pint into the back pocket of his jeans, leans down, and lifts her body over his shoulder.

Twenty minutes later, exhausted and drenched with sweat, he lays her on her back on the shoulder of the two-lane highway. A small circle of blood appears under her head as she lay unconscious. She will appear the victim of a hit-and-run accident. He draws the back of his hand across his forehead to remove the sweat. He remembers the pint, pulls it from his pocket, and holds it up to the light. Just about one or two good drinks left. He takes a drink, turns, and begins his walk back toward the mobile home. Minutes later, at three in the morning, Ringler is found lying on the road, unconscious. The partygoers, including Larry Souter, race to the scene of what appears a hit-and-run accident. Along the way, he tosses the pint whiskey bottle into the ditch by the side of the road. Souter's plan appears to have worked. Later that morning, Ringler dies of her head injury.

The prosecution came to the trial armed with a good deal of evidence, albeit circumstantial evidence, to prove this scenario. One of the truck drivers testified that when he came upon the body he was surprised at how clean Ringler's clothes appeared, noting that her shirt remained tucked into her jeans. Detective Charles Foster, the chief investigator in the case, also found suspicious the lack of blood and dirt on the victim's clothes.[7]

Except for a small puddle under Ringler's head, several witnesses stated that they noticed very little blood on her clothes, suggesting that she may have been placed at the scene. The prosecution was unable to present Ringler's clothes during the trial (they were not available after more than twelve years; they had been lost).[8]

Three physicians testified as expert witnesses that the five-inch gash on Ringler's head was consistent with someone striking her with a bottle like the one Souter possessed that night: Dr. Bauserman, who conducted Ringler's original autopsy in 1979; Dr. Graeser, who examined the evidence, including autopsy slides and the bottle; and I, who acted as a forensic consultant (and the only board-certified forensic pathologist of the group).

The prosecution did have the bottle, retrieved from the ditch where Souter tossed it that night when Kristy Ringler sustained her fatal head injury. Dr. Graeser testified that over time the bottle lost its sharp edge, but in 1979 the bottle definitely had a sharp edge that could have created the lacerations found on Ringler's head.[9]

Souter's defense scripted a different scene:

> *The two meet at the Lamplight Inn, where she is celebrating her nineteenth birthday. As the Lamplight closes, the two decide to continue the party at a friend's home down the road. The two find themselves locked into each other's arms in the yard, when she decides she does not want to continue. She stands, announces that she is going home, turns, and walks away.*
>
> *He pleads with her to come back; he will drive her home. He follows her for a short distance and stops, watching her fade into the black night. He shrugs at the missed opportunity and laments the curt ending of their private party. Behind him, voices emanate from the house party, and he decides to rejoin the fun.*
>
> *She stumbles down the road. The driver does not see her until it's too late . . . the night is dark and he's tired. The bone-cracking knock as the car sideswipes her and the side mirror smashes into her head startles the driver, and in his rear-view mirror he sees something fall on the road. The driver wants to stop, but he cannot take his foot off of the gas pedal, as if instinct has taken over. He speeds away into the distance.*
>
> *A few minutes later, word reaches the Carpenter home that two truck drivers found Ringler sprawled out, unconscious, down the road. The partygoers race to the scene. On the way, Souter tosses the pint bottle into the ditch beside the highway.*

Souter's defense had reason to believe it could create reasonable doubt in the jury: three people witnessed Souter's return to the Carpenter home. One of them, Marvin Carpenter, testified that Souter did not appear to act suspiciously and was not sweating or out of breath, which he would have been if traumatized by committing a murder and/or carrying Ringler's body nine hundred feet from the Carpenter house where she was found.[10]

Deputy Sheriff John Sutton, who interviewed Souter at the scene, testified at the trial that he did not see blood on Souter.[11] The bottle that represented the alleged murder weapon contained blood on the label. Souter explained the source of this blood: he cut his finger on a sharp doorknob at the Carpenter home.[12] Since both he and the victim shared the type A blood found on the bottle's label, the presence of the blood does not indicate that it came from Ringler—a notion underlined by the fact that so many Americans share the same blood type.

Neither the bottle nor Souter's boots, collected by the police the next day, contained any of the victim's hair.

A forensic pathologist consulted by the police, Dr. Laurence Simson (who testified for the defense), believed that the pint whiskey bottle could not have been the murder weapon because it did not have a sharp edge that could have caused the gashes on the victim's head. Instead, he maintained, Ringler most likely was hit by a car.[13]

Despite the evidence presented by the defense, on March 13, 1992, the jury convicted Souter of second-degree murder. He received a sentence of twenty to sixty years in prison for the senseless, brutal murder of Ringler. The story did not end here, however; Souter's drama had just begun.

During the next four years, several appeals followed. Souter argued that the twelve-and-a-half-year lapse between Ringler's death and his arrest represented a prejudice and violated his right to due process of law. The Michigan Court of Appeals rejected Souter's argument and supported the lower court's decision. The Michigan Supreme Court deferred the matter to the trial court to conduct a hearing as to whether the delay violated Souter's due process rights. On December 30, 1996, the trial court found that it did not. Souter, it seemed, was all out of appeals and would remain behind bars for what looked like the rest of his life.

Undeterred, over the next few years, Souter collected new evidence to support his innocence, and more appeals followed. In 1999 he appealed to the Newaygo Circuit Court for a new trial, but the court denied his request for a new trial because it maintained that the new evidence was in fact not new and existed at the time of the 1992 trial, and the new evidence he wished to present would most likely not lead to an acquittal. Eight months later, the Michigan Court of Appeals denied his application because he failed to meet the one-year deadline between the time he discovered the new evidence and the date of his application. On January 30, 2001, the Michigan Supreme Court confirmed the lower courts' decision. No one, it seemed, wanted to consider Larry Souter's new evidence and his possible innocence.

In 2002 the relentless Souter filed a petition for a writ of habeas corpus with the United States District Court for the Western District of Michigan. His defense team argued that denying him a new trial based on the new evidence amounted to a violation of Souter's due process rights. The evidence presented as support for his petition consisted of five key pieces that Larry Souter had amassed over the years, five formidable new "witnesses" for the defense: four affidavits from forensics experts indicating that the whiskey bottle may not have caused Ringler's injuries, and photographs of Ringler's clothes showing significant amounts of dark spots that could be blood (recall that the lack of blood on her clothes created some of the suspicion that a car did not hit Ringler). The foundations of Larry Souter's conviction, these five pieces of evidence suggested, had been built on sand and were now crumbling.

The three photographs of the clothes Kristi Ringler wore when she was killed, showing what could be blood, provided a convincing piece of reasonable doubt that Larry Souter murdered Kristi Ringler. The photographs, which Souter claimed were unavailable at the 1992 trial, show the back of Ringler's clothes stained with dark red material. Remember, the lack of blood at the scene caused speculation in 1979 that Ringler was murdered elsewhere and placed in the road to appear the victim of a hit-and-run accident. Yet no blood appeared on Larry Souter, either, and if he killed Ringler, wouldn't spots of blood have appeared on his clothes?

At Souter's 1992 trial, the state presented a convincing answer to this question: the State posited that the lack of blood on Ringler accounted for the lack of blood on Souter. In other words, if her wounds did not bleed profusely, he could have avoided bloodstains when he murdered and/or transported her. The presence of blood-soaked clothes, however, would not only counter this speculation, but it would also raise an interesting question: If her head wounds did bleed profusely, how could Souter have murdered Ringler and carried her body nine hundred feet to the scene without obtaining any spots of visible blood on his clothes or boots? The photographs seemed to support the possibility that a car struck Ringler as she walked home that night.

While Souter had negotiated the rapids of the justice system, the bottle that helped to convict him reemerged and resulted in the other four pieces of evidence, in the form of affidavits, presented to the US District Court. At the 1992 trial, the prosecution argued that the bottle contained a message that proved Souter's guilt; the bottle's sharp edge caused Ringler's wounds, and the blood on its label matched her blood type. In the years since his conviction, though, the bottle began to tell a different story, as the experts who testified at the original murder trial became engaged in a bizarre case of spin the bottle.

Through a private investigator, Stephen Pletcher, Souter interviewed officials from the manufacturer of the bottle, Hiram Walker and Sons, Ltd., who maintained that the manufacturing process made the existence of a sharp edge a very unlikely possibility. Hiram Walker and Sons, Ltd., had sold over one hundred million bottles of the same type as the one Souter possessed, and the company had never received a complain about an edge sharp enough to cut a person's fingers.[14] This fact would make the bottle Souter possessed one in a million, if it contained a sharp edge as Dr. Graeser maintained at the 1992 trial.

A forensic scientist, Thomas Kubic, examined the bottle and claimed that the bottle did not currently have a sharp edge, and it never did.[15] But Kubic examined the bottle years after the alleged murder. Perhaps, as Dr. Graeser maintained (though he did not explain how), the sharp edge became worn in the succeeding years. After all, a quarter of a century passed since that morning in August 1979. Yet, in another affidavit, Edward Gundy, a police laboratory technician who examined the bottle during the original investigation, stated that the bottle he examined in 1979 did not have the sharp edge described by Dr. Graeser.[16]

Still, during the 1992 trial the prosecution had three expert witnesses, all of whom agreed that the bottle could have caused Kristy Ringler's fatal head injuries. By the time Souter filed his appeal to the US District Court in January 2002, though, two of the three would reverse their opinions.

In 1992 Dr. Graeser asked me a hypothetical question: Could a sharp-edged bottle have caused Kristi Ringler's wounds? I replied that, if the bottle had a sharp rim, it could have caused the wounds.

After learning that the bottle could not have had a sharp edge and after viewing autopsy slides not available to me in 1992, I reversed the opinion that I gave in the trial; now, I stated in an affidavit, as evidence appeared that indicated the bottle did not contain a sharp edge in 1979, I believed it unlikely that the bottle could have inflicted the wounds on Kristy Ringler's head. When I studied the bottle in 1992, it did not contain a sharp edge, but I based my opinion that it could have been the murder weapon on Dr. Graeser's claim that in 1979 the bottle did contain a sharp edge.

Dr. Bauserman, who conducted the autopsy in 1979, also reversed his opinion, and deferred the matter to me. In his affidavit, Bauserman also attacked Dr. Graeser's forensic expertise and suggested that Graeser, who had been not only my former student but also a former student of Dr. Bauserman, struggled in his studies.[17]

At the 1979 trial, the bottle represented the only physical evidence that connected Souter to Ringler's death. Two of the three expert witnesses now doubted that connection.

This new evidence, Souter's defense maintained, indicated his innocence and as such created an exception to the statute of limitations to file the habeas corpus petition. The district court, however, disagreed that the evidence proved Souter's innocence because none of the five pieces ruled out the possibility that the bottle could have caused Ringler's injuries, so Souter went one step higher on the ladder of judicial appeals.

The US Court of Appeals for the Sixth Circuit considered his case in September 2004. Finally, Souter found an audience that would consider his new evidence for what it represented: the likelihood that the system had failed Larry Souter and had sent an innocent man to prison. Once again, discussion revolved around the pint whiskey bottle he carried the morning Kristy Ringler died—a bottle that would not go away.

Although the US Court of Appeals judges agreed with the lower courts that Souter failed to meet the deadline for his habeas corpus petition, they found that the new evidence called into question the 1992 verdict of guilty. After the United States Court of Appeals for the Sixth Circuit decided in his favor, it looked like Larry Souter would get his second "day" in court, but then his case took a shocking, unforeseen twist.

The evidence cast doubt on Souter's guilt, but it raised a disturbing question: If Souter didn't murder Kristy Ringler, what happened to her? It seemed like Ringler's death would end in a file of unsolved homicides—again.

Someone who could answer this question read about Souter's appeals. And then she came forward—again. Carla Dimkoff contacted John Smietanka and Anne Buckleitner, two attorneys on Souter's defense team, and told her story about that night in 1979.

Dimkoff's father appeared at the Lamplight Inn that night; he had come from Tennessee, where he lived. He stayed late before leaving for his daughter's house, which would have placed his Dodge Champion motor home on the road that morning.

The next morning, she noticed her father replacing a broken side mirror. He evaded her questions about the mirror, finished replacing the broken one, and rather than discarding the damaged one, took it with him when he left. Since Kristi Ringler was two and a half inches taller than the side mirror on the motor home, her injuries could have occurred when she was struck by the mirror's edge.[18] This possibility also fits the forensic evidence; the sharp edges of the mirror could have caused the two gashes on Ringler's head.

Despite the fact that her statements could implicate her father in a hit-and-run homicide, Dimkoff approached police, who listened to her story. Investigators contacted her father in Tennessee, but apparently decided not to pursue the lead, though they did file a report, which remained buried until Souter's attorneys filed a Freedom of Information Request with the Newaygo sheriff's department. The attorneys found evidence that corroborated Dimkoff's claims that she contacted and told her story to Newaygo police. Why didn't she come forward earlier? Dimkoff said she didn't know about Souter's 1992 trial, and only learned about his conviction from news reports years later.[19]

In early April 2005, United States District Court judge Gordon Quist ordered Souter's release from prison after the fifty-three-year-old man had been incarcerated for thirteen years.

Dimkoff's story provides a clearer picture of what may have happened that night. As the Lamplight closed, Souter and Ringler left the bar at 2:20 AM and went to the Carpenter residence, where they fooled around for a few minutes before Ringler decided to walk home. Perhaps it took her twenty minutes to walk the nine hundred feet where she was found at approximately 3:00 AM. Sometime between 2:20 and 3:00 AM, Dimkoff boarded his motor home and started for his daughter's residence. His route placed him on a collision course with Ringler.

Of course, without Dimkoff to corroborate his daughter's statements—without his version of the events that occurred on the morning of August 25, 1979—no one can know for sure what happened to Kristy Ringler. Since Dimkoff had passed away five years before his daughter came forward in the spring of 2005, his possible role in Ringler's untimely demise will remain speculative.

What is certain is that there was a message in the bottle: the justice system failed to bring to light what happened to Ringler, and it failed Larry Souter—an innocent man who spent thirteen years of his life in a cage. The bottle struck the justice system in the face, giving it a black eye—actually, two black eyes, a broken nose, and a fractured jaw.

*****

Thirty minutes after leaving Spectrum Health's Blodgett Campus, we arrive at the Ottawa County Courthouse. It is a blustery day with a high of one degree Fahrenheit and a wind that effectively brings the temperature to about ten below zero. To the west, a dark gray tone to the cloud cover over Lake Michigan tells of a storm that will hit west Michigan tonight, bringing with it an expected half a foot of sleet and snow. In the courtroom on the third floor, where the death of one man is explored and the fate of another lies in the balance, the temperature is much warmer—literally and figuratively.

Inside the courthouse, people queue to walk through the door-shaped metal detector, and the temperature rises when the machine "notices" the small penknife on my keychain. Under no circumstances, the Ottawa County sheriff's deputy monitoring the metal detector explains, can she allow me to enter with the small Swiss Army knife. But we're at least a half an hour late.

> Can I give her the knife?
> No.
> Can I leave the knife?
> No.
> But I'm thirty minutes late, can't I . . .
> No.
> But . . .
> No.
> Well . . .
> NO!

After a brief argument and at the officer's insistence, I return the knife to my car as Jill Jennings and Tobin wait for me in the prosecutor's office; I arrive at the office a few minutes later. When we open the door, one member of the prosecutor's office, already aware of the scuffle (the deputy called her), greets us with a nervous smile. "We don't want to upset our star witness." Too late!

"You two kids will want to go up to the trial. You . . . " I turn to the prosecutor's clerk, "I have a bone to pick with you."

Jill and Tobin take the stairs to the third floor, where the court will write the last chapter in the tragedy of Richard Sullivan.

The courtroom is small, with three pewlike benches—the audience gallery—sitting perpendicular to the jury box. The benches are filled with bereaved family members of the defendant and the decedent and journalists scrawling notes into tiny notebooks—all eyes fixed on Sullivan's roommate, who found Sullivan's body and is now in the witness box giving testimony. The defendant, Michael Brancaccio, dressed in a sweater over an off-white shirt and flanked by his two lawyers, sits three rows in front of the medical students and Tobin, who will see me in my courtroom role this afternoon. Brancaccio watches, focused intently on the roommate's testimony. His face is long and thin with an aquiline nose and hazel eyes buried under a slightly jutting brow ridge. He is in his midthirties.

As he surveys the gallery of faces, Tobin realizes that this is the human element to last August's autopsy. This is *pathos*, and some of the faces in the courtroom today, like a painter's canvas, illustrate a picture of human pain and suffering, of tragedy—not the kind that is simulated for the stage or filtered for television, but real tragedy. A woman sitting in the gallery a few rows behind the defendant cuddles with her teenaged daughter, her arm around the girl's shoulders. Her bloodshot, swollen eyes suggest that she has been crying. Murders create tsunamis that engulf everyone involved. The public tends to see court cases with winners and losers. While someone will ultimately win this case, both sides have already lost something.

In this courtroom will be written the final chapter in the sordid murder of Richard Sullivan, who, at fifty-five years of age, died before his time. The twelve members of the jury will attempt to answer one very important question: What motivated the murder of Richard Sullivan? This is not a "whodunit," since the defendant confessed to murdering Richard Sullivan, but rather a "whydunit"?

Brancaccio claims that the decedent made a homosexual pass, and in a fit of rage, he killed Sullivan by strangling him with a shoelace. And his lawyer will attempt to convince the jury that this "heat of passion" killing justifies a second-degree murder conviction or possibly manslaughter with a sentence of three to about twenty years in prison. This argument will be a difficult one to establish since Sullivan's hands were bound behind his back with a second shoelace, which suggests a degree of premeditation.

The prosecutor wants to convince the jury that something more insidious, more calculated occurred—that the defendant, fueled by a "drug lust" for heroin and a need for cash to satisfy his craving, befriended Sullivan, whom he met at a local outlet mall. The two returned to Sullivan's home, where Brancaccio strangled Sullivan with a shoelace. The defendant, the prosecutor will attempt to show, strangled Sullivan twice: the first time was with his hands until his victim lost consciousness. He returned later, bound Sullivan's hands with a shoestring, and fatally strangled him with the lace from the other shoe. The second incident, the prosecution believes, represents premeditation—in other words, first-degree murder and a much, much longer sentence of life without parole.

This is the scenario the prosecution will attempt to prove, and my testimony will provide a crucial piece of evidence in his case: the Sullivan autopsy uncovered forensic evidence that supports the prosecution's theory like a pillar. Without this evidence and an expert witness to back it, the prosecution's case for first-degree murder will collapse. For this reason, I anticipate a contentious cross-examination.

Ottawa County prosecutor Ron Frantz uses the roommate's testimony to establish a material link between the perpetrator and Sullivan's home in order to prove that robbery motivated the crime. On the afternoon of the murder, Riverside police arrested the defendant; at the time of his arrest, he was driving Sullivan's Pontiac Aztec and possessed items taken from the house. With the roommate's testimony, Frantz can establish the victim's ownership of the items—rings, a watch, and two cameras.

Following the testimony of Sullivan's roommate, a parade of witnesses, all sheriff's deputies, provide testimony about the crime scene and the disposition of the body, some pointing to various places on a large poster-sized layout of Sullivan's house on an easel behind the witness box. Did they see any evidence of forced entry? Did they see any evidence of robbery? There was no evidence of forced entry, which helps the defense's case, since the defendant claimed he came to the home after Sullivan invited him, only to make a homosexual pass after they entered the house.

The prosecution calls Wavelet Thompson, the Ottawa County medicolegal death investigator (who performed the death scene investigation) and autopsy assistant. Her black suit matches her raven black hair tied in the back with a large, black bow. At the prosecutor's prompting, she gives a list of qualifications, and characterizes her job as "his eyes"— the medical examiner's eyes at the scene of the crime.

Thompson is personable and aware that the twelve people in the jury box will make the ultimate decision in this case; she looks at them while she answers the prosecutor's questions.

How many autopsies have you seen or assisted? The prosecutor wants to establish her credibility before delving into the specifics of the crime scene.

Hundreds, she answers. Thompson is the opener, warming the stage for the featured act, who has conducted autopsies in the thousands. In her testimony, she details the crime scene, the disposition of Sullivan's body, the position of the shoelace and shoe around Sullivan's neck, and the procedure for moving and transporting his body to the Kent County Morgue in Grand Rapids.

The defense attorney, an elderly man with snow white hair and a slight stoop when he walks, questions Thompson. Anyone involved in crime scene investigation and autopsies meets with tremendous scrutiny in court. One false step and . . .

The judge calls a fifteen-minute recess.

At about three thirty, the prosecution calls me to the stand.

First, the prosecution must establish my credibility, so my testimony begins with answers to a series of questions about my professional background. At Ron Frantz's prompting, I outline my qualifications, a verbal rendition of the résumé hanging in my office in the form of various diplomas: University of Missouri medical school; chief resident at Baylor College of Medicine; forensic pathology training at The University of Texas—Southwestern Medical School Institute of Forensic Sciences. Twenty-two years as forensic pathologist for Kent County; one year as chief medical examiner of Kent County; forensic pathologist for a number of other Michigan counties.

"How many autopsies have you conducted?" Frantz asks.

"About five thousand."

Although to Tobin, who watches intently from the gallery, these credentials may appear to make me a virtually unimpeachable witness, experts can always be impeached. In court their professional credentials represent their armor, their protection against accusations of error, malpractice, and subterfuge. The court declares me an "expert witness"—my armor is strong.

Like a teacher instructing a class of twelve, I look directly at the jury while I explain the role of the forensic pathologist and medical examiner in a homicide investigation. After countless court appearances, I realize that the fate of the case lies in the minds of twelve people whose knowledge of forensic science may extend only as far as the last episode of *CSI* or *Law & Order* they viewed, so I explain in "layperson's language" the job and its jurisdiction. Without jargon or technical language, I explain that the forensic pathologist studies victims of violent death, causes of natural death, and correlates injuries/marks on body with what inflicted injury.

With credibility and job description established, Frantz turns to a pile of one-inch-thick white posterboards, each approximately thirty-six inches tall, mounted onto which are photographs of Sullivan's body. One at a time, he hands the posterboards to me and asks me to describe the injuries on the victim's body as they were studied in the Kent County Morgue. To facilitate the testimony and to present a clearer picture of the forensic story the photographs tell, I stand in front of the jury, holding the oversized photographs, and point to the various injuries: the deep groove in Sullivan's neck left by the shoestring . . . a blister on Sullivan's right wrist. To the layperson, the blister may go unnoticed, but to the trained forensic pathologist, such a seemingly irrelevant detail represents a vital clue: the blister was most likely caused by friction from the shoelace that bound Sullivan's hands as he struggled to free himself. Frantz asks if this suggests that Sullivan was alive when bound, and I confirm that it does. The forensic evidence creates a vivid picture of Sullivan's final moments.

Various scrapes on Sullivan's body occurred before he died. I explain to the jury the difference between premortem scrapes, or those occurring before death, and postmortem scrapes, those occurring after death. Scrapes that occur before death, when the heart still pumps blood through the system, will often appear red on a body. After death, scrapes tend to appear yellow—the color of the underlying fat. Sullivan's scrapes are red. They occurred before death. They suggest a struggle.

A "white mucoid material" was found on Sullivan's upper thigh, which tests confirmed was semen, but its presence does not necessarily indicate any sexual activity occurred. Upon death, the body muscles stiffen—a process called rigor mortis—and the stiffening of the smooth muscle of the prostate gland can sometimes result in the release of semen.

After establishing the nature of the external injuries, prosecutor Frantz begins a line of questions intended to describe to the jury the key internal injury discovered in the August 14 autopsy—a key piece of evidence that could prove premeditation: the fractured c-o-r-n-u (I spell out the word for the court reporter). There are two three-quarter-inch cornua (or horns) located on each side of the thyroid cartilage, or Adam's apple. One or both of these can be fractured from the pressure of the fingers digging into the neck during manual strangulation but fractures are much less commonly seen in ligature strangulations. This physical evidence suggests that Sullivan was choked before being killed with a shoelace. The hemorrhaging or bleeding in the throat structures indicates that this damage occurred before the victim died.

I outline my theory based on the forensic evidence: two strangulations occurred—one that rendered Sullivan unconscious and another that ended his life. A minute and a half without blood flow would suffice to render a victim unconscious; three to four minutes would prove fatal.

Satisfied with the forensic picture of Sullivan's death provided in response to his questions, Frantz rests. Now for the defense.

When facing a brick wall, the defense realizes that it should not throw punches; attacking a well-credentialed expert could suggest to the jury that the defense has a weak case and no other option but an attempt to discredit the prosecution's witnesses. In other words, the defense will appear desperate. Realizing this, the defense attorney asks only a few specific questions. He asks about the semen on the victim's thigh. Did it result from ejaculation or slow leaking? I responded that it could be either; therefore, one could not conclude that he had sexual activity before death.

After a short, noncontentious cross-examination by defense counsel, during redirect, Prosecutor Frantz queries about the series of scrapes, which I explain Sullivan likely received when he rubbed against a surface such as a carpet, perhaps during a struggle.

After a few questions, the defense has finished with me, and my role in the case comes to an end.

Four days later, on a Friday, after three hours of deliberation, the jury returned their verdict: first-degree murder and a life sentence. At thirty-five, the defendant is a young man and a father. He will have some time to contemplate his crime and his victim. Or rather, his victims, if all the lives affected by the crime are taken into account.

Those standing close to Sullivan's roommate heard him utter, after hearing the verdict, "Oh, Rick, finally it's over."[20] But for a victim's loved ones, does the ordeal ever end? The crime leaves a wound on their psyches—one that will perhaps heal in time but will no doubt leave a permanent scar.

The same could be said for those victimized by the crime: Brancaccio's children.

No one wins. . . . No one.

CONCLUSION: MORGUE POETRY AND WINTERGREEN MINTS

Late Winter 2005
Spectrum Health, Blodgett Campus
East Grand Rapids, Michigan

Eight months later, Tobin's tour of the gritty world of the medical examiner is now complete. In the autopsy room of the morgue suite, visitors often notice a yellowed and faded piece of blue-lined paper taped to the beige tile; the paper contains a poem written by a pathology intern some years before Tobin entered the morgue for the first time, but its contents provides a neat summary of Tobin's experience. Future visitors to the Kent County Morgue may notice the sheet and its contents and consider its presence somewhat out of place, like a keg of beer at a funeral, but its contents are anything but anomalous.

The paper contains something one would least expect taped to the wall of a morgue: a poem that summarizes what occurs here.

An Ode to Forensic Pathology
Well, it's goodbye to forensic pathology,
My time here is done,
It's goodbye to bodies, homicides, and

307

A unique blend of fun.
No more slicing and dicing with Paul and his knife,
No more Jason and Jeff and extinction of life.
No more lights, camera, action for John and his slides,
No more "Autopsy's clear—so how did he die?"
It's the end of depositions and visits to court,
Au revoir to all the vital facts that are sought.
Suicide or murder or driving too fast,
Rich, colourful lives consigned to the past.
It's an end to ASCVD, skull fractures, and infarcts;
No more transected aortas and tears to the heart.
No more four done before lunch, with Dr. D. Start,
Or one done all day (Sorry, Dr. Cohle)—each to his art.

In the remainder of the poem, the author, an English intern who penned these catchy lines after completing a cycle in pathology, praises forensic pathology as a science and a potential career path. One can understand her enthusiasm; the world of forensic pathology is as addicting as it is fascinating. It is the study of the human organism.

Yet these lines do far more than provide a creative and heartfelt goodbye to the personalities that frequent the morgue; they offer a snapshot of life in the Kent County Morgue and the daily work of the medical examiner, and they subsequently provide a fitting summation of the experiences documented in this book.

A year ago, Tobin may have understood none of the specific references in the poem, but after his travels in the world of the medical examiner, he now knows not only the meaning of the acronym ASCVD, but much more; in fact, he's seen an infarct, and he understands the author's gentle gibe—a good-humored needling, a gentle index finger in the rib of the Kent County medical examiner that Paul Davison would understand better than anyone alive: "Or one done all day (Sorry, Dr. Cohle)—each to his art."

The poem's upbeat tone and rhythm belies the sorrow and grief—the human tragedy—at the center of this world, yet this playful verse that seems so incongruous to the *pathos* experienced each day in this place perfectly represents the clinical objectivity that envelops anyone who spends an appreciable amount of time among the deceased. Each day, the medical examiner rolls up his or her sleeves and thrusts both arms into human tragedy and investigates "Rich, colourful lives consigned to the past." Only with a dose of objectivity and a unique sense of humor does a forensic pathologist avoid a cell with padded walls and a straightjacket, or a prescription for Halcion, or worse.

Yet each victim's story *is* a tragedy, a life-altering, life-shattering tragedy for someone, because victims many times have siblings or children of their own, and they all have parents. In short, underlying each case is the reality that someone sometime someplace feels a tremendous sense of loss.

In the lobby of Spectrum Hospital one morning while awaiting my arrival, Tobin witnessed a curious scene: a mother and her young daughter sitting on one of the couches, waiting and waiting. The little girl, perhaps four years old, had spread her dolls' paraphernalia across the carpet; she undressed and dressed the dolls in various outfits.

If this scene occurred in a novel, it could be interpreted as symbolism. The little girl represents the fact that much of the drama, indeed much of the trauma of experiencing life in the world of the medical examiner, lies in the fact that at any given time any one of us can become a victim— even the little girl herself. Shakespeare characterized life as a stage play with humans merely acting parts prescribed to them. Watching the little girl pull off a polka-dot blouse and blue jeans from one of her dolls and then replace it with a pink and purple evening gown, one has to wonder what fate awaits any of us. What will occur in the final act of our lives? And in hers?

Tobin stands up to stretch his legs, and decides to take a walk around the hospital lobby. He spots another mother, cradling a newborn in her arms. Inside a pink and white striped bundle, she is lying on her back, the middle and index fingers of her left hand wedged in her mouth, her right hand clutching a bright pink plush doll. She is the image of peace, a wondrous image that seems to represent the cycles of nature and the whirlpool of life in which people float—one leaves, one arrives . . . one dies, one is born.

Outside the hospital lobby, swirls of wind howl. Winter has arrived in Michigan and Demeter has unleashed her sorrow onto the world as she mourns for her daughter Persephone. This ancient Greek tragedy provides a fitting epilogue to my efforts at helping readers better understand the world of a medical examiner and the impact we have on the lives of others.

The god of the underworld, Hades, fell in love with Persephone, who didn't feel the same way. Her mother, Demeter, Mother Earth, didn't approve of her daughter marrying someone from "the other side of the tracks," but Hades' brother, Zeus, did. With Zeus's help, Hades kidnapped Persephone and took her to the underworld.

Demeter, distraught, searched the earth for her daughter but to no avail. She mourned and humans suffered as she caused a plight during which crops wouldn't grow. Fearing that people would die of famine, Zeus forced Hades into allowing Persephone to return to Demeter. Yet before he relinquished his bride, the wily Hades tricked Persephone into eating some pomegranate seeds. According to Greek myth, those who dine on the food of the dead belong to Hades and must remain in the underworld, so the pomegranate seeds Persephone ate ensured her periodic return to his kingdom.

Reunited with her daughter, Demeter rejoiced, thus lifting the plight on humans. Crops flourished, ensuring the survival of humanity. Yet whenever Persephone returns to the underworld, Demeter mourns and the earth once again grows cold. For the Greeks, this myth explained the existence of the seasons. Persephone's return to Hades and her mother's subsequent sorrow marks winter when crops go dormant; her reemergence from the underworld and Demeter's resultant joy represents spring and summer when the crops flourish.

Like Persephone, Tobin has eaten pomegranate seeds in the underworld, "doomed" to return periodically, drawn back by its intriguing characters and compelling plot lines and, most of all, by the vivid images indelibly impressed into his mind. Perhaps he will again visit the morgue (as a tourist *with a two-way ticket*!!), but for certain he will revisit his experience.

Like a write-only CD-ROM, his mind has recorded images that

cannot be erased, images of moments that flash across his consciousness triggered by certain stimuli, such as a scene in a *CSI* episode. So powerful are these images that he can close his eyes and see them parade before him . . . little Aaron Michael Edwards and his blanket stuffed with plush toys . . . Patty Fredericks, with half of her face missing . . . Sarah Coleman, her head concealed behind a red plastic shopping bag . . . Richard Sullivan, a running shoe dangling from the shoelace-noose around his neck, and others.

And the smells—he will revisit them each time he detects the faintest odor of wintergreen, latex, and certain soaps similar in scent to those used in the morgue restroom to scrub away any potential droplet of blood and his paranoia. In fact, he will find that he has developed an odd, psychosomatic disgust for wintergreen mints.

If there is one lesson for Tobin to learn in the morgue regarding the human condition (anatomy aside), it would be that the use and misuse of substances can prove lethal. Revisiting his experiences over the past eight months, he will find that most of the victims he met arrived to the morgue as a consequence of substance use and abuse: a victim who overdosed on oxycodone and booze and fell into a lake; two victims who in alcoholic stupors sustained lethal head injuries; a victim who consumed a mixed drug cocktail of prescription narcotics, and the physician who through the prescriptions mixed it for her; even the most innocent victim (when one dismisses the child victims), Richard Sullivan, came to the morgue not the consequence of his addiction but of his killer's thirst for heroin. For many, the genie that can grant happiness lies within a syringe or a bottle of spirits. While he proudly proclaims a "drug-free" life, Tobin admits to enjoying a periodic binge of whiskey, but the genie released when he opens the next bottle will whisper something different in his ear . . . remember.

A return in his mind to his experience in the morgue is certain, but perhaps one day he will return to the real place.

But for now, he must leave and return to the world of the living, while he still can. And maybe one day, he'll again be able to eat wintergreen mints.

ACKNOWLEDGMENTS

For their role in making this work a reality, the authors would like to thank the following:

For sharing their experiences and their work, the Kent County medical examination team: Paul Davison, Kent County death scene investigator and autopsy assistant; Jason Chatman, autopsy assistant; Joel Talsma, autopsy assistant; John Connolly, death scene investigator, "semiretired"; Dick Washburn, body conveyance specialist; Sue Atwood, Dr. Cohle's "right brain"; and Forensic Administrative Assistant Jodi Patton.

For navigating the difficult channels of publication, literary agent Mike Hamilburg and his assistant Joanie Kern. For making the connection between authors and agent, Sue Gutierrez and Joe Declan Moran.

For information about *The People v. Ernest Stiller*, Berrien County prosecutor and chief trial attorney Mike Sepic.

For information about Richard Dunn and his untimely passing, Barbara Dunn.

The various law enforcement personnel who must periodically venture into the underworld and who provided key insight into various aspects of forensic science and detection: *you truly fight the "good" fight.* In particular, members of the Kent and Ottawa County sheriff's departments and the United States Federal Bureau of Investigation.

For the information on forensic entomology, Dr. M. Lee Goff, distinguished professor of entomology at Chaminade University in Honolulu, Hawaii, for fascinating information about the art and science of forensic entomology and all that insects can tell crime scene investigators.

For his help in turning draft into final product, Steven L. Mitchell, editor in chief of Prometheus Books, Chris Kramer, director of production, and cover artist Grace Zilsberger.

And most of all, we would like to thank our families, who provided insight, guidance, and above all, the antidote to the *pathos* in this drama.

NOTES AND SOURCES

INTRODUCTION: SCENES

1. Suicide statistics from the National Center for Injury Prevention and Control, *WISQARS Fatal Injury and Leading Cause of Death Report, 2003.* http://webaypa.cdc.gov/sasweb/ncipc/leadcaus.html (accessed April 4, 2006).

CHAPTER 1: DECOMPRESSION

1. American Heart Association, *Heart Disease and Stroke Statistics 2005 Update,* http://www.americanheart.org/downloadable/heart/1105390918119HDS Stats2005Update.pdf#search='The%20American%20Heart%20Association %20%20Heart%20Disease%20and%20Stroke%20Statistics%202005%20Update (accessed March 27, 2006).

CHAPTER 2: CONTRASTS

1. National Center for Health Statistics (NCHS), "Self-Inflicted Injury/Suicide Fast Stats," http://www.cdc.gov/nchs/fastats/suicide.htm (accessed March 27, 2006).

2. Robert Wilkins, *Death: A History of Man's Obsession and Fears* (New York: Barnes & Noble Books, 1990), p. 229.

3. Colin Wilson, *The Mammoth Book of True Crime* (New York: Carroll and Graf, 1988), p. 556.

4. Sandy Banks, "Choking Game Takes Toll on Teens," *Grand Rapids Press*, December 11, 2005, p. A22.

5. Henry Erb, "Death Behind Bars," WoodTV.com, http://woodtv.com/Global/story.asp?S=1258895 (accessed December 8, 2005).

6. Suzy Platt, ed., *Respectfully Quoted: A Dictionary of Quotations Requested from the Congressional Research Service* (Washington, DC: Library of Congress, 1989).

CHAPTER 3: WHAT KILLED HARRY FREIBURG?

1. Dr. M. Lee Goff, forensic entomologist, telephone interview with Tobin T. Buhk, October 20, 2004.

2. Ibid.

3. Ibid.

4. Ibid.

5. Ibid.

6. Ibid.

7. Ibid.

8. Ibid.

9. Ibid.

10. Ibid.

11. Edgar Allen Poe, "Premature Burial," 4Literature.com, http://www.4literature.net/Edgar_Allan_Poe/Premature_Burial/ (accessed March 28, 2006).

12. Ibid.

CHAPTER 4: RED SKY IN THE MORNING

1. Ed White and Theresa D. Mcclellan, "The 'Truth' Hurts," *Grand Rapids Press*, March 2, 2002, p. A1.

2. Ed White, "Gabrion Guilty; Death-Penalty Hearing Next," *Grand Rapids Press*, March 5, 2002, p. A1.

3. *People v. Briggs*, Mich. App. 241568; 1,3 (2003); unpublished, http://courtofappeals.mijud.net (accessed December 12, 2005).

4. *People v. Goecke*, 457 Mich. 442, 464; 579 NW.2d 868 (1998).

5. Ibid.

6. *People v. Aldridge*, 246 Mich. App 101, 123; 631 NW.2d 67 (2001).

7. John Tunison, "Murder Suspect Confessed, Records Reveal," *Grand Rapids Press*, August 24, 2004, p. C1.

CHAPTER 6: ACCIDENTS

1. *People v. Selwa*, 214 Mich App 451; 543 NW.2d 321 (1995).

2. Ibid.

CHAPTER 8: BLUE HIGHWAY

1. James Prichard, "Judge Weighs 2 Trials in FSU Alcohol Death," *Detroit Free Press*, August 23, 2000.

2. Ben Schmitt, "Father Seeks Justice in Son's Death," *Detroit Free Press*, March 27, 2000.

3. Higher Education Center, "HEC News: Three Plead Guilty in College Death," Associated Press, June 8, 2000, http://www.edc.org/hec/news/hecnews/events/000609d.html (accessed April 16, 2006).

CHAPTER 9: BROKEN HEARTS

1. "Beyond the Rubber Bullet," *Time*, http://www.time.com/time/nation/article/0,8599,322588,00.html (accessed December 21, 2005).

2. Robert Herrick, "Upon a Child: An Epitaph," in *Works of Robert Herrick: Volume I*, ed. Alfred Pollack (London: Lawrence and Bullen, 1894).

CHAPTER 10: OF ZEBRAS AND HORSES

1. Arthur Conan Doyle, *Sign of the Four* (1900; Penguin Classics Edition, New York: Penguin Books, 2001).

2. Bob Evans, "How a Company Cashed in on Anthrax," dailypress.com, December 4, 2002, http://www.dailypress.com/news/dp-anthraxseries,0,6168344 .storygallery?coll=dp-widget-news (accessed November 21, 2005).

3. Ibid.

4. Ibid.

5. Ibid.

6. Barbara Dunn, interview with Tobin T. Buhk, January 16, 2006.

7. Ibid.

8. Ibid.

9. Ibid.

10. Ibid.

11. Ibid.

12. Evans, "How a Company Cashed in on Anthrax."

13. Bob Evans, "Young Men Got Lou Gehrig's Disease," dailypress.com, December 5, 2005, http://www.dailypress.com/news/dp-anthrax-series, 0,6168344 .storygallery?coll=dp-widget-news (accessed November 21, 2005).

14. Bob Evans, "'I'd Known That Kid . . . That Wasn't Him,'" dailypress .com, December 5, 2005, http://www.dailypress.com/news/dp-anthrax-series,0,6168344 .storygallery?coll=dp-widget-news (accessed November 21, 2005).

15. Barbara Dunn, interview with Tobin T. Buhk, January 16, 2006.

CHAPTER 11: ENDINGS

1. Ken Kolker and Tanda Gmiter, "Police Say Death Not Suicide," *Grand Rapids Press*, September 19, 2000, p. A1.

2. Ibid.

3. Doug Guthrie, "Doctor Describes Sandra Duyst's Depression. He Says She Had Changed Drugs and Was Improving during the Six Months before her Death," *Grand Rapids Press*, March 21, 2001, p. A16.

4. Doug Guthrie, "Defense Video Shows Duyst's Side of Story. The Prosecutor Complains the Dramatic Re-creation of Events Is 'Simply Not Accurate,'" *Grand Rapids Press*, March 23, 2001, p. A1.

5. Doug Guthrie, "Death Scenario Re-created. A Blood Spatter Expert, Testifying for the Prosecution, Says There Is No Way Sandra Duyst Could Have Committed Suicide," *Grand Rapids Press*, March 15, 2001, p. A25.

6. Pat Shellenbarger, "No Easy Way out for Convicted Husband," *Grand Rapids Press*, April 16, 2006, p. A1.

7. Ibid.

CHAPTER 12: HORSEPLAY

1. Aaron J. Mead, prosecutor's brief, counterstatement of facts, *People of the State of Michigan v Ernest William Stiller* in the State of Michigan Court of Appeals, p. 6.

2. Ibid., p. 21.

3. Ibid., p. 6.

4. *People v. Stiller*, 242 Mich. App. 38,42; 617 NW.2d 697 (2000).

5. Mead, prosecutor's brief, counterstatement of facts, appendix B.

6. *Stiller*, 242 Mich. App. at 38, 44; 697.

7. Mead, prosecutor's brief, counterstatement of facts, appendix A.

8. Ibid., pp. 4, 11.

9. Ibid., p. 15.

10. Ibid., p. 5.

11. Ibid; Aaron J. Mead, argument, *People of the State of Michigan v. Ernest William Stiller* in the State of Michigan Court of Appeals, p. 38.

12. Ibid., p. 20.

13. Ibid., p. 22.

14. Ibid., p. 22.

15. *Stiller*, 242 Mich. App. at 38, 49; 697.

16. *Id.* at 38, 52; 697.

17. Ibid.

18. Ibid.

19. *Stiller*, 242 Mich. App. at 38, 53; 697.

20. Mead, prosecutor's brief, counterstatement of facts, p. 13.

21. Michael J. Sepic, Berrien County chief trial attorney, telephone interview with Tobin T. Buhk, January 13, 2006.

22. Ibid.

CHAPTER 13: THE LAST CHAPTER: LIFE

1. Flynn McRoberts et al., "Fact or Fiction? The Jury Is Still Out on the *CSI* Effect," *Chicago Tribune*, June 5, 2005.

2. *Souter v. Jones*, 395 F.3d 577, 582; 2005 FED App. 0027P (6th Cir.).

3. *Id.* at 577, 585.

4. *Id.* at 577, 583.

5. *Id.*

6. Quoted in *id.*

7. *Id.*

8. John Agar, "Murder Suspect 'Was Done Wrong,'" *Grand Rapids Press*, July 6, 2005, p. A1.

9. *Souter*, 395 F.3d at 577, 584.

10. *Id.* at 577, 582.

11. *Id.*

12. *Id.*

13. *Id.*

14. *Id.* at 577, 592.

15. *Id.*

16. *Id.*

17. *Id.*

18. Ed White, "New Witness Sets Man Free," *Grand Rapids Press*, April 2, 2005, p. A1.

19. John Agar, "26 Years Later, Somebody Listened," *Grand Rapids Press*, April 7, 2005, p. A1.

20. John Tunison, "Verdict Comes Swiftly in Murder Trial," *Grand Rapids Press*, January 22, 2005, p. A1.

Sources

INTRODUCTION: SCENES

National Center for Injury Prevention and Control. *WISQARS Fatal Injury and Leading Cause of Death Report, 2003.* http://webaypa.cdc.gov/sasweb/ ncipc/leadcaus.html (accessed April 4, 2006).

CHAPTER 1: DECOMPRESSION

American Heart Association. *Heart Disease and Stroke Statistics 2005 Update.* http://www.americanheart.org/downloadable/heart/1105390918119HDSStats 25Update.pdf#search='The%20American%20Heart%20Associa-tion%20%20Heart %20Disease%20and%20Stroke%20Statistics%202005% 20Update (accessed March 27, 2006).

Nolte, Kurt B., MD, David G. Taylor, PhD, and Jonathan Y. Richmond, PhD. "Biosafety Considerations for Autopsy." *American Journal of Forensic Medicine and Pathology* 23, no. 2 (2002): 107–22.

CHAPTER 2: CONTRASTS

Banks, Sandy. "Choking Game Takes Toll on Teens." *Grand Rapids Press*, December 11, 2005, p. A22.

Bartlett, John. *Bartlett's Familiar Quotations.* 16th ed. Edited by Justin Kaplan. Boston: Little, Brown and Company, 1992.

Erb, Henry. "Death Behind Bars." WoodTV.com.http://woodtv.com/Global/story.asp?S=1258895 (accessed December 8, 2005).

National Center for Health Statistics (NCHS). "Self-Inflicted Injury/Suicide Fast Stats." http://www.cdc.gov/nchs/fastats/suicide.htm (accessed March 27, 2006).

Platt, Suzy, ed. *Respectfully Quoted: A Dictionary of Quotations Requested from the Congressional Research Service.* Washington, DC: Library of Congress, 1989. Bartleby Online Edition, 2003. www.bartleby.com/br/73/1782.html (accessed April 16, 2006).

Wilkins, Robert. *Death: A History of Man's Obsession and Fears.* New York: Barnes & Noble Books, 1990.

Wilson, Colin. *The Mammoth Book of True Crime.* New York: Carroll and Graf, 1988.

CHAPTER 3: WHAT KILLED HARRY FREIBURG?

Goff, Dr. M. Lee, forensic entomologist. Telephone interview with Tobin T. Buhk, October 20, 2004.
Poe, Edgar Allen. "Premature Burial." 4Literature.com. http://www.4literature .net/Edgar_Allan_Poe/Premature_Burial/ (accessed March 28, 2006).

CHAPTER 4: RED SKY IN THE MORNING

People v. Aldridge, 246 Mich. App. 101, 123; 631 NW.2d 67 (2001).
People v. Briggs, Mich. App. 241568; 1; (2003); unpublished, http://courtof appeals.mijud.net (accessed December 12, 2005).
People v. Goecke, 457 Mich 442, 464; 579 NW.2d 868 (1998).
Tunison, John. "Murder Suspect Claims Victim Made Pass." *Grand Rapids Press*, September 2, 2004, p. A1.
———. "Murder Suspect Confessed, Records Reveal." *Grand Rapids Press*, August 24, 2004, p. C1.
White, Ed. "Gabrion Guilty; Death-Penalty Hearing Next." *Grand Rapids Press*, March 5, 2002, p. A1.
———. "Juror Gives Details about Deliberations in Death Penalty Case." *Grand Rapids Press*, March 26, 2002, p. A1.
———. "Lawyers Make Final Points; Jurors Take Over." *Grand Rapids Press*, March 5, 2002, p. A1.
White, Ed, and Theresa D. Mcclellan. "The 'Truth' Hurts." *Grand Rapids Press*, March 2, 2002, p. A1.

CHAPTER 6: ACCIDENTS

People v. French, Mich. App. 242564; 1; (2003); unpublished, http://courtofappeals .mijud.net (accessed December 12, 2005).
People v. Selwa, 214 Mich. App. 451; 543 NW.2d 321 (1995).

CHAPTER 8: BLUE HIGHWAY

Higher Education Center. "HEC News: Three Plead Guilty in College Death." Associated Press, June 8, 2000. http://www.edc.org/hec/news/hecnews/ events/000609d.html (accessed April 16, 2006).

Prichard, James. "Judge Weighs 2 Trials in FSU Alcohol Death." *Detroit Free Press*, August 23, 2000.

Schmitt, Ben. "Father Seeks Justice in Son's Death." *Detroit Free Press*, March 27, 2000.

CHAPTER 9: BROKEN HEARTS

"Beyond the Rubber Bullet." *Time.com*. http://www.time.com/time /nation/article/0,8599,322588,00.html (accessed December 21, 2005).

Herrick, Robert. "Upon a Child: An Epitaph." In *Works of Robert Herrick: Volume I*. Edited by Alfred Pollack. London: Lawrence and Bullen, 1894.

CHAPTER 10: OF ZEBRAS AND HORSES

"Britain's 'Anthrax Island.'" BBC News. http://news.bbc.co.uk/1/hi/scotland/ 1457035.stm (accessed November 22, 2005).

"Cause of Anthrax Vaccine Worker's Death Debated." CNN.com. http://archives .cnn.com/2000/US/09/29/anthrax.death.01 (accessed November 21, 2005).

Doyle, Arthur Conan. *The Sign of the Four*. Penguin Classics Edition. New York: Penguin Books, 2001.

Dunn, Barbara. Telephone interview with Tobin T. Buhk, January 16, 2006.

Evans, Bob. "How a Company Cashed in on Anthrax." dailypress.com, December 5, 2005. http://www.dailypress.com/news/dp-anthrax-series,0,6168344.story gallery?coll=dp-widget-news (accessed November 21, 2005).

———. " 'I'd Known That Kid . . . That Wasn't Him.'" dailypress.com, December 5, 2005. http://www.dailypress.com/news/dp-anthrax-series,0,6168344.story gallery?coll=dp-widget-news (accessed November 21, 2005).

———. "An Incomplete Picture." dailypress.com, December 4, 2005. http://www.dailypress.com/news/dp-anthrax-series,0,6168344.storygallery ?coll=dp-widget-news (accessed November 21, 2005).

————. "Young Men Got Lou Gehrig's Disease." dailypress.com, December 5, 2005. http://www.dailypress.com/news/dp-anthrax-series,0,6168344.story gallery?coll=dp-widget-news (accessed November 21, 2005).

State of Michigan Worker's Compensation Apellate Commission, *Richard Dunn Decedent, Barbara Dunn, Plaintiff v. Bioport Corporation and Citizens Insurance Company of America*; Michigan Department of Health, Self-Insured, Opinion on Remand; 2003 ACO #291; Docket #03-0014.

CHAPTER 11: ENDINGS

Guthrie, Doug. "Death Scenario Re-created. A Blood Spatter Expert, Testifying for the Prosecution, Says There Is No Way Sandra Duyst Could Have Committed Suicide." *Grand Rapids Press*, March 15, 2001, p. A25.

————. "Defense Video Shows Duyst's Side of Story. The Prosecutor Complains the Dramatic Re-creation of Events Is 'Simply Not Accurate.'" *Grand Rapids Press*, March 23, 2001, p. A1.

————. "Doctor Describes Sandra Duyst's Depression. He Says She Had Changed Drugs and Was Improving during the Six Months before Her Death." *Grand Rapids Press*, March 21, 2001, p. A16.

————. "Handgun Couldn't Have Fired Twice by Accident, Jurors Told. A Weapons Expert Says There Were No Broken Parts on the Gun That Put Two Bullets in Sandra Duyst's Head." *Grand Rapids Press*, March 13, 2001, p. A16.

————. "Husband 4 Feet Away When Shots Were Fired, Blood Expert Testifies. He Says Blood Droplets Found on David Duyst's Shirt Are the Kind That Result from Being Nearby When a Shooting Happens." *Grand Rapids Press*, March 14, 2001, p. D1.

————. "'My Life Is Over,' Shooting Victim's Message Says Jurors Hear Sandra Duyst's Voice Mail Message, Telling Her Husband to 'Enjoy Your Life.'" *Grand Rapids Press*, March 9, 2001, p. C1.

Kolker, Ken, and Tanda Gmiter. "Duyst Jury Swayed by Second Shot. All Eventually Decided That Sandra Duyst Could Not Have Shot Herself in the Head Twice. The result: David Duyst Was Convicted of Murder." *Grand Rapids Press*, March 31, 2001, p. A1.

————. "Police Say Death Not Suicide." *Grand Rapids Press*, September 19, 2000, p. A1.

Parish, James Robert. *The Hollywood Book of Death: The Bizarre, Often Sordid, Passions of More than 125 American Movie and TV Idols*. Chicago: Cotemporary Books, 2002.

Shellenbarger, Pat. "No Easy Way Out for Convicted Husband." *Grand Rapids Press*, April 16, 2006, p. A1.

CHAPTER 12: HORSEPLAY

Mead, Aaron J. Argument, *The People of the State of Michigan v. Ernest William Stiller* in the State of Michigan Court of Appeals.

————. Prosecutor's brief, counterstatement of facts. *The People of the State of Michigan v. Ernest William Stiller* in the State of Michigan Court of Appeals.

Michael J. Sepic, Berrien County chief trial attorney, telephone interview with Tobin T. Buhk, January 13, 2006.

People v. Stiller. 242 Mich. App. 38; 617 NW.2d 697 (2000).

CHAPTER 13: THE LAST CHAPTER: LIFE

Agar, John. "Murder Suspect 'Was Done Wrong'; Attorney General Says Larry Souter Never Should Have Been Brought to Trial." *Grand Rapids Press*, July 6, 2005, p. A1.

————. "26 Years Later, Somebody Listened." *Grand Rapids Press*, April 7, 2005, p. A1.

McRoberts, Flynn, Steve Mills, and Maurice Possley. "Fact or fiction? The Jury Is Still Out on the *CSI* Effect." *Chicago Tribune*, June 5, 2005, Perspective Section, p. 3.

Souter v. Jones. 395 F.3d 577; 2005 FED App. 0027P (6th Cir.).

White, Ed. "New Witness Sets Man Free." *Grand Rapids Press*, April 2, 2005, p. A1.

INDEX